Praise for ~~Not~~ *Today*

"I had the honor of calling Ari one of my friends. He inspired me every time we were together with his toughness, spirit and grit. I'm certain his story, shared in this book, will inspire you."

—Brad Stevens, head coach of the Boston Celtics

"~~Not~~ *Today* is a memorable and inspiring book. We all have a lot to learn from Ari and the Schultz family about how to face adversity with love, courage, and optimism."

—Senator Joseph I. Lieberman

"Personal, actionable and generous, this is a book about the choices that each of us makes, every single day, and the light we're capable of sharing."

—Seth Godin, author of *This Is Marketing*

"Ari fought a battle no child should be faced with and he did it with such a brave face, constantly surrounded by his all-star family. We're all proud to call Ari and the Schultz family our friends and a huge inspiration."

—David Ortiz, three-time World Series Champion

"Problems are the nectar of life—they challenge us to grow. In this book, ~~Not~~ *Today*, we see a perfect example of the tremendous strength we all carry deep inside."

—Michael A. Singer, #1 *New York Times* bestselling author of *The Untethered Soul*

"I'm bombarded routinely with books promising to make you more productive. They're loaded with charts and ridiculous claims. This book is totally different and refreshingly so. It's rooted in one of the most difficult life experiences imaginable and the efforts of the authors to cope and thrive simultaneously. There is no way that you can avoid taking away important productivity and life skills while reading an incredible story!"

—Len Schlesinger, Baker Foundation professor at Harvard Business School and president of Emeritus-Babson College

"Poignant, personal, and practical. You definitely need to take the T.I.M.E to read this, and be rewarded to boot!"

—Barry Z. Posner, PhD, coauthor of *The Leadership Challenge* and *Everyday People, Extraordinary Leadership*

"Ari Schultz was a global media sensation, but behind the story of this remarkable little boy were his parents struggling to live their lives and find their path in the face of seemingly insurmountable obstacles. Through ~~Not~~ *Today*, everyone will be inspired by Ari, and learn invaluable lessons about how to thrive when life throws you curveballs."

—Dan Rea, host of NightSide, WBZ News Radio 1030

"~~Not~~ *Today* is a must-read if you want the secrets to a more balanced life. Starting my day with my GIA is an absolute game changer and will be for you, too."

—Sarah Johnston, founder of The Briefcase Coach

"Ari's spirit was infectious, and the devotion Mike and Erica showed to Ari, each other, and their business through the most challenging circumstances, is inspiring. Are you spending your time the way that you want? Writing from the heart, and with world-class business sense, Mike and Erica help all of us consider how we want to answer that important question."

—Mike Reiss, Patriots reporter for ESPN

"A must-read for everyone. It will make you cry, laugh, and think. It's a blueprint for optimism, hope, confidence, and happiness."

—Steve Fisher, former head coach of the
Michigan Fab Five and SDSU Basketball

"This book is pure gold! If you want to be more productive and happier, then dig in because you are about to learn that when you know your *why*, it transforms *how* you do your work and life, and this opens the doors to *what* you have always wanted to do."

—Tom Ziglar, CEO of Ziglar Corporation

"If you read only one book on productivity in your life, ~~Not~~ *Today* is the one. Not only does this have the best and most well-researched productivity advice of any productivity book ever written, but you also *need to read this story*. Both will change your life."

—Gina Gallagher, author of *Shut Up About Your Perfect Kid:
A Survival Guide for Ordinary Parents of Special Children*

~~NOT~~ TODAY

Also by Mike Schultz

Insight Selling: Surprising Research on What Sales Winners Do Differently (coauthored with John E. Doerr)

Professional Services Marketing: How the Best Firms Build Premier Brands, Thriving Lead Generation Engines, and Cultures of Business Development Success (coauthored with John E. Doerr and Lee W. Frederiksen, PhD)

Rainmaking Conversations: Influence, Persuade, and Sell in Any Situation (coauthored with John E. Doerr)

Virtual Selling: How to Build Relationships, Differentiate, and Win Sales Remotely (coauthored with Dave Shaby and Andy Springer)

Take Control of Your TIME,
Achieve Your Goals,
Become Unstoppable

~~NOT~~ TODAY

THE 9 HABITS OF
EXTREME PRODUCTIVITY

Erica & Mike Schultz

Matt Holt Books
An Imprint of BenBella Books, Inc.
Dallas, TX

BenBella Books, Inc.
10440 N. Central Expressway
Suite 800
Dallas, TX 75231
www.benbellabooks.com
Send feedback to feedback@benbellabooks.com

BenBella is a federally registered trademark.
Matt Holt and logo are trademarks of BenBella Books.

Printed in the United States of America
10 9 8 7 6 5 4 3 2 1

Library of Congress Location Number: 2020056714
ISBN 9781950665976

Editing by Mary Flaherty and Claire Schulz
Copyediting by James Fraleigh
Proofreading by Jenny Bridges and Sarah Vostok
Indexing by Amy Murphy
Text design by PD&PS
Composition by PerfecType
Cover design by Sarah Avinger and AuthorImprints.com
Printed by Lake Book Manufacturing

CONTENTS

Foreword   xi

Prologue   xv

Introduction: The Gift of Time   xxix

Not Today   I

A New Mindset About TIME   13

The Productivity Code Key #1: Manufacture Motivation

Habit I: Recruit Your Drive   27

Habit 2: Ignite Your Proactivity   47

Habit 3: Reengineer Your Habits   65

The Productivity Code Key # 2: Control Your TIME

Habit 4: Obsess over TIME   87

Habit 5: Say No   I05

Habit 6: Play Hard to Get   II9

The Productivity Code Key #3: Execute in the Zone

Habit 7: Sprint into the Zone   I35

CONTENTS

Habit 8: Fuel Your Energy   **149**

Habit 9: Right the Ship   **165**

Epilogue   179

Acknowledgments   183

Appendix A: Your Personal 90-Day Productivity
Code Challenge   185

Appendix B: Research Note   197

Notes   217

Index   225

If You Want to Continue Your Journey with Us   232

About the Authors   233

About RAIN Group   235

FOREWORD

W*hat did you endure?"*
It sounds so simple, but who asks such a question? And what might the answer contain? Often, our family is too close, our friends too caring, for such an inquiry. And then, to hear the reply in all its dimension: strength and pain, hope and loss, fear and anger, exhaustion and doubt, joy and surprise, hope and grief. Who could bear to hear it and know the weight of experience behind it all?

Without any right or relationship, any established history or deep connection, it's a question I asked in August 2017 of two strangers sitting in the living room of their house in Stow, Massachusetts. I asked each of them separately, and then waited. Each looked at me and then away, pausing and reflecting. And then, each took a breath, and answered.

That Mike and Erica Schultz had the strength to respond at all was a testament to their collective will, their astounding persistence, and to something deeper. The power of what each shared that day shapes, in many ways, the message they share in this book.

I've been a reporter, serving different networks and platforms, for the majority of my career. For more than twenty years now I've covered sports, mostly at ESPN. Without hyperbole, it's a job that feels closer to a lottery win than any kind of labor. I've had the chance to work the side-lines at the Rose Bowl, to interview the winner at the Masters, to pro-vide play-by-play at Wimbledon, and to conduct the trophy ceremony on court at the US Open.

But the deepest and richest part of the job has been the chance to tell stories—of teams revered and obscure, of people famous and unknown, and of moments often rooted in the same sacred ground: family.

That's what led our producers Mike Farrell and Toby Hershkowitz to the Schultzes' door, through the wondrous portal of YouTube. Toby came across a video on the platform, posted March 6, 2017, a clip so magical it spread far and wide across the web. The clip features a father, off camera, sharing a piece of news with his five-year-old son. It's the news their family has been waiting for at Boston Children's Hospital, every second, for 211 days.

"I was talking to the doctors a few minutes ago," the father says. "You know how they've been looking for a heart for a long time?"

"Yes," the boy says immediately. He's spirited and blond and beautiful.

"I think they found one, and it might be perfect for you."

"They found one?" the boy says, and smiles with a joy as pure as grace itself. He's holding a plastic bat, and swings it. "Great!" he says. His only question is when. When will he get it? And the question he doesn't ask, but his father knows he's thinking is:

After I get it, when can I go to Fenway Park and see my Red Sox?

Toby shared the clip with our bosses, and they had the same reac-tion he did. We needed to share the story that led to this infectious and joyous moment, and, if the family would be willing, to chronicle what might come after.

By the time I sat with Mike and Erica, almost six months after the video was posted, Ari and his parents had shared, withstood, and persisted through more than any of us could have ever imagined.

There were soaring highs and crushing lows, instances of such self-less love that they recast our definition of what a parent is capable of—in devotion, commitment, and energy.

In the time producers Mike and Toby spent with the family, our cameras also captured scenes around the house, showing how a mother and father somehow found ways to give everything they had to their son, and then find to give—to their two younger children, to their business, to emergency rebuilding after the loss of their home, to each other.

Evidence of their sheer capability that stays with me comes from that June, after Ari returned home with his new, transplanted heart. Leaving the hospital was a goal the doctors and the family had worked so hard for, and the celebration filled the hallways, with the staff cheering Ari as he made his way out the doors.

But beyond the celebration lay the daunting task of managing Ari's care, a full-time job in itself. The picture I see is the tableau of Mike and Erica at their kitchen table, its surface covered with rows and columns of ziplock bags, arranged with color coded Post-it Notes alongside. Ari was sent home with twenty-three different medications, each with its own exact dosage and to-the-minute schedule. The regimen would've overwhelmed any set of caregivers short of a staff of veteran nurses.

Mike and Erica were the staff. "If we make a mistake," Erica said, "we could really hurt our son." Without any room for error, they made none. They created a system, organized the medications, developed the schedule, and administered the medicines.

How? With the highest stakes possible, how did they manage it all? How did they stay on task without surrendering to the fatigue or collapsing under the burden? I marveled at it then and still do.

But Mike and Erica did more than bear it, more than carry on and get by. They made it through—through the greatest loss conceivable, yet intact and connected. Productive and purposeful.

This is the story of their *how*.

Ultimately, I asked them the wrong question.

What I understand now, through Mike and Erica's story, is that their aim was never simply to endure—not when they first learned of Ari's heart defect, nor when he survived two surgeries before he was born, nor when they waited for a heart transplant, nor when his body rejected it, nor when they lay with him in his final hours.

Their goal was greater, through it all. Their mission was to remain fully and resolutely alive—in intention and action, motivation and result—in all the ways they needed to be, through challenge unfathom-able and immediate.

They know, and continue to prove, that enduring gains its greater meaning as a step toward a much higher ideal.

Prevailing.

Tom Rinaldi
December 2020

PROLOGUE

Happiness can be found in the darkest of times,
if one only remembers to turn on the light.

—Albus Dumbledore, *Harry Potter
and the Prisoner of Azkaban*

MIKE

There are moments in your life that change you. Defining moments. Sometimes a moment prints its stamp on your life instantly—your eyes meet across the crowded room, you land your dream job, the doctor says "cancer." Other times the seed of that moment takes years to bloom, but looking in the rearview mirror, you can trace its growth back to a turning point. Ours was September 28, 2011.

*

In the days before we were happily married with children, we were happily married with Toby, the bagel-crazed, foul-breathed Cavalier King Charles Spaniel. (Married to each other, that is, not the dog—though he might have argued otherwise.)

Life was fairly quiet when we started to cruise open houses on Sundays. We weren't really looking to buy, but you know what happens when you go out shopping "just to look" every weekend.

One brisk, sunny May morning we walked into a house that looked tired and shabby from the outside. Once inside, we couldn't get out fast enough. The musty smell was overwhelming, and the spotted, wavy ceilings looked like they could collapse any minute.

Eleven years later, this is where we live. Sorta.

The dubious ceilings and stale smell didn't detract from the lovely location on Lake Boon in tiny, bucolic Stow, Massachusetts, and we were told the bones of the house were fine. No kids? Plenty of time on the weekends?

Renovation!

It took about a year, but soon enough we'd transformed the funky fishing lodge into our homey lake house, with a rustic stone fireplace, wide pine floors, huge screen porch, and a wall of windows overlooking the "narrows," a stretch of water between two basins of the lake.

On the work front, our then-small business had survived the Great Recession largely intact. We had just launched a major strategy pivot because we saw a growth opportunity too good to pass up, though it required completely reinventing the company. The business had three service-offering areas, and we were gung-ho to grow only one of them—the smallest one.

Difficult as it was, we said "no" to the other two, and renamed the company RAIN Group and focused on sales training. Even though its revenue was the smallest of the three areas, we thought it had the greatest long-term potential.

We were crazy busy at home and crazy busy at work, but somehow we still had time. So we added some crazy fun and hobbies. We'd show up to work by 8 AM and wrap up around 6 PM. Afterward, we'd relax with a Seirenkai Jujitsu class from 6:45 to 8:15 PM, followed by a challenging ninety-minute Seirenkai Karate workout. Then we'd finish up with drinks with our friends from class and return home around 11 PM. If it wasn't a martial arts night, we'd go to a Celtics or Red Sox game, a movie, or some other shindig. We kept ourselves moving.*

---

* Lest you think poor Toby the dog was neglected, note that we took him to work with us every day. We literally wrote him into the office lease. He had plenty of companionship and bagels.

❋

By most measures we were successful. Living the good life for sure.

New house, successful business, busy social life . . . pretty much everything was going well for us. All except adding a third member to the human part of the family.

We tried. And tried.

We struggled.

After ten long months, it happened: we were pregnant!

The following week Erica had a miscarriage.

We had tried so hard, for so long. Now, understanding we could lose our baby at any moment, we were paralyzed. Even when Erica was physically okay to try again, we weren't ready.

Finally, after months of emotional agony, we were ready to try.

In a hot minute we were pregnant again.

ERICA

On September 28, 2011, we arrived at Mass General at 11 AM for our eighteen-week ultrasound. We had made it through the first trimester and breathed a sigh of relief.

The eighteen-week ultrasound is a big one: the fetal survey, as the doctors call it. They check on all sorts of things, but all we wanted to know was if we were having a boy or girl. Big pending decision: How to decorate the nursery? Just the week before, we announced on Facebook we were pregnant. The news was out there.

As I lay on the hospital bed with the gooey wand gliding across my belly, we saw ten fingers. We saw ten toes. It looked like the baby was sucking its thumb. Its profile . . . perfection.

The technician looked at us and asked if we wanted to know the sex. We nodded.

She smiled warmly and said, "It's a boy."

Tears streamed down my face. A boy. I felt pure joy.

She continued the survey, taking picture after picture, running measurements and logging numbers.

And running measurements and logging numbers.

And more measurements and numbers.

Okay, this is taking forever, we thought at each other with a glance. *That's a lot of pictures of his heart. Let's move on now.* Right?

Wrong. My joy turned to fear.

"Is everything okay?" I asked.

"I just need to take a few more pictures," the technician replied.

She handed me a towel and said the doctor would be in shortly to have a look. I was shaking as I wiped the gel off my belly.

She saw something. Something's wrong. She's getting the doctor.

The doctor came into the room, picked up the wand without a word, and started taking more pictures. Of our baby's heart. Only his heart.

I don't know how long he spent taking all those pictures and measurements. All I remember is when he was done, he said, "Let's go across the hall and talk."

I now know that whenever a doctor asks to meet you in another room, or picks up a pen to draw something, you're screwed.

Once we were seated in his office, he said, "I think your baby has critical aortic stenosis, a serious congenital heart defect."

Then came the vocabulary lesson: "Hypoplastic left heart syndrome," also called HLHS. "Fetal echocardiogram." "In utero aortic valvuloplasty." "Possible fetal demise." "Probable three palliative surgeries: the Norwood, the Fontan—and that one in the middle that I can't remember."

He might not have remembered at the time, but we came to know it all too well. Though our son never had "that one in the middle" (the Glenn), we were about to spend the better part of a decade deeply enmeshed in the world of ultra-complex pediatric cardiology.

The way the doctor explained it, our son's aortic valve—which opens and closes to allow blood to flow from the heart and through the body—had narrowed, causing a backup, high pressure, and damage to his left ventricle, the pumping chamber.

Most fetal ultrasounds are done in black and white. However, there's a nifty little switch on the Samsung UGEO you can flip that turns the color on. The color shows the direction of blood flow in the heart. With each beat of the baby's heart it should look like this:

<Beat> = Blue/Red

<Beat> = Blue/Red

<Beat> = Blue/Red

What we saw, however, was:

\<Beat\> = Red/Blue/Red/Blue swish swish

\<Beat\> = swish Blue/Red swish swish Red

\<Beat\> = Blue swish Red/Blue Blue/Red swish

It was surreal. Time froze. Time whizzed by. We had no idea how to feel. We had no idea what to do. We were lost.

Wednesday turned into Friday and an emergency visit to Fetal Cardiology at Mass General Hospital. A pediatric cardiology imaging specialist took about an hour's worth of pictures and video of our son's heart. The idea was to learn what exactly was wrong, what it meant, and what to do about it.

It didn't look good.

They confirmed that his aortic valve was closing and told us that *if* he survived to term, there was a 99 percent chance our son would be born with HLHS, a severe congenital heart defect where essentially the baby is born with half a heart.

We were devastated.

*

Mass General told us to get to Boston Children's Hospital *immediately* to see Dr. Wayne Tworetzky, director of the Fetal Cardiology Program and associate professor of pediatrics at Harvard Medical School. We had never heard of him and had no idea how to pronounce his last name. We could spell it, though. So we looked him up.

The first result that came up on Google was the *New York Times* article "Operation on Fetus's Heart Valve Called a 'Science Fiction' Success."[1] A few years before, Dr. Tworetzky had invented a new surgery to prevent HLHS. The science fiction line was not exactly comforting, but into his office we headed like a clattering train in the dark—not knowing if, on the other side of the pass, there were tracks to safety or a cliff to the abyss.

Friday turned to Monday, 7:30 AM. There we sat for the first time at the Advanced Fetal Care Center in the Farley Building, at the far end of the second floor. For our not-yet-born son, Ari, this was his first visit to Boston Children's Hospital (BCH). We'd like to say that BCH became

Ari's second home, but for long stints it *was* his home—even more than our house in Stow.

It was that morning, for the first time since receiving the diagnosis, we were given hope he could be born with a whole, functional heart.

South African by birth, Dr. Tworetzky has a warm yet intense manner and a winsome smile that says, "I think I'm funny, but I realize most normal people don't"—which, given our own debatable normalness, struck a reassuring note with us. He walked us through the options for treating critical aortic stenosis and evolving HLHS. One option was an experimental in utero fetal balloon valvuloplasty. (Say that three times fast.) As it turned out, we were good candidates for this surgery.

He explained the procedure: they would stick a needle through my belly, into Ari, through his chest cavity, into his heart (which was the size of a grape at the time), and into the valve, which should have been open three millimeters, but was only open one. Once there, they would string a balloon through the needle and inflate it to open the valve. All of this is done with only ultrasound for guidance. Essentially, they're trying to hit the end of a ballpoint pen with a practically microscopic needle while blindfolded. Oh, and the pen is floating in water.

To this day, I admire the doctor's confidence in pulling off this incredibly complicated procedure and the precision and steadiness needed to perform it. (As for me, I can barely hit a foul shot.)

If it worked, we were given a 70 to 80 percent chance Ari would not develop HLHS—meaning they'd be able to save his left ventricle. This would be winning the jackpot. (We were also given a 10 percent chance Ari would not survive the surgery.) While there is a set of three palliative surgeries for HLHS that are done over the course of several years, the outcomes are often challenging, and too often devastating. Even after the surgeries, the five-year survival rate is a not-exactly-reassuring 65 percent.[2]

At the time there had been around one hundred cases (anytime, anywhere) of the in utero surgery, which Dr. Tworetzky himself invented. He and his team had done eighty-nine of them. We were going to be number ninety.

*

On October 11 at 8:45 AM, I steeled myself for surgery. I would have an epidural and be awake during the procedure. When I entered the room, there were upward of thirty-five people standing there, all in scrubs and masks. Shaking uncontrollably, I didn't recognize a single one of them. My nurse-chaperone took one look at my face, turned to the mob, and shouted, "If you don't need to be in this room right now, get out!" Two-thirds did. Still, there were multiple anesthesiologists for me, multiple anesthesiologists for Ari, several interventional cardiologists, imaging doctors, imaging techs, maternal fetal medicine doctors, a Neonatal Intensive Care Unit (NICU) team, nurses, nurse practitioners—oh, and the team of pediatric cardiologists from Texas Children's Hospital learning to do the procedure.

I took a deep breath. They settled me on the bed.

The procedure itself takes only a few seconds. Manipulating my belly and Ari? That took an uncomfortable few hours preceding those few seconds. They had to move Ari into the correct position, make sure I was in the right position, then give Ari anesthesia so he wouldn't move during the procedure.

The day went as well as it could have. The surgery was a "technical success," which means they got in, inflated the balloon in the right spot, and got out with both Ari and me doing okay. As for whether the valve would stay open . . . time would tell.

*

We spent the next four months on a roller coaster with no governor and no safety bar. We visited the Advanced Fetal Care Center every Monday morning for a fetal echo to check on Ari's heart.

One Monday in November, Dr. Tworetzky told us, "The valve is closing again." He continued, "We've seen this happen before, but this valve is closing very quickly, causing more pressure on the ventricle. I think we need to do the surgery again."

Shit.

Mike asked, "Have you ever done it twice?"

"No," he replied. "I'd like to say we've done it time and again. In this case, however, we'll be doing it time. After you, the next case will be again, and then I'll be able to say it." (See what we mean—funny, not funny?) "You sit tight. I'll go find Jim and see what he says." Jim, by the way, was James Lock, the cardiologist-in-chief at Boston Children's Hospital, which had the number-one pediatric cardiology and cardiac surgery program in the world. He's like the Steve Jobs of pediatric cardiology.

(Though, in terms of personality, he was more like a stew of Steve Jobs, George Patton, and Kramer from *Seinfeld*. Fun guy to chat with.)

Dr. T. strolled back in about an hour later and said, "We are set to go for Wednesday. Check in at Brigham and Women's first thing in the morning."

Two days later, the day before Thanksgiving, we went back in. (Big thank you to Auntie Pat for hosting the thirty-five people who were on their way to our now fully renovated house on the lake for turkey and cranberry sauce.)

Again, the surgery was a technical success. However, from there on out, it was far from smooth sailing. There were endless doctor appointments, a tour of the NICU at Brigham and Women's Hospital, a tour of the cardiac ICU at Boston Children's Hospital, and visits with the hospital social workers to prepare us for what life in the hospital would be like after Ari was born.

And worry. So much worry.

We had no idea what would happen once Ari was born. With a baby in utero, the mom does all the cardiac work. As soon as Ari made his grand entrance, the training wheels would come off his heart. He would be put to the test. Would he be born blue? Would he be able to breathe on his own? If his heart worked at all, would it be able to sustain him?

Would he make it?

*

On February 16, 2012, at 12:58 AM, Ari Francis "Danger" Schultz made his big debut. He came out screaming. He was perfect. We all sighed in relief. The delivery team let us snuggle with him for five minutes before whisking him off to the NICU. From there, Mike and a cardiology team escorted him over the bridge that connects Brigham and Women's Hospital to Boston Children's Hospital. Ari would have a few hours to adjust to life on the outside . . . and to prepare for his first surgery in a few hours. No rest for the weary.

In the first seven months of Ari's life, we spent barely five weeks at home with him. He underwent two major open-heart surgeries to replace three of his four heart valves. It was a long road, but we were able to save his left ventricle, giving him whole-heart circulation. Jackpot!

But the game was far from over. What was behind curtain number one could be either a trophy or a bear trap waiting to be tripped—or something in between. Damage had been done in utero to the ventricle we were trying so hard to save. Muscle tissue fought for space with scar tissue. The hope was that as Ari got bigger and stronger, so would his heart. That as he grew, muscle tissue would grow, making the scar tissue insignificant.

That didn't happen.

MIKE

Any parent of a young child will tell you how remarkable and uniquely talented their child is—but there truly was something special about Ari. From the get-go, he was all in. He was a sports savant, born with a golf club in his hand and spikes on his feet.

Baseball, basketball, football, hockey, and golf were Ari's big five, and he was deeply fanatical about all of them. When he picked up a ball, any ball, he knew what to do with it. As first-time parents, we didn't see it as unusual. People would tell us, "Wow, he's really talented!" We just shrugged it off.

We should have known he was off the charts when the dads gathered around him as he drained hoops at the playground *as a one-year-old*.

Just before Ari's third birthday, Make-A-Wish volunteers came by to grant him his wish. When they asked what he wanted, he told them, "I want a basketball court in my backyard." You could see them thinking, "Yeah, right, sure you do, kid." He then proceeded to play basketball in front of them for two hours, calling out, "Paul Pierce for three . . . got it!" and showing them his Dirk Nowitzki moves: "Back to the basket, shake and bake, fall away, and SWISH!"

Ari was a boy on the move, packing action into every minute of his life. Over the course of five and a half years after Ari was born, he spent about 430 nights in the hospital. This meant we (one or both of us together) also spent 430 nights at the hospital.

While we were going through all of this with Ari, it would have been nice to have been able to take a leave of absence from work—even if unpaid—and then pick it up when we got back. We've since learned this isn't how it works for most families, and it sure isn't how it worked for us.

Remember the part about reinventing our business in 2011? Yeah, that meant we needed to keep at it or there wouldn't be any business to get back to.

If we took a leave of absence from the business, the business would have taken a leave of absence from the planet. This would have been a particularly bad time for health insurance to take a leave of absence from our lives. By the time Ari was two, his medical bill topped three million dollars. Not to mention, as we were dealing with Ari's medical challenges and every other craziness in our lives during these years, we also had two more children, Lexi and Eli.

We couldn't lose health insurance. We couldn't let the business fail.

*

Now, lest you think, "What the hell kind of people are they? Their son is in the hospital and they're off somewhere else working on growing their business?" That's not exactly how it went. Lots of days we lived a hot war: all of us gearing up for surgery, Ari waking up from surgery, Ari not doing well, and so on. But there were also quiet days: say, the week after a big surgery when he was still a baby. The doctors would tell us, "He looks good. We're going to keep him sedated and let him rest for the day. You guys take a breather. Nothing is likely to happen for a while."

There we were, on 8 South, the Cardiac Intensive Care Unit (CICU), with a sleeping, recovering, sedated baby boy and sixteen hours to kill at his bedside or down the hall. So . . . get some work done! Right?

Eh, not that easy. For those of you who haven't spent any time in an intensive care unit, it's a combat zone. There's a constant hustle and bustle of visits. Nurses, nurse practitioners, pharmacists, social workers, administrators, clergy of various denominations, doctors of varying types—residents, fellows, attendings, chiefs; then cardiology, cardiac surgery, cardiac intensivists, cardiac interventionists (no, they're not the same), anesthesia, rehabilitation, pain, gastroenterology, nephrology, neurology, psychology, hospital medicine, interventional radiology . . . okay, we'll stop here but it would be easy enough to keep going.

Then there's the constant flow of families—talking, laughing, crying. Beeps: alarms, infusion pumps, reminders, errors, and general use noises. And the phone: calls, messages, emails, social media. Always medical emergencies and codes where the war was happening around us—not *at* us, but still it would shake us to our core.

It never. Ever. Ever. Stopped.

On the bright side, we could work *from* the hospital.

Could we, however, work *at* the hospital? Could we actually get anything done there? Saying cardiac intensive care is a distracting place is like saying the sun is on the warm side.

As far as getting work done went, it wasn't just the hospital environment, it was the environment between our ears and in our hearts. Could we work when our emotions were whipping from devastated to hopeful to afraid to terrified to angry and back to hopeful again—every fifteen minutes?

It was draining. But when things were quietish with Ari, we had no choice. We couldn't just tinker around and get some work done. We had to produce . . . deliver . . . achieve, or our lives would crash and burn in another area. We had one dumpster fire burning in our living room. We didn't think we could handle a second one.

So to work we went: from the bedside, the hallway, the family room, the cafeteria, the lobby. (It was nice of them to let us use the hospital as an office for free, as long as we were "renting" CICU bed space 2 for $10,000 a day between $200,000 surgeries. Very accommodating.)

ERICA

Why do we spend our time doing what we do? How can we get the most out of our time? What's truly important? How do we want to live?

On September 28, 2011, our turning point, we started a new journey that—though we had no idea of it at the time—would lead us to obsess over these questions, as life and death hung in the balance. Many times.

Until this date, we lived rather formulaic lives. We worked hard in school and got good grades. Excelled in sports. Went to good colleges. By all measures we were succeeding. We got married, bought a house, rebuilt it almost from scratch, started a successful business.

We subscribed to the formula:

$$\text{Effort} = \text{Achievement} = \text{Happiness}$$

We made effort. We achieved. But were we happy?

Happyish, we'd say.

But then we got knocked down, again and again. Remember when we worked all day, worked out all night, and did fun things on the weekends? Hah! Us, too. Vaguely.

When Ari was diagnosed, we did everything we could to learn about and understand his condition. We questioned the doctors, talked to other heart parents, and consumed every piece of information we could find. I immersed myself in the therapies that would help him. My days were filled with physical therapy, occupational therapy, feeding therapy, playgroups, and individualized education programs. I thought that if I could learn enough, I could control what was going on and I could control the outcome. After all, that's how everything else in my life had gone. I worked hard and good things happened. I thought I could "effort" through anything. I thought I could save him.

I could not save him.

On July 21, 2017, at just five years, five months, and five days old, Ari died.

The brightest light went dark. When he died, we did too. And when we realized we were still, in fact, alive, we wished we weren't. We didn't understand how he could have gone through so much, and we could have tried so hard, only to fail. This was *not supposed to happen*.

Walking out of that hospital without Ari was one of the hardest things I've ever had to do. We got home and picked his Red Sox shirt up off the living room floor. Silenced the alarm that told us it was time for his 9 PM meds. Closed his copy of *Harry Potter and the Prisoner of Azkaban* on page 213. Forever.

How could we go on? Would we ever feel anything but misery? Stabbing, suffocating, every-moment misery? Would we someday accept that he was gone? Would we ever be able to forgive ourselves? Would we ever stop feeling deep failure, shame, and guilt over his death? Would we be able to show back up for Lexi and Eli?

Would we ever get through this?

At times I didn't want to get through it if it meant having to let go of Ari in any way. Finding joy. Finding happiness. Finding peace. Finding our way back to living life. These weren't even considerations. We fell into a very dark place.

Rediscovery of light in our lives was not a foregone conclusion. For the first year after Ari's death, and a bit beyond, the struggle tore us down. Yet suffering led to a path we did not expect.

Deep down, we knew Ari wouldn't want this for us. He would want us to be happy. He would want us to live—because he had lived each day to the fullest. And then some. He'd want us to fill our days with baseball diamonds, Harry Potter, Luke Skywalker, and eighteen holes. Ari was still our bright light, cutting through our darkness, showing us the way.

And we had a lot to live for. Two amazing children, though they also struggled with the death of their brother and the loss of their house. (Right. Should have mentioned, we found ourselves unexpectedly homeless while living full time at the hospital as Ari fought for his life.) Wonderful family and friends who supported us through incredibly challenging times. A successful business that continued to grow and thrive.

Eventually we found we had purpose.

That purpose includes sharing our story and teaching others what we learned and how we learned it, with the hope that it will make their lives better. And that's why we're writing this book—so you can live better, too. Richer. More successful. More fulfilled. Happier.

Starting ~~not~~ today.

INTRODUCTION:
THE GIFT OF TIME

If you were aware of how precious today
is, you could hardly live through it. Unless
you are aware of how precious it is, you
can hardly be said to be living at all.

—Frederick Buechner

Since Ari died, we've been especially mindful of the gifts he gave us. There are so many gifts. The greatest one was his time. We had five years, five months, and five days with him. We'd give all our tomorrows for one more yesterday with Ari, but we know we can't. We are so incredibly grateful for the time we had. We would not trade any of it—the good times and the struggles—for anything.

Everyone says that time is our most precious gift.

But from what we observe, we're not sure most people know what this actually means. When we were young and had all the time in the world for work and play, we didn't think about time that much. It was only when everything changed that time became precious and scarce.

We knew we needed to change how we spent our time, but we didn't have a guide for how to do that. So we built one.

In ~~Not~~ Today we share a model of how to think about time that, when taken to heart, will transform the way you live. This model is proven not only to help people become more productive and effective; it has helped them to live happier, more satisfied lives.

You might think, *That's kind of an odd intention given how this story began*, but as you read on, we think you'll see how it makes sense. When we had all the time in the world, we were successful and busy, but we weren't necessarily happy. Aware. Present.

When our lives became a constant fire drill, time was at a premium. We had to be very deliberate about how we spent it. We needed to find time for Ari and his medical needs, and our growing family, while staying productive enough to get a new business off the ground.

And we needed to not feel like hell while we were doing it all.

Happy and productive with time at a premium: this was our quest. When we started talking to people about this, we had no idea what kind of chord we were about to strike. Turns out it was a pretty loud one, so we kept striking.

Now, many people think of productivity as working harder, working smarter, and getting more done. But it's not about working harder, it's about working wholeheartedly: working on things that fill you up, that fulfill your purpose, that *mean something important to you.*

It's not about getting more done, it's about choosing what you get done and what you don't. It's about setting boundaries and learning when and how to say no. You may get the same number of things done, but they'll be the right things.

And when it comes to working smarter, that's actually the point. However, as our client at Terrapure Environmental told us, "My entire career I'd been told to work smarter. RAIN Group's Extreme Productivity Challenge training was the first time anyone actually showed me how. The program taught me how to take control of my time and get the most important things done, and also provided me with the tools to make lasting changes that have already contributed to my professional success."

We didn't know what was most important to us, so we didn't know what to do to fill us up. When we woke to the fact that life is indeed short and precious, everything changed. Then we were faced with a fresh challenge: getting into the mindset of continually defining what was important to us so we could remain constant on our journey.

These were hard changes for us to make, and they will be for you, too. But if you aren't willing to do this upfront work, you can try all the productivity tips, tricks, and hacks in the world and just end up feeling drained, like you're still not doing enough. Feeling like you, yourself, aren't enough.

It all begins with TIME. Everything you do, each minute and second of your day, falls into one of the four levels of TIME:

> Level 4: T stands for **Treasured time**. This is time you cherish. Time you hold dear, that fills you up, when you do things you love with people you love.
>
> Level 3: I is for **Investment time**. This is time you spend that generates outsized returns. It's when you work toward your goals and priorities.
>
> Level 2: M is for **Mandatory time**. This is time you spend on things you feel like you must do.
>
> Level 1: E is for **Empty time**. This is time that you waste.

Once you know what's truly important to you, you can start on the path to choosing how you spend your time. You'll be able to take Treasured time to fill you up, spend work time on high-return Investment activities, learn to delegate Mandatory activities, and eliminate the Empty ones. (We like to think: Take Treasured, Increase Investment, Minimize Mandatory, and Eliminate Empty. More on this later in the book, which brings us to our next topic.)

In This Book

When everything hit the fan in 2011, we could barely respond to a single email. Getting almost anything done, literally finding the energy to go to the cafeteria and grab a coffee, felt like a chore.

This brings us to our turning point, the turning point of how we worked and how we lived. It all came down to how we spent our time.

As days turned to weeks, weeks to months, and months to years, we started to figure out the productivity part of the equation. It became an obsession, albeit an obsession of necessity (remember, we needed that health insurance), to figure out how to execute tasks and accomplish objectives in the environment least conducive for anyone to work, and with us in the least-conducive mindset to getting anything done.

Somehow during this time, we:

- built a complete product and service set for our company from scratch
- wrote four books, one of them a *Wall Street Journal* bestseller, published now in seven languages
- joined our top competitors on several prestigious lists of the elite companies in our industry, knocking out some big-name companies in the process
- conducted and published six major research studies
- opened offices in Geneva, London, Mumbai, Sydney, Johannesburg, Toronto, Bogotá, Mexico City, and Seoul.

And welcomed into our family Lexi (in 2013) and Eli (in 2016) while we also lost our home to mold, right down to pulling the foundation out of the ground, and then rebuilt it from the dirt up (in 2017).

During the time Ari was in the hospital, we had to overcome the massive amount of distractions around us. We *needed* to focus. We started yelling, "Focus, Daniel-san!" at each other, but that didn't work, so we tried other things. Some worked, some didn't. Each time something did, we built on what we learned the time before. We also added more techniques (or hacks, as they're frequently called these days) to help us get more done each time we found ourselves living at the hospital again with Ari.

What we didn't expect was, when things were quiet-quiet (like when Ari was playing full holes on championship golf courses at age two; like when he was making friends with Celtics head coach Brad Stevens at age three; like when he was drafted onto a college baseball team at age four ... for real) and we were back at home and working at the office, how much more we would produce and achieve than ever before.

In one of these quiet times, we shared what was now our burgeoning productivity system with some of our colleagues. They wanted to know more, so we wrote it down.

Next thing we knew, some of our colleagues were teaching it to clients in Australia! Then it made its way into some of our training and coaching programs.

Clients started to send us their results, including:

- 200 percent account growth in four months
- 31 percent jump in sales activity
- $100,000,000 (yes, THAT one hundred million) increase in pipeline in ninety days

One client had had two years of down revenue; then, after the training program, revenue was up and the team was beating its plan by 20 percent. Another client—after twenty quarters of lackluster growth—had their best pipeline growth one quarter after the training, and their best quarter ever the quarter after that.

We were onto something.

Over the years, we found that some productivity concepts worked more consistently than others for broad groups of our clients. When that happened, we updated the system.

Then, to further and deepen our research, we began studying the work behaviors of people who were Extremely Productive (The XP) compared to The Rest (those who are not in The XP group). We began our initial analysis after collecting data on 2,377 professionals across industries, geographies, and career stages.

Our goals were to find out:

- what The XP do differently than everyone else
- which habits and hacks, if any, actually *drive* productivity
- whether people who use various productivity habits and hacks are top performers, satisfied with their jobs, and happy

Based on our own experiences and those of our colleagues and clients, we hypothesized that productivity went hand in hand with performance, job satisfaction, and happiness. Would the research bear that out? If so, to what extent?

Through a variety of statistical analysis techniques (e.g., multiple regression, ridge regression, key driver) and through interviews with hundreds of individuals and leaders, we discovered the habits, hacks, and behaviors that drive productivity and separate The XP from everyone else. We found that The XP were not only top performers but reported high levels of job satisfaction and overall happiness in their lives. What thrilled us was that these habits, hacks, and behaviors *can, indeed, be learned.*

By anyone.

In Not *Today*, we share the system to become one of The XP in detail.

As natural skeptics, we're aware that the claims we make—redefining the typical approach to productivity, creating a new model to allocate your time, finding happiness while achieving professionally, accomplishing stretch goals even in exceptionally trying circumstances—may come across as a bit (or a lot) of hyperbole.

We're not the first to write a book promising to help you make great strides in your professional and personal lives, and we won't be the last. However, many of these books are loosely researched at best (or they're based on techniques that may work for the author but may not translate to most readers).

As we've built The Productivity Code, and as we've written this book, we've been careful to be, well . . . careful: to produce a practical guide that is both supported by research and proven in real life.

Our goals for this book are as follows:

1. **Redefine the typical approach to productivity.** We share a new approach to productivity and a new model to manage your time for greatest effectiveness, fulfillment, and happiness.

2. **Share The Productivity Code's 9 Habits.** We explain each habit in detail and how you can integrate them into your life, allowing you to approach your days in a new way.

3. **Make it actionable with how-to tips and a process to get started.** We give you the concrete tips and exercises you need to move in a new direction—one that moves you away from the old formula of procrastination and frustration, and toward a more energetic and meaningful life.

Structurally, the book is broken down as follows: First is an overview of what we've found in our research on productivity with more than 2,300 participants. We'll share and cite various pieces of research throughout the book, but here we outline the meat of what we've found in our primary research.

The next nine chapters provide detail about The Productivity Code's 9 Habits and the hacks and tactics to employ. You'll note that the 9

Habits are grouped into 3 Keys: Manufacture Motivation, Control Your TIME, and Execute in the Zone.

Finally, in Appendix A we'll share a 90-Day Challenge to help you adopt the 9 Habits as part of your daily routine. This chapter will help you make tremendous progress toward achieving your goals and objectives. (If you're interested in seeing the results from our research, with the numbers in depth, check out Appendix B.)

9 Habits That Will Change the Way You Live, Work, and Feel

In the last ten years, more than any other time in our adult lives, we've grown and changed.

Ari was the catalyst. Without Ari we would never have learned . . . understood . . . *felt* so strongly and so forcefully that life is short and time is precious. That it can be filled with joy even in the most severe circumstances. That we could persevere. We also learned that we couldn't do it without support. Without the help of our family, colleagues, friends, and the community, we're not sure we could have made it through the dark night. This is no overstatement. It is with their help we made it through, and we are forever grateful.

It would, however, be an overstatement to say we couldn't have done it without the 9 Habits. We probably could have. It's likely, though, that how we felt, how we feel, and where we are now would be quite different. Maybe we'd have jobs and not be running and growing our own global business. Perhaps we'd live someplace other than on the shore of our beautiful lake, which has been our family home for more than a decade now. And quite possibly we'd be less happy and at least a tad bitter.

The truth is we all experience challenges and adversity in our lives. You have the choice to let it tear you down (we let that happen to us . . .) or to use it as a catalyst for growth and change. Eventually (and with a lot of help) we chose growth. You can too.

With the 9 Habits, we work better and we feel better. We live better. We can't let you borrow our family and friends, but we can give you, fully and freely, The Productivity Code's 9 Habits.

We look forward to sharing them, and a bit more of our story, on the pages that follow.

~~NOT~~ TODAY

---

*I don't always make a to-do list. But
when I do, it's already checked off.*

—The Most Interesting Man in the World

Nobody wants to be unproductive. Nobody wants to procrastinate. Nobody wants to fall short of their goals and see their dreams fade away.

Yet, when many people ask themselves, "Am I ready to stop putting off my future, make a plan, and change?" they all too commonly, if perhaps ever so faintly, deep within their psyches, answer, "Not today."

Why?

Because personal change is disquietingly scary and fantastically challenging. Even the idea of becoming more productive is draining. Since many of us feel drained *already*, it's often all we can do to find the time and energy to get through today's installment of our seemingly never-ending to-do list.

Drained though we are, we power on to power through, against the headwinds of our lives, and it comes to pass: we push, we push, and we push some more. Maybe the needle moves to an extent, but in the process, we find ourselves *exhausted.*

It doesn't, however, need to be like this.

In her ten guideposts for wholehearted living, researcher and author Dr. Brené Brown implores us to "let go of exhaustion as a status symbol and productivity as self-worth."[1] The point is well taken about exhaustion, but we think the conversation about productivity needs to change fundamentally. We all—pundits, researchers, workers, leaders—have overlooked a key piece of the productivity puzzle, one that's right there in the definition:

Productivity. Noun.[2]

I. The state or quality of producing something, especially crops.

2. The effectiveness of productive effort, especially in industry, as measured in terms of the rate of output per unit of input.

Productivity as a business phenomenon bloomed in the 1980s. The popularization of "lean manufacturing" through the Toyota Production System[3] inspired all of us in the workplace to think about the part of productivity that was "measured in terms of the rate of output per unit of input."

In the 1980s and 1990s, productivity was all about management getting the most from machines. Eventually, management lined up in their crosshairs a new type of productivity: human. Well intended as it might have been, this often made people feel treated as if they were themselves machines. For a lot of people, especially when the mandate for their personal productivity came from the bosses on high, it made them feel low.

The pursuit of human productivity is, in fact, noble. Yet too often, the approach has been wrongheaded. Or, perhaps more accurately, wronghearted. Interestingly, the key to unleashing human productivity is right there in the definition. See the part where it says "especially crops"? It's easy to miss, yet it makes all the difference.

Most people do, indeed, miss it, including the majority of human-productivity advice givers. The great body of popular productivity guidance is all about stepping on the gas, yet never about filling the tank. All about yielding fruit, but rarely about planting seeds, and the time and often delicate and careful tending needed for their growth.

Planting the seeds and tending to them the right way, we've learned, produces not only the most impressive productivity, but also durable and sustainable productivity throughout our lives.

In the early years of my (Erica's) career, I worked in a cubicle with a window overlooking a Middlesex Savings Bank and a parking lot. Nothing like seeing the same 1997 Ford Aspire parked there every day. When I daydreamed, I'd see the Aspire and think, "Aspire. Aspire. The Aspire is taunting me again. Aspire . . . but to what?"

I might not have known where I was going, but I was certainly headed there in a hurry. At the office, I wasn't like the other recent college graduates. Each morning I would come in, pour a cup (or three) of coffee, fire up my computer, and start the grind, tuning out the incessant "How was your weekend?" chatter around me. I wasn't interested. I'm a pretty friendly person, but when it came time to work, I leaned in (before leaning in was even a thing). My parents owned a small inn with cottages on Route 1 in Wells, Maine. They rubbed two nickels together and bought it when I was two years old. From my earliest days, I learned that starting the working day meant "time to paint the railings," not "time to chitchat."

Thus, when I arrived at the cottages of my own career, hard at the railings I went. I considered myself highly productive. I pushed projects forward. I handled whatever was thrown at me.

And I succeeded. I climbed the corporate ladder, ran a division of the company, and assembled a team of my own. Mike and I met and we married, bought a house on a lake, and life looked good.

But I felt unfulfilled.

I was judging my success based on external markers, by the gauges of a machine of somebody else's design—one that reported I was well-calibrated, delivering at maximum efficiency. I thought I wanted the powerhouse job, the nice house, the shaggy dog, the Italian holiday. I never, however, stopped to ask myself, *Why? Why are these things important to me? Hang on a minute—are they important to me?*

While I was certainly "productive," my productivity didn't fill me up. I was delivering output, but I wasn't, for myself, bearing the fruit I wanted to bear. And that's what the definition of productivity was missing for me: meaning.

I found my meaning the hard way, ping-ponging about through nightmare episodes of my double-take-inspiring personal story. What

I came to learn is this: I could help others find their meaning without their having to suffer the catastrophes I remarkably survived, and without seeing their lives pass by before they learned what I learned through Ari's devastating loss before my fortieth birthday.

Making Meaning

Sitting in a fluorescent-lit examination room at Massachusetts General Hospital in 2011, we began a journey that would lead us to obsess over one question that we had never explicitly considered:

Why do we spend our time the way we do?

As we started working from the hospital soon thereafter, then from home, with a mostly high-maintenance (sometimes off-the-charts high) special needs child, and then with one infant after another, the hacks and habits we adopted meant we got much more done in what became severely limited time. They helped us when we needed to focus on critical priorities and needed to keep our life-ship afloat through constant distraction and often paralyzing circumstances.

At first these changes were about survival, but then something unexpected happened.

We began to feel better.

The habits and hacks that became The Productivity Code led us to question everything about what we did with our time and why. We looked at other so-called time management systems and found them to be (often overwhelmingly) brimming with tips, hacks, and tactics to be productive from moment to moment. Never did we find much exploration of what we now believe to be essential for truly durable productivity: purpose.

Everything we read was about managing to-do lists, flow-charting your day, color-coding calendars, and filtering out the constant "ding" of alerts and emails. Some of it focused on accomplishing larger objectives versus smaller ones.

Some focused on the *what*, some on the *how*—but when it came to *why*? Silence.

Unless you can tie the actions (the what) and tactics (the how) to what you really want (the why), it feels empty.

Here's what it looks like when you take any one of the three components out of the equation:

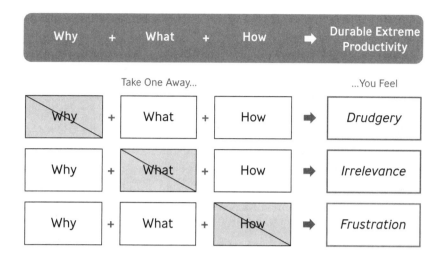

You need all three—the why, what, and how—to achieve any kind of durable productivity.

At least *we* needed it, especially when our lives were flipped ass over teakettle, and then sideways, with such force it would have been a comedy if it wasn't true. The gods of torment granted us no quarter.

Why, though, were we working so hard? We had a short-term *why* (not to lose health insurance and to keep putting food on the table), but we didn't have visibility beyond fending off disaster and making it through each night. Without the long-term *why*, our work accomplishments felt empty.

Happiness, we came to believe, wasn't about achieving something specific. Before we began living our lives in the upside down, before Ari came along and then so often got so sick, we both thought, "Get this job, and I'll be happy. Move to a bigger house, and I'll be happy. Make 10 percent more money, and I'll be happy." You could say we had reasonably achieved all of this and more. None of it filled our souls. Not then. Not now.

It may sound cliché, but even this productivity system didn't fire us up until—right in the middle of making it part of our life rhythm—something remarkable happened. As the pieces of the system came together—before we even had a name for it—we started to feel better. We weren't sure why at the time, but when we realized what had made the difference, everything became clear for us.

The Productivity Code had added meaning to our get-it-done madness. It added the "why" to our "what" and our "how."

It was then that we realized we had to share this system with everyone.

What the Numbers Tell Us

Productivity is a curious thing: it's driven, or hampered, by our mindsets and our habits. A habit, Merriam-Webster's online dictionary says, is "a settled tendency or usual manner of behavior; an acquired mode of behavior that has become nearly or completely involuntary."[4]

Some habits seem innocuous. Kicking off the workday with some watercooler chat, then plowing through emails and other messaging. Keeping our phones on our desks so we can keep an eye out for incoming messages. Catching up on social media—and everything else—in between meetings.

Yet as Annie Dillard says in *The Writing Life*, "How we spend our days is, of course, how we spend our lives." A few minutes here and there add up to hours each week, which add up to days each year. Before we know it, years have rolled by, and we still haven't accomplished the things that matter most to us.

But somehow, we can keep up with Facebook, LinkedIn, and Instagram.

From our own experience, we know that changing our "settled tendencies" made a phenomenal, life-changing difference not only in how much we got done, but how we felt. The days, weeks, and months we spent in the hospital with Ari taught us that even though time is finite, there is always enough time to do the things that matter most.

Was it just us? we wondered. Or was there a broader pattern here? Did other people feel like they got things done, yet it (and we) never felt like enough?

For decades in our business, we had studied what top sellers do to achieve sales success. We learned a lot about how those top sellers lead masterful sales conversations, prospect, and drive account growth. We knew that the right skills drive performance. If you don't have the skills, you won't have the success. But there was something more. Many people do have the skills—and yet they still don't succeed.

As a result of our earlier research, we learned how top sellers *sell*. Now we wanted to know: Do those who achieve—those who get the most done—approach work differently? And is it the same in sales as in other roles, from management to finance to technology, from engineers to entrepreneurs and everyone in between?

If the most productive people do approach work differently, what exactly are their habits, their "settled tendencies"? How are these habits different from everyone else's?

Also, are productive people more likely to be happy people? Are some happier than others because of how they approach productivity? Do extreme productivity, top performance, job satisfaction, and happiness ride up and down together?

And can those who are not yet extremely productive adopt new habits and become extremely productive?

From that kernel of curiosity, we set a team to work on a major global human-productivity research study. We wanted to understand how to help people get the best results from their time and efforts at work—and achieve the highest levels of motivation and accountability. And, dare we say, happiness.

The sample needed to be big enough and broad enough to withstand all the poking and prodding we were going to inflict on it. Over several months our team collected data from 2,377 confidential assessments (as of this writing, now 5,000) from respondents across the Americas, Europe, the Middle East, Africa, and the Asia-Pacific region. The assessment measured thirty-six productivity attributes, behaviors, and habits, and how they affect performance. We continue to use the same assessment tool with our corporate clients as part of 9 Habits of Extreme Productivity workshops and online learning programs (see page 235).

We analyzed the data in multiple demographic slices, including job function (sales versus non-sales), role, industry, annual company revenue, and geographic region. We found that there were no significant differences in productivity by role in an organization, sales versus non-sales, or any position at all. There were slight variations in productivity by geography that could be accounted for by nuances in the survey sample.

In other words, the findings and recommendations in this book are generally applicable regardless of what industry you work in, what your role is, how high up the corporate ladder you are, how large or small a company you work for, whether you are an entrepreneur or student, or where you call home.

Before and after the quantitative portion of the study, we held over 250 conversations with company leaders about the productivity habits and performance of their teams. These conversations enabled us to vet and validate all of the assumptions and quantitative conclusions.

We ran the data through multiple lenses to answer several questions:

- What do The Extremely Productive people do differently than The Rest?
- Which behaviors are correlated with productivity?
- Which behaviors and habits are likely to have the greatest impact on productivity?

And to get the fullest view possible of what productivity could look and feel like in people's lives, we analyzed productivity with regard to job performance, job satisfaction, and overall happiness.

Some of our findings were about as surprising as finding that elite athletes train a lot. Extremely Productive people are very proactive, they write down their goals, and when events derail their day, they bounce back fast. (See? Shocking.)

What we didn't expect was (A) the chasm between Extremely Productive people and the rest of our sample, and (B) how The Extremely Productive exhibit sometimes obvious but hard-to-achieve behaviors as a matter of course. We came up with the groupings we introduced you to in the Introduction: **The XP (Extremely Productive)** and **The Rest.***

The XP rated themselves on the question "I am extremely productive" with 5 out of 5—"very much like me." Self-reported data can, however, be biased. So, with permission, we reviewed performer groups at companies with their management to confirm that those who labeled themselves as top performers and extremely productive compared to their peers were categorized similarly by their managers. It turns out people answered the study questions honestly and accurately.

We also identified a subgroup of The XP who spent very little time during a typical workday on non-value-add activities. They do not waste time. We call these people "**XP TIME Champions.**"

---

* We've spared those of you who don't geek out over data the way we do by putting additional detail about the analysis in Appendix B: Research Note (page 197).

"I am extremely productive."

14% The Extremely Productive (5 out of 5)

86% The Rest (4 or below out of 5) **3%** XP TIME Champions

Reading this book, you might be wondering, "How do I compare to The Rest, The XP, and XP TIME Champions?"

Enter the concept of a Productivity Quotient.

Your **Productivity Quotient** (PQ)* is a score from 36 to 180 that measures how productive you are or your team is, based on the cumulative score of your productivity attributes and habits. The average PQ of all respondents in our sample is 129. The Rest average 126. The XP average 144, and XP TIME Champions average 154.

Productivity Quotients

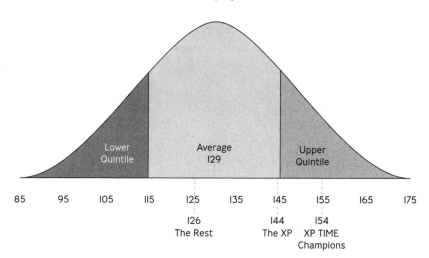

Possible score range is minimum of 36, maximum of 180. If you're looking at an assessment report, 129=72%, 144=80%, 126=70%, 154=86%.

When you take the Extreme Productivity Assessment (see the TIME for Action box at the end of this chapter), you will discover what your PQ is. Be aware that your PQ is a snapshot in time, one you can change and improve by implementing the 9 Habits.

---

* Read more about the Productivity Quotient in Appendix B: Research Note (page 197).

PQ not only correlates to productivity, but also top performance, job satisfaction, and happiness. It's something that we experienced in our own lives, and now this research meant others could experience it, too. We'll cover this more throughout the book, but it warrants repeating: if you approach productivity following The Productivity Code, it's more likely you will perform better in your job, enjoy your job more, and be happier overall.

The Productivity Code

The XP and XP TIME Champions use 3 Keys and 9 Habits to drive durable extreme productivity. The chart below shows how they all fit together. Don't worry about what the details of the habits are just yet, or how to implement them. That's what we cover in the rest of the book.

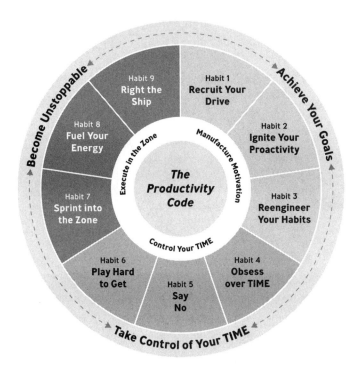

For now, it's enough to note that, big picture, achieving extreme productivity is straightforward. Just 9 Habits.

Productivity Can Be Learned

What is it about The XP that allows them to be so much more productive than The Rest? It turns out that the number-one attribute that most distinguishes The XP is that they have "productive work habits" overall. In fact, The XP are more than five times as likely to have productive work habits than The Rest. Moreover, this is one of The XPs' most frequently exhibited behaviors, with almost two-thirds of them strongly agreeing they have productive work habits.

For the most part, however, productive people are not born this way. They *learn* productive work habits.

Following our 9 Habits of Extreme Productivity training sessions, designed to teach people to adopt productive work habits, we've seen substantial increases in participants' productivity quotients. For example, one recent client team went from an average PQ of 124 to 142. And we typically see dramatic changes to key company success metrics. When it comes to training teams in the system, we are regularly blown away by the "before" and "after" pictures of results.

$100,000,000 Growth in the Sales Pipeline

We worked with a large telecommunications company that had challenges growing its pipeline (sales in process that have yet to close) from one quarter to the next. After several years of minimal pipeline growth, we trained the new business development team in the 9 Habits and ran a 90-Day Extreme Productivity Challenge.

Four months later, the company's weighted average pipeline grew by $100,000,000. Yes, that's a hundred million dollars! The next quarter was their best quarter in twenty quarters.

This example, among many others, demonstrates that productivity can be learned and improved over time with the right guidance.

We also found that The XP are far more likely than The Rest to recover quickly when derailed from being productive. Even the most productive people lose focus every once in a while. The XP, however, recognize when things go off the rails more quickly and can get back on track without delay.

When you become more mindful of your productivity and employ productive habits, you'll have the skills and tools needed to recognize when unproductive behaviors creep back in and be equipped to change them.

Learning about and applying the 9 Habits, however, starts with deep introspection into how we spend our time, and why. Let's get started ...

Not Today. 3 ... 2 ... 1 ... Go!

TIME FOR ACTION

How do you stack up compared to The XP? What's your PQ? Which habits offer the greatest areas of improvement for *you*? Get started by taking the Extreme Productivity Assessment to give yourself a benchmark of where you are today. Go to MyProductivityCode.com/booktools.

A NEW MINDSET
ABOUT TIME

When you change the way you look at
things, the things you look at change.

—Dr. Wayne W. Dyer

Long ago, there was a wise Zen master. People traveled from far and wide to seek his counsel. Many asked him to show them the way to enlightenment. He seldom turned anyone away.

One day, an esteemed scholar came to visit the master. "I have come to ask you to teach me about Zen. Open my mind and show me the way." This scholar was used to being in command, so his manner and voice were forceful.

The Zen master smiled and said they should discuss the matter over a cup of tea. When the tea was brought out, the master poured his visitor a cup. He poured and he poured. The tea rose to the rim and began to spill over the table, onto the floor, and finally splashed onto the scholar's robes. The scholar cried, "Stop! The cup is full already. Can't you see?"

"Exactly," the Zen master replied with a smile. "You are like this cup—so full of your own opinions that nothing more will fit in. Come back to me with an empty cup."

At first, exploring productivity was, for us—and we guess it might be for many people—about getting more things done on top of an already full cup. Tasks flowed like tea from an ever-pouring pot. Our Sisyphean focus was readying our cups to hold as much tea as possible, clear them with alacrity, and make way for more. It worked to an extent, but it wasn't sustainable.

Having studied martial arts from our own wise master, Seirenkai Karate and Jujitsu founder Dan Cohen, for close to a collective thirty years, we had a bit of wisdom to draw from that might just help us change the dynamics of the whole situation.

We were initially focused on the principle of *seiryoku-zenyo*, or maximum efficiency. That was helpful to deal with the flowing tea that we, like everybody else, always seemed to have. What we needed to do was stem the flow entirely and change the substance of the tea itself. So we took a page from both masters' books, became willing to leave behind what we thought we already knew, and adopted *shoshin*, a beginner's mind.

Once we did, the questions all kept coming back to "why." Why are we working so hard? Why are we trying to achieve?

Why do we spend our time the way that we do?

How we spend our time, after all, is how we spend our lives.

TIME Changes Everything

We were pushing to find our path to professional success. Pushing to get a business off the ground as we cared for Ari, and then Lexi and Eli. Pushing ourselves to produce and to become leaders. We had a lot to learn, though, and we learned it all the hard way.

One thing we learned is that existing time management systems focused too much on *seiryoku-zenyo* to get things done, but not *ikigai*, or reason for being.

This needed to change. For everyone. It was time to put *ikigai* in the spotlight. After years of struggling to sort it out, we've come to think of time in the following four levels: Treasured, Investment, Mandatory, and Empty.

Level	Description	Examples	Action
Level 4: Treasured	Time you hold dear	Vacations, hobbies, sports/games, time with family	Take some now, maximize for future
Level 3: Investment	Time that generates outsized return	Starting day with Greatest Impact Activity, working on top priorities	Increase: prioritize, calendar, maximize
Level 2: Mandatory	Time you feel you must spend	Administrative tasks, unimportant correspondence	Minimize/ outsource
Level I: Empty	Time you waste	Aimless web surfing, online shopping, non-work social media, overall procrastination	Eliminate/ minimize

The four levels form an elegant mnemonic: T (Treasured), I (Investment), M (Mandatory), E (Empty). TIME.

Our TIME cups were full of old tea brewed decades before without considering what it all meant or the consequences for our lives. We had to empty them, re-brew the tea, and refill our cups anew if we wanted to feel differently.

At the start, we almost completely stemmed the flow of **Empty time**: time that led us nowhere. Sure, we still value downtime (that's different . . . we all need to recharge), but wasting time couldn't happen anymore for us.

This helped, but it was just the start.

When we still felt like we needed more time to get our business and careers moving where we wanted, we questioned everything we did. We asked ourselves if there was anything else we could cut out.

We began to Obsess over TIME (Habit 4). That's when we learned that some things we *felt like* we needed to do, we didn't actually *need* to do. Either they didn't need to happen at all, or they didn't need to be done by us.

We called this kind of time that felt necessary for us to do, but in reality wasn't necessary, **Mandatory time**. This definition might seem like a paradox . . . time we feel we need to spend, but don't actually? It's not. So much of our nonessential time could be outsourced or minimized—for example, activities such as proofreading and creating PowerPoint presentations. Figuring out what was Mandatory time took effort and questioning of every activity. Sometimes it meant questioning deep-seated beliefs of what we should and shouldn't do. With this questioning and self-reflection, we found a lot more time could be redirected and better used.

It's often here, when the two of us question with someone else whether a chunk of their time is Mandatory or not, that we meet with emotion and stonewalling. Most of the time, if the person is willing to stick with the discussion, the result is some sort of revelation. More on this in Habit 4: Obsess over TIME, but it's enough to note here that after some introspection, most people come to realize that much of the time they *think* they need to spend on certain activities, they actually don't.

Mandatory Versus Investment Time

When you're looking to advance within your organization, you have to closely examine the difference between Mandatory time and Investment time. Taking a tedious task off your boss's plate may feel like Mandatory time, but it's actually Investment time because it can pay off for you. Of course, a step better is taking it off your boss's plate and also finding a way to take it off yours (like automating it), but that may not always be within your control.

Where did we redirect this time? At first, it was to **Investment time**: time that would yield outsized returns. For us, that meant activities such as leading, writing, and recruiting. Investment time is the ultimate goal of most time management systems. However, we still didn't *feel good*. Most systems' ultimate goals are devoted to their concept of Investment time, whatever they chose to name it. Maximizing Investment time wasn't enough for us, and is among the major reasons we felt we needed to create our own system.

Ultimately, we discovered that we needed more of one special kind of time in our cups. More T in our tea. Time in our cups that filled *us* up. Time we held dear. For us, that meant time with our children. Time with each other. Time with friends. Time at the yoga studio and on the golf course. *Ikigai.* **Treasured time.**

The XP Spend Time Differently . . . *Very* Differently

A lot of the time-management literature advises people to focus only on Investment time *now* in order to maximize Treasured time *in the future.* To Treasured time, they say, "Not today." That might work for some people, but we needed Treasured time now. Not today needed to become ~~not~~ today. We knew we needed to maximize our Investment time to fulfill our professional potential and free up even more time for some yet unknown future period. But to fill our hearts and fuel our tanks, we needed to be present in our lives for things other than work and chores.

With all the trials we'd been through, we learned, cliché though it sounds, that life is precious and short. Without healthy doses of Treasured time in our lives, nothing felt quite right. But with Treasured time on our everyday radar, everything else started to fall into place.

In studying the habits of The XP and The Rest, we found that our burgeoning beliefs about time aligned very closely with how The XP behave. When it comes to spending time where it matters most for success and life, XP TIME Champions—that subgroup of The XP who waste practically no time—are the gold standard.

Compared to The Rest, The XP and XP TIME Champions spend, on average, 46 percent and 77 percent more hours per day, respectively, on high-return, value-add Investment time, and 21 percent and 37 percent less time per day on Mandatory and Empty time.

It turns out that all of us could do better, though: nearly half of *all* respondents spend a significant amount of time on activities that either add no value (Mandatory) or outright waste time (Empty) *during a typical workday.*

Yes, during a typical workday.

It makes sense, then, that across the board, all respondents say they have the potential to increase the average time they spend on Investment activities: the XP can increase it by about a quarter. The least productive people can *more than double* their Investment time.

No matter what your productivity levels are right now, there's a meaningful opportunity to improve.

Finally, nearly two-thirds of The XP reported they spend the amount of time they want on Treasured activities, while less than half of The Rest do. We wondered if it might be the opposite, that the most productive people would be focused on more Investment time now so they could take Treasured time later, but this wasn't the case.

Rather, it seems The XP maximize *both* Investment and Treasured time. It's no wonder, then, that they can sustain their productivity. It's not just a time-saving hack here and there. It's life changing. It's durable.

And, indeed, it's learnable.

Manufacturing More Time

The XP report spending nearly six hours per day on Investment activities, compared to less than four hours for The Rest. (In a five-day workweek, that represents about thirty hours on Investment activities for The XP, under twenty hours for The Rest.)

Imagine you're among The Rest and, starting now, you find time to spend nine more hours a week on the activities that get you an outsized return.

Nine more hours for being proactive and driving your priorities.

Nine more hours to lead and inspire.

Nine more hours of studying.

Nine more hours to build a strategy to impress leadership.

Nine more hours of prospecting.

Nine more hours of coaching your team to greatness.

Nine more hours to drive growth in big accounts.

Nine more hours to think big picture.

Nine more hours per week, every week, to make the magic happen. Without working one extra minute.

Manufacturing Time for Your Team

Here's one more for you team leaders out there. Let's say you have a group of one hundred people. That nine more hours? Make that *900 more hours worked on Investment activities each week, every week, to blow the doors off your team's goals.*

It would be like gaining 46 percent more output from your team without adding a single person to your head count. Assuming you follow the principles in the 9 Habits of Extreme Productivity to get there, they will feel like people, not machines; be able to sustain it long term; and be *much more likely to be satisfied with their jobs.*

In fact, The XP are more than twice as likely to be satisfied in their jobs as The Rest.

What does people being "more satisfied in their jobs" mean for an organization? A lot! According to research by the Gallup Organization, the most satisfied employees are the most engaged employees. The link between engaged employees and business results is staggering.

From *Fast Company*: "The most 'engaged' workplaces [. . .] were 50% more likely to have lower turnover, 56% more likely to have higher-than-average customer loyalty, 38% more likely to have above-average productivity, and 27% more likely to report higher profitability."[1]

If you want engaged employees, The Productivity Code is the path.

TIME as a Mindset

TIME. It's an organizing framework for managing how you spend your days, but it's also a mindset.

How you define activities within the framework is deeply personal. It's also dynamic—it changes depending on where you are and what you need in the moment.

For a long time, I (Erica) dreaded making school lunches for the kids. After a long day at work, arriving home at 6 PM to a whirlwind of children hugging, screaming, and hanging off me while I made dinner, cleaned up, picked up toys, bathed everyone, and read "just one more" story (while Mike watched the Celtics and smoked cigars . . . kidding; Mike's a peach and a very involved dad), the last thing I wanted to do was open the refrigerator and start peeling and slicing apples.

That is, until I went through the exercise of defining my goals, examining what's *really* important to me, and finding my why. Among my goals is living a healthy lifestyle for myself and teaching my children to develop healthy eating habits.

Suddenly, making the kids lunches went from feeling like draining, to-do list drudgery at the end of each day, to feeling more like an accomplishment. My lunch-making mindset went from something Mandatory that I had to do, to an Investment in living a healthy lifestyle. I was more motivated, and it made me feel better to be working toward my goal. Netflix could wait.

The next step in my mommy lunch-making journey came months later when I realized *I did not need to be the one making these healthy lunches*. So I asked our babysitter to make them. It turned out she was happy to help. (We'll talk more about this, and some of the mindset hurdles people need to jump in order to change how they spend their Mandatory time, in Habit 4: Obsess over TIME.)

As another example, some days binge-watching *Grey's Anatomy* is exactly what I need to recharge. It's Treasured TIME. However, if I did that every day it wouldn't have the same effect—it wouldn't feel good anymore. The line of demarcation between Treasured and Empty time can be fuzzy. *And it changes.*

When does it change the most? When you examine it.

Accepting the TIME framework, and viewing each day, hour, and minute through this lens, is incredibly powerful. It's transformational.

This is no exaggeration.

Begin to view everything you do through the lens of TIME. Be mindful of how you spend it. Examine your cup to see where you are. Ponder, then plan to fulfill, your *ikigai*. Not only will you find more time for your work priorities, you'll create time *for yourself.*

It's Your Time—N̶o̶t̶ Today

Can I change?

People ask us (and themselves) this question all the time. They tell us they've tried and tried, but it hasn't worked, and they wonder if they should give up and resign themselves to the status quo.

If you're wondering whether it's your time to change, think about this oldie (but goodie):

Q. How many psychologists does it take to change a light bulb?

A. Just one, but the light bulb has to want to change.

In other words, to give yourself the chance of changing, really changing, you have to want it.

Do you want it?

Really want it?

If you do, great. You're starting from the right spot.

＊　　＊　　＊

It's tempting at this point to skip ahead and go straight to the productivity tips we share in later habits. But it's important to begin getting a sense of how you actually spend your time. The TIME for Action exercise below will help you get started. It's also important that you more fully explore what's most important to you. Take some time to find your *why*. In the next chapter, Habit 1: Recruit Your Drive, we'll help you find your purpose and build your *why* as strong as possible. It'll make all the difference. After that, we'll dig in to the *what* and the *how*.

TIME FOR ACTION

If you want to be extremely productive, you first need to understand how you spend your time. You can't answer the question about why you spend your time how you do, until you answer the prerequisite question, "How do I actually spend my time?"

Note that the word *actually* is placed deliberately into the question. How people *think* they spend their time and how they *actually* spend their time are usually different. You'll only find out for real where your time goes when you track it meticulously for a few days. We're going to talk more about why and how to track your time in Habit 4: Obsess over TIME, but you can get started right now.

Print three copies of the time tracker you'll find at MyProductivity Code.com/booktools. Complete it for at least three days to get a realistic picture of how you spend your TIME. (And use a stopwatch and track in real time as your day happens. Most people estimate incorrectly even how they spent their morning if they don't log it until the afternoon.)

Tracking your time in a log might sound mundane, but it's easy enough to do—and it works!

THE PRODUCTIVITY CODE
KEY #1:

MANUFACTURE MOTIVATION

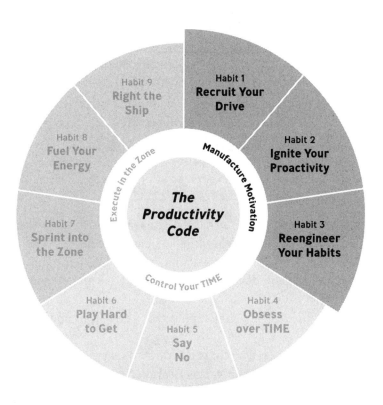

Motivation is often thought of as innate and binary: people either have it or they don't. They're either go-getters or they're not. Self-starters or procrastinators. Proactive or lazy. Even psychologists thought like this until recently.

Motivation and its causes have been hot topics of debate among psychologists for well over a century. In the 1890s, William James made the case that motivation was mostly instinctive.[1] By the 1920s, the instinctive approach was largely shelved when Sigmund Freud suggested that unconscious psychological forces shape our behavior the most. Still, motivation was thought to be essentially out of our control.

Now, not so much.

Starting in the 1960s, research began to indicate that motivation might be *learnable*. It's only been in the 2010s, however, that studies have largely concluded that motivation is less an innate, immutable attribute and more like a skill: something that can be learned, practiced, and strengthened.[2]

Motivation: Internal and external factors that stimulate desire and energy in people to be continually interested and committed to a job, role, or subject, or to make an effort to attain a goal.[3]

In *Talent Is Overrated*, Geoff Colvin answers the "what drives people" question this way: "World-class achievers are driven to improve, but most of them didn't start out that way. Most significant, we've seen that the passion develops, rather than emerging suddenly and fully formed."[4]

"Passion develops." That's phrased as if it happens *to you*, spontaneously.

Our productivity research has motivated us (see how we did that) to think about this differently. Don't think, "Passion develops," think, "Develop passion!" Make the process active. Develop it. Build it. Do it *systematically*.

Indeed, you can manufacture your own motivation. Get organized, and you can literally produce it regardless of how far away from you it might feel at the moment.

Thus, we have the first Key of Extreme Productivity: Manufacture Motivation. In this section, you will get acquainted with the first three of the 9 Habits:

1. Recruit Your Drive
2. Ignite Your Proactivity
3. Reengineer Your Habits

Together, these three habits will enable you to find and turbocharge your motivation.

RECRUIT YOUR DRIVE

THE YEN

If you want to be happy, set a goal that
commands your thoughts, liberates your
energy, and inspires your hopes.

—Andrew Carnegie

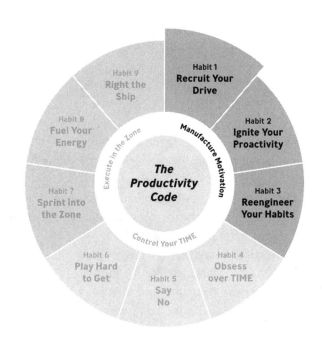

When Ari was twelve weeks old, he had been home only a few weeks from the hospital and was looking the best he ever had. One morning at 6:50 AM, we left Stow for the cardiology clinic at BCH, expecting to get an echocardiogram, some medication adjustments, and a few high fives. The plan: be home by lunch.

We underestimated how early we should leave. Because of heavy Massachusetts Turnpike traffic, we didn't check in at the clinic until two hours later. Now we figured we might not make it home for lunch. We were a little off on that calculation, as well.

We didn't get home for another 120 days.

The logistics of this unplanned four-month BCH camping trip had us spinning. Depending on Ari's health status, one of us would sleep in his room with him on the Cardiac floor or in Cardiac Intensive Care. The other would go home to sleep, then leave the house at 6:20 AM to drive back to the hospital, and head home again around 9 PM. The next day we'd switch.

Ari's health concerns were, of course, paramount. But to say the driving, parking, unexpected 12,000-mile additions to our car leases, and never eating a family meal at home were altogether annoying is pretty accurate.

For Ari, there were (too many) hot bursts of intense, life-threatening ambushes and long weeks of cold sieges. During one of the sieges a few months in, I (Mike) was talking to Sherry, the West Virginia mom of Mighty Mark, a two-year-old whose sieges had been, to this point, longer than ours. I had met her husband, Jack, earlier that day, and later saw Sherry around 8:30 PM at the BCH Au Bon Pain. Jack wasn't there so I asked where he was staying. She said, "Oh, he sleeps in the car. Parking is expensive around here, but it beats the $300-a-night hospital rate we get at the local hotels. For better or worse, right now, he's my Jack-in-a-box."

We never complained about the drive again.

Every time I met a new out-of-town family coming to the hospital, I'd think about Jack, sleeping in the car, for what I learned later was around two hundred nights before Mighty Mark fell.

Fast-forward three years. Ari's home, holding the cardiac-stability line. No ambushes for a year or so. Most evenings after work the two of us made dinner, put the kids to bed, and then poured a glass of wine and turned on *Grey's Anatomy*.* Finally, a lighter-stress, quiet period.

---

* One evening, we turned on *Grey's* only to find Geena Davis as Dr. Nicole Herman, a fictionalized version of Dr. Louise Wilkins-Haug, Erica's OB and one of the lead doctors who performed both fetal surgeries on Ari. Come on, *Grey's Anatomy*, couldn't you give us even a little break?

On one of those evenings I turned to Erica and said, "I wonder who's sleeping in the hospital parking garage right now." We started talking about Sherry, Jack, and Mark, wondering if we could do anything for the families who we knew, right then, were doing the math on how much a hotel would set them back for a night, a week, a month versus sleeping in the car, and how many years it would take them to dig out of the financial hole once they resumed their at-home lives.

While we, you know, watched TV and drank wine in the living room by the fire.

Shortly after, we reached out to the Ethan M. Lindberg Foundation, a charity that at the time funded an apartment within walking distance from the hospital for families who need to travel to Boston to get cardiac care for their children, to see if they were interested in us hosting, running, and fundraising for them through a yet-unplanned, yet-unnamed golf tournament.

A charity golf tournament and fundraising . . . things we knew nothing about.

A week later, we picked a golf course and delivered a down-payment check. Full-time jobs running a business now just starting to go global? Managing Ari and two-year-old baby Lexi? Didn't seem like much compared to sleeping in cars and fighting for your child's life at the hospital.

A week after we plunked down the cash to hold the course, we learned that baby Schultz number three was on the way, due one month before the tournament. And Erica was the event operations leader. Yikes! Still, we charged forward. I mean, what could possibly go wrong?

We scheduled "Ari's Tournament" for September 10, 2016, and went to work. By midsummer we had thirty sponsors lined up, sixty volunteers, more than one hundred golfers, and a few hundred people for the dinner, programming, and auction.

Two months before tee-off, in the middle of the tournament-organizing frenzy, Ari was diagnosed with congestive heart failure. This sucker punch completely blindsided us. He needed a heart transplant, and we didn't know if he would qualify for one. It would take the better part of a month of appointments and invasive inpatient testing to find out if he was even a candidate.

We almost canceled the tournament. Ari was our priority. We didn't think we had the mental bandwidth for anything else. But when we talked to Ari about it, he was crestfallen there was even a chance he wouldn't be able to play in his own golf tournament. Then he asked us, "If we don't have the tournament, how will we help Jack get out of the box?"

No canceling now.

What Is Your Yen?

Mike's dad, whom everyone calls Zayde, has sometimes quipped, "If you have the yen, buy a Yamaha!" Sure, get it? The yen is money. But the wit is in the double meaning: *yen* also means longing or yearning. Yen is a nice blend of feeling-inspired motivation. Inspiration that moves you to action.

In other words, drive.

For us, we were driven to move forward with the golf tournament, inspired by the hospital families and Ari. At other times in our lives, however, we've felt virtually incapable of mobilizing to do anything.

Have you ever felt like you're not driven? Or been told (shamed?) by others that you are not driven? Are you fated to being a couch potato for the rest of your life? Not necessarily. More to the point, not if you don't want to be. What you did (or didn't do) a year ago, a week ago, or a minute ago is old news. Yesterday is not today. You can manufacture your own motivation. Drive is in there somewhere. You can recruit it, mobilize it, and bring it forth—if you know how.

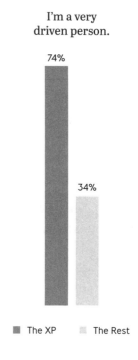

Let's look at The Extremely Productive (The XP) for clues. The XP are more than twice as likely to be very driven compared to The Rest. They agree with the statement "I am a very driven person"—one of the components that makes up Habit 1: Recruit Your Drive, which is positively correlated with productivity, AND a key driver of productivity. It's also among the widest percentage-point differences between The XP and The Rest.

The XP largely weren't born driven. Either their passion develops on its own, as Colvin said, or, as we've seen, they adopt certain habits to *develop passion*. They recruit their drive. Take a look at the research findings, and the corresponding hacks, of Recruit Your Drive when comparing The XP and The Rest:

Research Findings	Motivation and Productivity Hack
The XP are much more likely (40% vs. 12%) to have written goals.	Choose Your New Reality
The XP are much more likely (49% vs. 17%) to plan priorities and work activities weekly.	Plan Actions Weekly
The XP are much more likely (76% vs. 34%) to hold themselves accountable for what they told themselves they were going to do.	Track Progress Weekly

Here we can see the power of drive and the hacks that go with it.

1. Choose Your New Reality (written goals): Helps you define *what you want* because of *your why*.

2. Plan Actions Weekly: Helps you *know clearly what to do* and *what not to do* at any given time. So your *drive knows where to point*.

3. Track Progress Weekly: Helps you, for yourself and with other people, strengthen your emotional commitment to *doing what you committed to do each week*.

Figuring out what you want long term and clearly seeing the short-term path to reaching that destination, combined with increasing your commitment to take action, are, we've learned, exceptionally motivating when done together.

Moreover, our research found that being driven is the number-two most frequently exhibited productivity attribute of the happiest people. This is important to note because some people who are described as driven are also sometimes labeled as unhappy workaholics. In fact, if you recruit your drive and apply it the right way, happiness tends to go with it.

Here's how you can put the three hacks together to recruit your drive:

I. Choose Your New Reality

Don't you hate when it feels like you *have to do something* versus *choosing to do it*? Like going to the gym because your doctor told you to lose weight instead of choosing to move your body for your own sense of well-being? Slogging through a task that someone else decides you should do, or doing something that feels mandatory, is deflating.

Often this is because what you're doing doesn't feel *personally meaningful*. It's not connected to *ikigai*; it doesn't feel like what you're doing will get you where you want to go. Even if it will, if you perceive the task as part of someone else's agenda, you don't have psychological ownership over it. It's their task, not yours, so the odds you will attack it with passion, intensity, and consistency are predictably low.

There are two parts to Choosing Your New Reality: the choice itself and the New Reality. Choice alone is crucial to revving up drive. In fact, an analysis of forty-one different studies on the effect of choice on motivation found that "choice enhanced intrinsic motivation, task performance, and perceived competence."[1]

In one of our favorite studies, Columbia Business School professor Sheena Iyengar concluded choice plays a significant role in motivation and performance. Iyengar explains, "We often think that the act of choosing is just picking—which one of these soda pops do I want, etc. But that's not really where the real power of choice comes from. The real power of choice comes from understanding what your needs are, and creating the meaningful option."[2]

If you want to make work meaningful to you, you need to choose something specific: your **New Reality**. A New Reality is the place you'll be when things change for the better. It's your desired future state. It's your measurable change in status.

It's what your needs are. For your life.

It's the *what your life will look like* and *where you will be* that align with, support, and help you pursue *your why*.

Your New Reality can also be short or medium term. It's simply a way to view the status quo and ask yourself, "Do I want this *to be different*?"

If you're happy with the status quo, any status quo, you don't need to do anything differently. If you want to be in a different place from where you are now (and if you're reading this book, that's most likely true, either for yourself, your family, or your work team), you need to define that different place clearly.

To help you think about your New Reality, use our New Reality exercise at MyProductivityCode.com/booktools.

Here's what your New Reality might look like in the straightforward context of Extreme Productivity:

	Current State	New Reality
Motivation	• Lack of motivation • Reactive • Procrastination	• Maximum self-started motivation • Major switch from reactive to proactive • Less procrastination, more action
Focus	• Unsure of what to work on • Scattered, too many priorities • Constant and ever-increasing distraction	• Always clear on Greatest Impact Activities (GIA)* • Few priorities tackled with obsessed focus • Distraction systematically eliminated
Execution	• Unproductive habits, massive wasted time • Rarely in the zone on important activities • Lack of accountability	• Productive habits minimize wasted time • Achieve maximum output per work hour • Major increase in accountability

Once you've defined your New Reality for productivity or your life, team, business, career, family—anything—write it down. The simple act of writing your goals is significant and powerful. Our colleague John Doerr, the estimable cofounder of RAIN Group, has seen its effect in the 9 Habits of Extreme Productivity workshops he runs. "Most people don't tend to reflect on their big-picture goals. When they do, it usually triggers a very emotional response," he says. "The sad truth is

---

* We introduce Greatest Impact Activity, or GIA, as part of Habit 2: Ignite Your Proactivity.

that maybe 97 percent of us don't think about our goals, we just drift along day to day. Then you get to a point where you wonder, what's it all about?"

John recalls one participant whose revelations led her to a dramatic shift in her personal as well as professional life:

> We were working through the Big Picture Goals exercise during our workshop. This is often a struggle for most people, but all seemed to be going well. That's when I noticed one woman staring at her paper with tears in her eyes. I walked over, sat down next to her, and asked if I could help in any way. She answered, "I have never done this before, and all my personal stuff is getting in the way. I just don't know where to begin." I suggested she could begin anywhere as these were her goals and hers alone. I also suggested she take a break and come back to the exercise when she was ready.
>
> Later in the workshop, I checked in to see how she was doing. "I just started to write, and the words flowed out rather quickly. I have never truly seen what I wanted for me on a page. Thank you."
>
> I never asked what the personal stuff was as that was beyond my purview, but I did check in weeks later to discover she had made great strides in her sales activities and success.

Too many people think that the next thing—the promotion, the new job, the dramatic weight loss—is what will make them happy. Instead, ask yourself, "What can I do today that will help me feel better?" Do that and you can make the journey itself more fulfilling, rather than putting too much stock in everything changing someday because you've reached some targeted destination.

In any case, if you want to feel better, fulfill your *ikigai*, and start to enjoy the journey more, writing down your goals will help you get there. Writing helps you clarify. Writing helps you think. Writing helps you feel.

It's not surprising, then, that The XP are more than three times likelier than The Rest to have written goals. In fact, having written goals is a key driver of Extreme Productivity.

I have clearly defined,
written goals.*

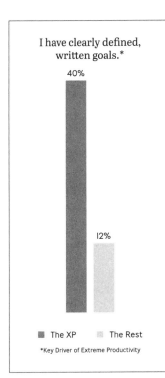

40%

12%

The XP The Rest

*Key Driver of Extreme Productivity

Goals Framework

As you think about your goals, use this three-part framework as a guide. (See the end of the chapter for a link to our Goal Setting Worksheet.)

1. **Big Picture Goal:** Where you're ultimately heading.
2. **Three-Year Goals:** What it looks like when it's not that far off from now, yet you've made great strides toward your Big Picture Goal.
3. **Annual Goals:** What you need to accomplish *this year* to make a dent in your three-year goals.

For years, I (Mike) struggled to articulate what my Big Picture Goal was. I just couldn't figure it out. What was it I wanted out of life?

The charity golf tournament sparked a change in all that. From the funds we raised, the Ethan M. Lindberg Foundation was able to rent a second apartment for families coming to Boston for their children's cardiology care. Is this what I wanted? To do charity work?

I wrote in the Big Picture Goal part of my Extreme Productivity Planner, "I want to be a full-time philanthropist." I thought about that, then I added the *why*: "I'm working hard to build my company and to make enough money that someday I can spend the majority of my time raising money for charity and giving my own money away so I can make a difference in the lives of others."

I didn't tell anyone about it for months. This was for me. In a way, I was trying it on like a pair of sneakers; I wore it for a while and decided it fit. That's my goal, and I'm working my way to get there. Don't get me wrong, I know I need to take Treasured TIME now and work on charity pursuits n̶o̶t̶ today, but this is my motivation to dive into work whole-heartedly at 5 ᴀᴍ.

As Friedrich Nietzsche wrote, "Those who have a 'why' to live can bear with almost any 'how'."

What's your New Reality? What's your *why*?

You want more money, a promotion, a bigger house . . . why? Why do you want these things? Until you answer, the pursuits will feel empty. When you get something like the money, promotion, house, or whatever, it feels great for a little while, then the excitement fades away and you're still left with yourself and your feelings.

Why do you want the money? To feel fulfilled? To be able to provide your children an education so they have a few breaks that you didn't? To make a difference in the lives of others? To be beholden to no one for how you spend your time? To relax, take vacations, and enjoy being present while you explore the world? Or the golf course . . . every inch of it?

Figure out your *why*. Choose your New Reality and a whole new world will open up for you. Both the journey and the destination will be more meaningful.

2. Plan Actions Weekly

In July 2016, in the midst of planning the golf tournament, we thought Ari was doing well. After three open-heart surgeries in the first three years of his life, he'd gone a year and a half with no hospital overnights or interventions. He was thriving. Obsessed with sports . . . and we mean obsessed. He could name the entire lineup of the Boston Red Sox. He met and spent time with the Boston Celtics. He could hit a golf ball eighty yards and play eighteen holes on a championship golf course.

I (Erica) remember the morning of his annual big checkup and heart catheterization. A cath is an invasive procedure that gives the cardiologists a good look at the heart and allows them to measure cardiac function. The chief cardiologist at BCH stopped by to visit Ari before the procedure. He took one look at Ari as he ran up and down the hallways, Gronk-spiking his football, and said, "This kid is too healthy. He doesn't need a cath—just look at him."

The barber himself just said Ari didn't need a haircut. We breathed a sigh of relief.

Still, into the cath lab he went. Around 11 AM, after Ari's cath was complete, Dr. Tworetzky came out. I will never forget the way he looked at us and said, "Let's go in the conference room to talk."

We were screwed.

"Ari is in heart failure. It's time to talk to the transplant team," Dr. Tworetzky said.

These were the exact words we had feared hearing since his diagnosis in utero. We always knew transplant might be something we'd have to consider, but we were hoping to avoid it. A heart transplant is not a fix. You're essentially trading one heart disease for another. It requires lifelong immune-suppressant medications, including steroids—upward of two dozen different medications taken at multiple times during the day and biweekly clinic visits with infusions. Then there are the health challenges and risks. Rejection, infection, post-transplant lymphoma, coronary artery disease, stomach issues, medication side effects, kidney problems, and the list goes on. We knew transplant was a hard road, but now our backs were against the wall.

The doctors were in disbelief. We were in disbelief. No one could understand how he could look so good on the outside and be so sick on the inside. This picture did not add up. But with Ari, nothing ever added up medically.

We spent the most of the last ten months of Ari's life in the hospital with him, waiting for a heart, getting a heart, and standing by helplessly as his body rejected it.

Meanwhile we had three-year-old Lexi and newborn Eli at home, a business that required our leadership and attention, and a one-hour-plus commute each way to and from the hospital.

Most of the time in the hospital we were just waiting. While there each day, I had a small, one-hour window during Ari's afternoon rest time when I could focus on work. I would hole myself up in the back corner of his room, turn my computer on, and try to get stuff done.

The first few weeks were a disaster. My nerves were frayed by, well, everything. I would spend the first forty-five minutes responding to emails and text messages, reviewing and approving materials, reading the hundreds of social media messages from people asking how we were doing, and responding to whatever came across my screen. By the time I started in on what I actually needed to get done, my hour was up.

Ooof. Day after day and *nothing impactful* done.

I realized I needed to change my plan for this hour. I was already in the habit of planning my annual goals and quarterly priorities. What I needed to do was break these down into monthly objectives and a weekly plan. I identified a few activities that were aligned with my quarterly priorities, and set to work on them one by one.

It made all the difference. Instead of spending the first forty-five minutes thinking about what I needed to do and responding to everyone else, I was now spending the entire hour dedicated to the activities that would make the biggest difference.

Then I took it a step further. I started sharing my weekly plan with Mike. Together we would review what I was working on, then challenge each other to determine if these really were the most important tasks.

My motivation, my drive, my productivity, and my outlook on both work and life began to change. Despite everything that was painful in our lives, I was making a difference and feeling good about it. It was a small win, but a small win that I very much needed. Instead of focusing on all the things I wasn't getting to and being frustrated with myself, I was proud of all I was accomplishing, even in a war zone.

Little did I know at the time, the research bears out the motivating power of having clear short-term action plans. For example, a study published in the *Harvard Business Review* focused on what most motivates salespeople.[3] Researchers analyzed four factors:

1. Intrinsic factors: Whether people came to the job naturally highly motivated

2. Compensation and incentives: How people were paid, and how much

3. Management: Whether supervisors could fire up their teams

4. Task clarity: Whether people knew very specifically what to do with their time

Which was most motivating? Turns out it's 4: task clarity. Make the task clear (such as in a weekly action plan), and you'll be well on your way to Recruiting Your Drive.

Which brings us to our second hack in Habit 1, Plan Actions Weekly. Here's how:

This Is Your Four-Three-Four Plan

Once you know where you want to go, you need a road map.

In the previous hack (Choose Your New Reality), you set up your longer-term goals. Now the idea is to break down your annual goals into manageable chunks to make a plan to get there. Think four-three-four. (More on that below.)

As you think about your goals and priorities, consider what's truly important to you. What do you want? We think about priorities in four dimensions:

- Family and friends: relationships that are important to you
- Health: physical, mental, and spiritual
- Community: your local community, as well as any groups you're a part of, secular or religious (for us, this includes heart and bereavement groups).
- Work/career

Your goals may fall into any of these dimensions, or a completely different one.* Your priorities are the action-oriented activities within each of these that will help you reach your goals.

For each dimension in which you have priorities, **bold** your top priority in that category. That way you'll know your overall top priorities.

For example, one of my family goals is to be present with my children. This is a written goal in my planner, but not a quarterly priority because I'm not currently taking action on it. It is there as a reminder to continue a practice I already have in place. Another family goal is to invest in my relationship with Mike. One thing we have changed recently is to have a standing date night every Wednesday. This required change, time, money, and activation energy. It's worth it, and we did it, but we didn't do it until we prioritized it.

---

* If these aren't the right dimensions for you, or one isn't relevant, change them. These are what work for us. The idea is to get granular on what is truly important to you.

How Many Priorities Is Too Many?

Too often, advice givers say things like, "Make sure it's only three, or less than five, or just one." How many priorities should you have at any given time? In general, the fewer the priorities, the higher the likelihood you'll achieve them.[4] However, it's not so much a matter of limiting your priorities to a specific number as much as it is assessing each and determining what it will require from you to tackle them individually. Then, look at them as a whole and ask yourself, "Can I do all of these to the level I want?" Instead of thinking in terms of absolute numbers, consider:

- How much time will it take? (For example, "It will take X nights and weekends to finish renovating the basement.")
- How big of a change is this? (For example, "being more present with my children" may be a small change or a big change for different people.)
- How uncertain is the outcome? (For example, "I need to make this merger work, and need to keep having conversations, driving communication and clarity to make sure it comes together, and I don't know when I'll be finished until it either works or falls apart.")
- How much emotional energy will this take? (For example, if one of your priorities is "finalize the divorce," it's likely to take a ton of mental energy, and adding a variety of other priorities requiring mental energy right now probably isn't a good idea.)
- What resources will this take? (For example, a family priority like "take the kids to Disney" might require additional savings, or a work priority might mean additional Investment time or staff and related expenditures.)

The answers will help you see when you have the right amount. This usually plays out such that when people look at these together, and ask the questions, they say, "That's too many," and then pare the list down.

You'll find that your priorities shift and change. When we were running the charity golf tournament, involvement in the heart community was a high priority. When Ari was in the hospital, family priorities took precedence. At any given time, your priorities may be more heavily weighted in one dimension, and that's okay.

I often have four to five work priorities and one to two priorities in each of the other dimensions (with one top priority **bolded** in each dimension). However, a friend of mine often has only one work priority at any point in time, given the nature of her work and her other priorities.

Again, the actual number is less important than assessing the factors just noted and understanding for yourself what you should and shouldn't take on.

Here's how you can use the four-three-four process:

STEP 1: Divide the year by *four*—into quarters—and focus on the current quarter only. Add your priorities for the current quarter that will put you on the path to reach your annual goals. Keep lists for your goals and priorities based on the dimensions important to you. Ideally, you want as few priorities as possible. One of these priorities in each dimension should rise to the top as being the most important. On your plan, make your top priorities **bold**.

Your quarterly priorities are the linchpin that binds your goals framework together, bridging the gap between the long-term goals and the short-term actions you're going to take right now to achieve them. The ninety-day time frame is great because, when you set your mind to it, it's enough time to get amazing things done. It's also virtually immediate: the end date is not so far off that it seems like it'll take forever to get there.

Once you've written them down, ask, "What will it take to achieve my quarterly priorities?"

STEP 2: Divide the quarter by *three*—into months—and focus on the current month only. Review your quarterly priorities and define the important activities you need to tackle this month to achieve them. Keep in mind that you might not be able to focus on all your quarterly priorities this month. Focus on as few priorities each month as possible.

STEP 3: Divide the month by *four*—into weeks—and focus on the current week. Define for this week only what you need to do to put yourself on the path to reaching your monthly objectives—this is your

Investment time. Make it part of your routine to plan the week ahead
and review the week that just ended. For example, at 3 PM every Friday
afternoon, look at your plan for last week and grade yourself on how you
did with your priorities. Then write your plan for the week to come, and
share it with your accountability partner (more on that in the next section). It might look something like this:

Pat,

   Here are my priorities for the previous and upcoming weeks.

   Last week priorities:

   Grade: B, travel delay interrupted my week.

- *GIA: Conference and follow-up: The conference was good
  and I made some solid connections. Follow-up has not happened in a timely manner due to travel, so I knocked myself
  down a grade*
- *Pipeline movement: Move ACME to contracting: Done,
  other movement in pipeline is encouraging but not enough.
  Knocked myself down a grade here, need to do a round of
  follow-up*
- *Sprint for 2 hours of prospecting M-Thurs: Done, secured 3
  new meetings*

   This week priorities:

- *GIA: Conference follow-up: 35 personalized prospecting
  emails and calls*
- *Close ACME*
- *Account growth plan for Alpha Manufacturing*
- *Win Lab for ABC Co. and push forward*
- *Round of follow-up on all pipeline opportunities*

   Jordan

   The four-three-four plan worked for us in the hospital when we
needed a solid structure for our few hours of uninterrupted work time.
It will work for you, too, no matter what your circumstances.

Goals make work meaningful!
• More likely to be pursued
• Guide action
• Make you happy

We studied the four-three-four process and learned the strongest productivity boost is when you set a clear weekly action plan. The XP are almost three times more likely than The Rest to plan weekly actions. Fifteen minutes for planning the week is all most people need to help them get specific about their greatest-impact activities and fast-track achieving their goals.

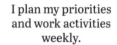

I plan my priorities and work activities weekly.

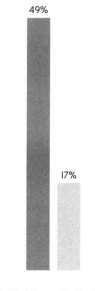

49%

17%

■ The XP   ▨ The Rest

As you go about your day, keep your quarterly priorities, monthly objectives, and weekly plan in a place where you'll see them regularly. You could put them at the top of your to-do list, print them out and post them on your wall, write them out in your planner, put them on a whiteboard—however you want to do it. Just make them visible.

One of our colleagues encouraged her high schooler to navigate the college admission process using weekly action plans and progress tracking. And what do you know—it worked. No more "Mom, stop nagging me!" from a student now matriculated at his top-choice university.

Four-three-four works as well at the office as at home. If you're a manager or leader, help your team develop weekly action plans. When you review them, guide your team members out of their comfort zones. Challenge them to focus only on what's most important. Then work with them to track progress weekly.

You might think, "Got it. Tracking progress will help me keep myself/my team/my child accountable." Yes, but it's more than that (and better)—tracking progress, itself, is motivating!

3. Track Progress Weekly

Accountability can get a bum rap if it's micromanage-y—for example, telling your team exactly what and how to do something and watching over them until it's done—but it doesn't have to be that way. Accountability should be a force for good and a powerful motivator. It's all about taking responsibility for your actions.

The importance of accountability can't be overstated. It is the most common behavior that The XP exhibit, and the number-one key driver of Extreme Productivity. The XP are much more likely to say that the statement "I hold myself accountable for doing what I tell myself I'm going to do" is "very much like me."

Accountability also represents the second-largest whole-percentage-point difference between The XP and The Rest. The XP are 2.2 times (76 percent versus 34 percent) more likely to hold themselves accountable and 3.4 times (44 percent versus 13 percent) more likely to track their progress weekly.

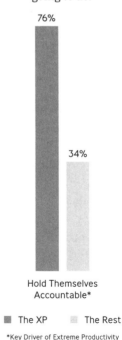

I hold myself accountable for doing what I tell myself I'm going to do.

Hold Themselves Accountable*

■ The XP   ▨ The Rest

*Key Driver of Extreme Productivity

Track Progress Weekly to Get Motivated

The act of writing your commitments and sharing them with others bolsters a sense of progress, so it is both motivating and drives accountability. We're not the only ones who found this. For their book *The Progress Principle*, Teresa Amabile and Steven Kramer surveyed more than six hundred managers and asked them to rank the impact of the following factors on employee motivation:[5]

1. Incentives

2. Clear goals

3. Interpersonal support

4. Recognition

5. Support for making progress

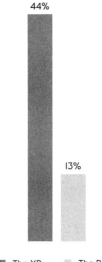

I track my progress weekly.

Managers most often guessed recognition was most important. They were wrong. In fact, support for making progress was the most motivating factor. As the authors wrote, "When workers sense they are making headway, their drive to succeed is at its peak."

In another study, researchers at Dominican University studied short-term goal achievement in the workplace.[6] Participants were split into five groups, each tasked with thinking about goals, writing their goals, writing action commitments, sharing both goals and action commitments with a friend, or providing a weekly progress report to a friend. More than 70 percent of the participants who sent weekly updates to a friend reported successful goal achievement, compared to 35 percent of those who kept their goals to themselves.

You can have a formal accountability relationship (such as with a manager) or seek out an accountability partner—someone you can check in with to share your upcoming weekly plan and review the previous week's plan. This can be a colleague, friend, family member, spouse, anyone.

If you follow our process, you'll already be creating and grading weekly plans. It takes only thirty seconds to send this via email to your accountability partner. As we mentioned in the previous hacks, create a set time for sharing (e.g., Friday at 3 PM), and calendar this time (more on the power of calendaring time in Habit 2).

Simply by sharing and reporting on weekly targets with someone, you're much more likely to take action and feel good about it. What's more motivating than that?

According to our research and others, not much.

*   *   *

Follow the TIME for Action steps listed at the end of this chapter to put yourself on the path to finding your purpose (your *why*) and figuring out what you must do to achieve your goals. In the next chapter, Habit 2: Ignite Your Proactivity, you'll learn how to get started on your most important activities, even when they're hard.

TIME FOR ACTION

Go to MyProductivityCode.com/booktools to download our Productivity Code Planner. You'll find a five-step process for creating a goal and action plan, complete with a goal-setting and action-planning template. This template will help you to:

- **Choose Your New Reality:** Fill out the goals section of the Productivity Code Planner. Struggle with them if you must and complete what you can. Just start writing. If you need help thinking them through, find a coach to talk to you about it.
- **Plan Actions Weekly:** Continue with the Productivity Code Planner, breaking down annual goals to quarterly, then weekly priorities. If you are not sure from a work perspective what to do, talk to your supervisor or someone you trust to help you think it through.
- **Track Progress Weekly:** Find an accountability partner, set a time (a recurring calendared meeting is best) each week to share your plan for the next week, and grade yourself on the previous week. Reach out to someone right now and ask them if they'll be your accountability partner.

IGNITE YOUR PROACTIVITY

THE SPARK

A journey of a thousand miles
begins with a single step.

—Laozi

W aiting for a transplant involves . . . waiting. A lot of waiting.

In the winter of Ari's wait, he was living full time on the eighth floor at BCH, relatively stable. We spent our time playing cards, reading Harry Potter, doing puzzles, playing board games and PS4, riding bikes through the lobby, transforming the hospital halls into hockey rinks and baseball diamonds, and reading all the countries on the massive map on the wall of the BCH Center for Families.

Erica would spend every morning at home with Lexi and baby Eli, then come to the hospital for the rest of the day with Ari and me (Mike), returning home in the dark of each evening. Her main focus was on being a mom in two locations every day to our three kids. Mine was keeping our business running while spending eighteen-hour days hanging out with Ari at the hospital. (And seeing Lexi and Eli as often as I could. But given that Eli was breastfeeding, he was happier than I was that Erica was home for him in the middle of the night.)

As the days wore on, quieted, and slowed, I had a conversation with my dad, Zayde, that proved to be the spark I needed to start shifting my focus onto work. He wanted to know how we were going to juggle time with Ari, our other two kids, and work (which we still needed to stay on top of if we wanted to keep that health insurance active).

"You could be waiting at the hospital for a year," he pointed out.

"I know. And I have to power through and keep the business going from here, no matter what," I said. "Erica is going to be mostly looking after Lexi and Eli, but we can't have both of us out of work."

I rubbed my eyes. "I need to figure out how to keep things together since this is open-ended. You're right, we have no idea how long we'll be waiting."

"What do you need?" he asked. (Ah, one of the toughest questions ever. If only we all knew what we needed and could ask for it.)

At least I had a start: "Well, I'm sure we'll do weekends at the hospital with the whole family when Ari is well enough, but on the weekdays, I need breaks during the day where I can try to get some work done." I added, "Then, when I actually have windows of work time, I need to figure out how stop wandering the halls here aimlessly, and, instead, get right to what I need to do."

"I can help with the first part of that," Zayde said.

"Which days can you come?"

"All of them," he replied. All of them.

Dad opened the door. The rest was up to me.

The Productivity Killer

Our minds are cognitive misers. Psychologists find that our brains take the path of least resistance between options.[1] We think and solve problems the easiest way possible, even if it's not the best way, rather than calling up our more sophisticated brain circuitry. The tendency is to choose fast over good. Ease over resistance. The path of resistance, however, is often the path that will yield the greatest return. Think studying versus watching TV.

What's the most difficult aspect of taking paths of mental resistance? Is it staying on the journey of a thousand miles? No, it's taking the first step. Getting started. Being proactive. If you put off proactivity when the option is available to you, that's procrastination. Proactivity drives productivity. Procrastination kills it.

Lest you think you're the lonely procrastination offender, you're not. Everyone procrastinates sometimes; in fact, 20 percent of people are chronic procrastinators, not starting things when we should or want to. (These folks even have a name among researchers: procs.[2]) The challenge of getting through procrastination is finding activation energy. It requires a lot of energy to get started on anything.

By the way, if you avoid getting started on difficult things, it doesn't mean you aren't *working*. Clear out your email in-box? No problem. Show up to the meetings on your calendar? Check.

But turning off your email, putting your phone in a drawer, and diving into your Greatest Impact Activity (GIA), which seems difficult to start? Not so easy. Yet The Extremely Productive largely have it figured out. The XP are much more likely than The Rest to:

- start their days focused on their GIA.

- put their GIAs in their calendars.

- stay focused on their GIA and, even when pressed, not react to other people's agendas. (In fact, only 4 percent of The XP feel like they react to other people's agendas instead of driving their own.)

Moreover, our research shows that proactivity overall, as well as habits of starting the day focused on GIAs and calendaring Investment activities, are key drivers of productivity.*

---

* See Appendix B: Research Note for statistics.

Greatest Impact Activity

Your GIA is the one activity each day that, should you do it consistently at high quality, will get you the greatest eventual return on your time. It's the number-one most important piece of Investment time you can ever spend. When you attend to your GIA, you make progress toward your goals.

Too often, however, people don't *feel* proactive. So the voice in their head tells them they're *not* proactive. If you think like this, there's good reason to consider changing that narrative, which goes even beyond productivity. Our research found that the happiest people are nearly two times more likely than everyone else to say they're proactive.

As we noted earlier, motivation, and by association proactivity, is more a skill than a fixed attribute. It's not "I am proactive" or "I'm not proactive." It's "I can be proactive if I can get organized about it."

Recall the definition of motivation on page 24. "Internal and external factors that stimulate desire and energy in people to be continually interested and committed to a job, role, or subject, or to make an effort to attain a goal."

Recruiting Your Drive stimulates desire and energy. Do so, and you'll be maximally ready, willing, and wanting to act. It's the yen.

Igniting Your Proactivity is setting the kindling, striking the match, and initiating the activity. It's the spark.

Applying Cluster Care to My Work

When Ari was a baby, I (Erica) learned about the concept of cluster care. This is when a nurse clusters, or batches, several routine care events rather than spacing them out over time. If Ari needed an echo, a dressing change, and a shot all in one day, the nurses would do their best to get it all done at the same time, while also taking care of the regular four-hour check of vitals that would so often interrupt his sleep. This allowed Ari longer periods of rest and has even been proven to improve patient care.[3]

I've applied this concept to my work. Emails, text messages, reviewing and approving communications, reporting . . . I cluster my activities. I am deliberate about when I choose to check and respond to messages. I don't let messages interrupt me every few minutes. Instead, I check them every few hours and batch my responses. It's so obvious that my colleagues have noted how they'll get a flurry of responses from me, followed by several hours of silence.

For most of us, very little of what we do at work is an emergency. Your boss may make a request, but you don't have to drop everything you're doing and answer instantly. If there is a true emergency, they can always pick up the phone and call you or swing by your desk.

Mostly, though, I've found it's okay to let people wait and to control when you respond so you can be more proactive on your priorities.

Spark Up

There's a concept in chemistry called activation energy. Activation energy is the minimum amount of energy required to get a chemical reaction started.

Let's say you want to cozy up to the fire in the evening with your General Foods International Coffee and a nice Nora Roberts novel. First order of business: light the fire. So you put on some logs and take a flamethrower to your fireplace. Right?

That would do the trick, but that's a lot of energy and expense to light a fire. On the other hand, lighting one match under a thick log doesn't provide enough energy by itself for the log to catch.

However, put some dry paper and a little kindling under the logs and light the paper, and soon the logs will catch fire, then burn for quite some time.

The paper is the catalyst that helps start the fire. Once it's started, the fire will keep burning without requiring much energy. A catalyst lowers activation energy requirements. In principle, you only need a fragment of catalyst to do the job.

Catalysts work in chemical reactions, but they also work with human behavior. Activation energy for people is the minimum amount of energy required to get started on a given task. What we need to do to ignite our proactivity is to understand activation energy and use catalysts to make the energy required that much smaller—once the fire is lit, it takes much less energy to keep it burning.

It all starts with the spark, that tiny flash of fire with the power to unleash energy at scale—like that conversation with Dad about how we were going to manage our lives while living in the hospital.

We've identified three catalysts—or hacks—that can help you tackle your high-impact but easy-to-avoid Investment activities by lowering the activation energy. Try them and you will ignite your proactivity regardless of your particular circumstances.

The three catalysts for proactivity are:

1. Calendar your Investment TIME

2. Talk to yourself

3. Say 3 . . . 2 . . . 1 . . . Go!

I. Calendar Your Investment TIME

For most of Ari's stay, Zayde came into the hospital five days a week—Monday through Friday. He would get there about eight in the morning and stay until midafternoon.

At 8 AM, we'd start to get Ari ready for the day and catch up. By 8:30 I (Mike) would be just about ready to leave the room to find a place to work, but inevitably someone would stop by to talk. Next thing I knew it was breakfast time, and I'd stay to help get Ari to eat.

Forty-five minutes later, I'd grab my computer to head out, only to see ten doctors on rounds two doors down. Knowing they'd be at Ari's room in a few minutes, I'd stay. (We tried to make rounds every day.) Thirty minutes would go by and they'd still be at the next door. Then I'd look up and they'd be gone because they were rounding today on odd room numbers first, and Ari was in room 8224.

At 10 AM it was time to work, and then . . . Zayde would go get coffee. I'd stay in the room. Around that time Ari would be in the middle of a few hours of extended hockey game summaries on NHL.com. While he usually did not mind spending some time alone in his room, we tried to make sure someone was always with him. I couldn't really concentrate there, so instead of diving into a project, I'd try to clean up emails or do something not particularly taxing.

Zayde would return to the room, and Ari would need an echo . . . or a chest X-ray . . . or a line change . . . or a shot . . . I'd stay for these just to be there.

I was taking care of Ari, but I certainly wasn't getting any work done.

After a few weeks of close to full-time support, somehow, I was still not getting any work done. Something had to change.

Two things helped. First, I was there with Ari full time, but I had to trust that someone else could hang out with him during an echo or something that, to Ari, was really no big deal. I had to allow myself mentally to leave him with Zayde for these, something neither of them minded.

Second, I started to put my top priority, my GIA, on my calendar for 8:30 AM every day. When Zayde would come in, unless something odd was up, I'd go straight to the family lounge twenty feet across the hall and start to work. I couldn't always get there by 8:30 AM because, you know, hospital life, but once I broke free I knew I had to buckle down and dive into a predetermined top Investment activity.

Before I started calendaring my investment time, I wasn't trying to procrastinate. I was, however, allowing circumstances to dictate how my mornings went, which in effect became procrastination. To change the dynamic and start being proactive, I had to intervene.

That intervention was calendaring my Investment time. It worked great for me. No matter what is keeping you from getting your work done—and for most people it likely pales in comparison to our situation—it can work for you, too.

Set Your Calendar on Fire

Later, as we looked into calendaring as a way to become more productive, we found that researchers had studied the effect of calendaring as a proactivity catalyst.

Sarah Milne, a psychologist at the University of Bath in the UK, and her colleagues analyzed the results of 248 people who committed to the following:[4]

During the next week, I will partake in at least 20 minutes of vigorous exercise on [DAY] at [TIME OF DAY] at/in [PLACE].

- Group 1 committed to "keep track" of whether they exercised.
- Group 2 committed to "keep track and read a pamphlet on the benefits of exercise."
- Group 3 committed to "keep track, read a pamphlet, and make a plan for when and where to exercise" (also known as *calendaring*).

In Group 1 (the control group), 38 percent of people exercised at least once per week. Group 2 (the motivation group) exercised weekly at a rate of 35 percent. Group 3 (the intention group) exercised weekly at a whopping rate of 91 percent.

Committing to a specific plan to perform an activity, including time and dates, not only makes us more likely to tackle the activity, but also frees up our cognitive resources so that we can function better.[5] In other words, if you know what you *are doing*, you are more at peace with what you *aren't doing.* The weight of everything you aren't doing will hang on you until you set the intention, and give yourself permission, to work on something else. Perhaps this is why the happiest people in our research were more than twice as likely than everyone else to calendar their Investment activities.

These outcomes have been proven time and again in different psychological studies, and we've seen the same results in our work with clients. We know this:

If you put it on your calendar, you're much more likely to get started.

For example, if you work in a management role, you might need to get a strategy in place for next year. But you keep putting it off because of the constant barrage coming at you. See in the sample calendar that follows how strategy time is calendared in several specific slots. Regardless of your job, there's always something you should do but you might not do if you didn't pick a time and put it on your calendar.

In the sample calendar, you'll see some Productivity Code concepts we haven't covered in detail yet. We'll get to them in upcoming chapters, but for now here are the basics:

- Investment Time: The time you spend that will get you outsized returns.

- Greatest Impact Activity (GIA): The single most important Investment Time activity for a given day.

- Sprinting: A form of timeboxing or focusing only on one pre-planned activity for a set period while tuning out all distractions. Sprinting helps you get in the zone and achieve maximum effort per work hour.

Sample Calendar

If you've gone through the goal- and action-planning process in Habit 1: Recruit Your Drive, you've already identified the Investment activities that will help you reach your goals. Now block off time in your calendar to work on them.

The XP are 2.7 times more likely than The Rest to block off time in their calendars every week to work on their GIAs. They're also nearly four times more likely to spend the maximum amount of time on activities that will drive the best results. Both of these behaviors represent key drivers of productivity.

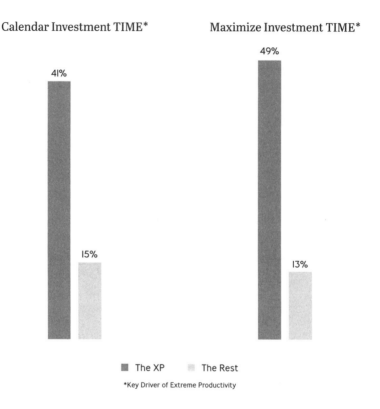

Like we said, when you put an activity in your calendar, you're much more likely to do it. (Then you'll make progress. Then you'll feel good. Then your motivation soars. Then you'll be proactive again tomorrow. See how this works?)

2. Talk to Yourself

Any decision you make for what you do with your time comes down to one moment. At that moment, which we call the Critical Decision Window, you are faced with choices, typically on a continuum from easy to challenging. If you want to make the challenging choice, you'll absolutely need one thing to help you get started: mental toughness.

At the critical moment, what you believe or don't believe, and how you feel about yourself, has an outsized impact on the choice you make—like telling yourself you're not proactive. Henry Ford's adage still holds true: whether you think you can or you think you can't, you're right. Specifically regarding proactivity, think of it like this: if you think you can't, you *won't even bother to start*. What's a girl to do then? (You too, Mike.)

Start working on mental toughness ~~not~~ today. Here's how.

The United States Navy's Sea, Air, and Land Teams, known more commonly as Navy SEALs, are universally renowned as an elite military unit. In the early 2000s, the military needed more SEALs but also needed to keep the elite standards for those they admitted to the program. They were afraid that too few would pass the required tests in order to maintain troop levels.

To maximize SEAL candidate success, the military developed a mental toughness program in which candidates learned essential skills. One of the key skills was positive self-talk. Passing rates for new SEAL recruits improved from 25 percent to a third, a 32 percent increase in passing rates without lowering standards.

If you think self-talk is a squishy, New Age point to skip past, consider this: the average person says between three hundred and one thousand words to themselves every minute.[6] That's a lot of coaching your inner voice gives you!

Your inner voice can be a real jackass, too. It can be a strict, disorganized, illogical, and self-destructive task master. Left to its own devices, your inner voice can be a real critic that holds you back, especially when it gets stuck in an endless negative loop: "I'm not good enough." "I didn't do enough." "I'm not enough." Your inner voice can also help you rationalize. "I'm really busy." "I'll get it done tomorrow." "I got a lot done yesterday."

The good thing for all of us is that nobody is in charge of our inner voices except us. We can change what we tell ourselves.* Own your mental narrative and you can change anything. Many people think that before you tell yourself something, you have to believe it. But we've found that simply changing what you say to yourself can change your beliefs. This might seem backward, but it's true. In this sense, "fake it

---

* More specifically, we can tell ourselves to change what we tell ourselves, though it's even more powerful to ask ourselves if we want to change what we tell ourselves (see page 73). Trippy, right?

till you make it" is good advice. The first step in changing that belief? Change how you talk to yourself.

Talking to yourself, of course, has positive implications beyond driving proactivity. In *The Soul of Money*, fundraiser and activist Lynne Twist observes:

> For me, and for many of us, our first waking thought of the day is "I didn't get enough sleep." The next one is, "I don't have enough time." Whether true or not, that thought of not enough occurs to us automatically before we even think to question or examine it. We spend most of the hours and the days of our lives hearing, explaining, complaining, or worrying about what we don't have enough of . . . This mind-set of scarcity lives at the very heart of our jealousies, our greed, our prejudice, and our arguments with life.[7]

Not long ago, I (Erica) had to attend a conference with a jam-packed agenda. I had meetings scheduled during many of the sessions and all of the breaks. I'd have to be "on" from six in the morning until ten at night. Yet here's the thing: I'm an introvert. Time to myself is essential, so the idea of this conference was overwhelming to me. The day before I got on the plane to attend the conference, I was in my therapist's office telling her about my anticipatory anxiety.

"If I can just find a half hour to myself, I think I'll be okay," I told her.

"Why a half hour?" she replied. "What if you have five minutes, and at the start of those five minutes, you tell yourself, 'This is the exact amount of time I need.' What do you think would happen then?"

Guess what? It worked! Since then, I've used that piece of advice nearly every day. When I wake up feeling like the amount of sleep I got was "not enough," I tell myself it was the exact amount I needed. When I'm speaking at an event and I feel I haven't rehearsed enough, I say to myself that I've done just the right amount of preparation.

This shift in my self-talk has boosted my ability to face the day, start difficult activities, and tackle whatever is in front of me.

Think about some of the ways your self-talk is holding you back and preventing you from being proactive, from just getting started. Here are some examples of negative self-talk and how you can flip those thoughts into positive messages. (In the positive examples, you're referring to yourself in the third person. That's intentional. See "You Can Do It, Steve!" on the next page.)

Negative Self-Talk	Positive Self-Talk
I can't get up early to exercise.	Steve, you can set your alarm tonight one hour earlier to exercise.
I'm terrible at leading sales meetings.	Mary, you need to learn what a great sales meeting looks like; then you can learn to lead one.
I'm not good at this and won't ever be.	Jeff, you're not good at it yet, but you can learn and get there.
I can't concentrate with all the distractions.	Emma, other people can tune out distractions, so can you; you need to research how [or . . . just keep going through our program].
If I try it, it won't work.	Dave, you tried it, and it hasn't worked, but you can learn to make it work.
I don't get this idea—I'm an idiot.	Jeanette, you don't understand this right now, but you can figure it out.
I'll never dig out of the pile on my desk, so I can't be proactive.	Andy, you haven't been able to dig out yet, but you can do it if you get help to manage your time and learn to say no.

As you might imagine, The XP are much more likely than The Rest to practice positive self-talk; 2.4 times more likely, to be exact. Moreover, the happiest people are 2.3 times more likely to use this hack, as well.

You Can Do It, Steve!

Psychology research gives us some clues about precisely the kind of language that is best to use in our self-talk. "You" statements are more powerful than "I" statements. Silently saying, "Steve, you can do it!" works better than "I can do it."

A study led by a joint Michigan State University–University of Michigan team found that third-person self-talk increases people's ability to control their thoughts, feelings, and behavior under stress, and is a relatively effortless form of self-control.[8]

Changing Your Self-Talk

Each of us has our own set of negative self-talk statements to overcome. Using the template at the end of this chapter, list some of the things you tell yourself that hold you back from achieving the things you want to do. Then flip those negative statements into positive ones. If you get stuck, look at the examples on page 59 for inspiration.

Oh, and by the way, if you're thinking this might be a bit of a challenge, say this out loud first:

<Insert your name here>, you can do this! 3 ... 2 ... 1 ... Go!

Sixty Self-Limiting Beliefs

Read the list and see if it sparks any ideas for you of self-talk you'd like to change.

1. I don't have enough time.
2. I just have bad luck.
3. It's better not to try than to be seen as a failure.
4. I can't start . . . I'm not ready.
5. I don't have enough experience.
6. I'm not educated/knowledgeable enough to do that.
7. I'm not likable or charming.
8. I'm not self-disciplined.
9. I'm not good at planning ahead.
10. Why try? I'll just fail.
11. I'm too old.
12. I'm too young.
13. I'm not creative enough to intrigue anyone.
14. I'm so awkward.
15. Their opinion of me is more important than my opinion of myself.
16. I'm being a nuisance.
17. I'm a mess.
18. I'm not lovable.
19. I'm such a screwup, I never do anything right.
20. I don't have enough connections.
21. People never accept meetings with me.
22. Decision makers don't want to engage with me.
23. They probably don't have the budget to buy from me.
24. That's a lot of money . . . this is a bigger money game than I play in.
25. I'll never be any good at [insert this or that].
26. I'll get hurt less if I don't put myself out there.

27. I'm not smart enough.
28. The economy is killing my ability to [succeed, get a job, get ahead, start a business, etc.].
29. I'm uncomfortable talking about money.
30. Our competitors are better than we are, they are winning more/ deserve to win more.
31. Getting rejected makes me so tired.
32. He/she is better than me.
33. I'd never get that promotion.
34. I'm too fat/skinny/tall/short.
35. I have to be perfect.
36. I'm a boring person, no one wants to listen to me.
37. It's my manager/company/team's fault I'm not succeeding more.
38. I need people to like me.
39. My to-do list is just too long to add anything.
40. I've never been able to concentrate.
41. There's no way to avoid distraction these days.
42. I don't have anything valuable to say.
43. I never get the day started right.
44. I don't have time to exercise.
45. I don't have time to relax.
46. I don't have time for [insert here what you don't have time for].
47. I don't have the right degree.
48. I can't find the energy.
49. I'll never be financially independent.
50. I'll never be happy.
51. My body/health/athletic ability just won't allow me to.
52. I'm not good at building relationships.
53. Other people have all the power.
54. Why get my hopes up? I'll just be disappointed.
55. I can't change.
56. I just don't have the self-discipline.
57. Why ask for what I want? I won't get it.
58. I'll just get rejected.
59. I can't trust myself with that.
60. I can do that, but Not Today.

3. Say "3 . . . 2 . . . 1 . . . Go!"

Here's what happens. You have your action plan and know your GIA and Investment activities. They're in your calendar. You've told yourself, "Jean, you can do this . . . you *will* do this . . ."

You're right there. Right at the precipice of getting started.

Then . . . squirrel!

Your mind switches to something else, and you don't get started on that Investment activity. Positive self-talk can get you in the success mindset. However, it's a particular kind of self-talk that will help you get started on significant activities. We call it Rapid Activation Talk.

Neuroscientist Antonio Damasio studies the impact on people's behavior of *rational* and *emotional* decision making.[9] He found that the "gut reaction" part of your brain has to be activated in the right way if you want to do something that otherwise would seem emotionally demanding. In fact, if those parts of your brain dedicated to gut reaction and emotions of punishment and reward (the prefrontal cortex and its orbitofrontal cortex) are damaged, you will be hamstrung when making even the most straightforward decisions.

It's not enough to have the logic; you need the right emotion to get started.

People tell themselves all the time they should work out right now, but they don't. That's because the thinking part of the brain is quickly overruled by the feeling part of the brain. When you're right there, you know what to do, it's time to do it, and you've told yourself to do it, but you still don't, it's usually the short-term-reward emotional center of your brain butting in and saying, "This is too hard. I don't want to do this. Something else is easier. I'll do the easier thing. I know what I need . . . a peanut butter cup!"

Your emotional brain sabotages your best-laid plans. It's doing its "cognitive miser" act, saving up the energy for later. To preempt the short-term-reward part of your brain from derailing your long-term desires, you need to head it off at the pass, and you only have a few seconds to do it.

Rapid Activation Talk is the solution. All you have to do—like any school-age child ready to start everyone racing—is say "3 . . . 2 . . . 1 . . . Go!" and immediately get started. This isn't a new idea. In *The 5 Second Rule*, Mel Robbins popularized the concept of acting fast on a countdown.[10] The idea is that the counting will focus you on the goal or commitment and distract you from the worries, thoughts, and excuses in your mind.

For example, while writing this book, I (Erica) had only a few pages left to review in one of the chapters when my calendar reminder went off—fifteen minutes to my next meeting. I snoozed the alarm and started checking email. But I knew if I powered through, I could finish the chapter in the next fifteen minutes. I said to myself, "3 . . . 2 . . . 1 . . . Go!" shut down email, and sprinted for the next fifteen minutes (more on sprinting in Habit 7). I focused intensely, finished the last two pages, and felt great. I was able to complete the chapter and feel accomplished. I didn't have the mental tax of it hanging on me, knowing I'd have to get back into it later. However, if I hadn't said to myself, "3 . . . 2 . . . 1 . . . Go!" I would have spent that fifteen minutes very differently, feeling less productive and not so great about what I got done that day.

For all the various researchers and authors who have their own versions of Rapid Activation Talk, the point is universally the same. You have a short amount of time to get started on an activity before your brain tells you, "That's too hard."

The XP are 3.5 times more likely than The Rest to immediately begin tasks that they know they should be doing, and the happiest people are nearly twice as likely as everyone else to do so. When you Recruit Your Drive (Habit 1), you inspire yourself to chase a long-term reward like getting into great shape. But to do that, you have to work out five days a week and eat healthy.

You know this intellectually. And you resolve to do it.

But then, at the very moment you should begin working out, the emotional part of your cognitive miser kicks in and says, "Right now I'd rather flip through social media on the couch with Cousin Brewski. Working out is so much effort. I don't have the right shoes. My hangnail will sting when I sweat. There could be a boll weevil infestation in the gym any minute and they'll eat right through my cotton socks. Better idea: I'll work out first thing tomorrow morning instead."

Fortunately, you can head these "don't make me get up" excuses off at the pass.

At the moment of truth, say "3 . . . 2 . . . 1 . . . Go!" and you'll be off the couch, and on the elliptical.

∗ ∗ ∗

Let the TIME for Action steps at the end of this chapter be the spark that gets you started on your greatest-impact activities. Then in the next chapter, Habit 3: Reengineer Your Habits, you'll learn how changing your habits can further help you harness your motivation and accomplish your goals. Go ahead and get started. You've got this.

TIME FOR ACTION

- **Calendar your Investment TIME:** Open your calendar and block off time for Investment activities over the next week. Say "3 . . . 2 . . . 1 . . . Go!" and get started right now.

- **Talk to yourself:** Turn negative thoughts and energy into positives to put you in the right frame of mind to get started. Complete the Self-Talk Exercise at MyProductivityCode.com/booktools. Write down the common negative beliefs you tell yourself and turn them into positive ones. Reference the examples earlier in this chapter for ideas.

- **Say 3 . . . 2 . . . 1 . . . Go!:** What should you be doing right now? Answer the question, then say "3 . . . 2 . . . 1 . . . Go!" and start.

REENGINEER YOUR HABITS

THE CHOICE

Now don't say you can't swear off drinking;
it's easy. I've done it a thousand times.

—W. C. Fields

As the months wore on in the hospital, Ari progressively got much better . . . at using the iPad. He'd watch basketball highlights, old baseball games, top ten golf-shot videos. He'd even watch this absolutely insane "Off-Season Softball League" series, which we still don't quite understand, yet millions of people—well, maybe hundreds of thousands—apparently do.

After a while Ari would wake up and ask for the iPad straightaway. When you have a generally healthy kid with a fever at home, at least in our home, all bets are off. If they want to watch TV and rest the day away, that's kosher. But when it became a habit for Ari to stay stuck in front of a screen each morning in room 8224 for too long, we began to notice ill effects. He'd be more sluggish than usual. He'd seem down, his energy low. The longer he stayed in bed, the harder it was to get him out of bed.

Something had to change. For the days he was feeling well enough, we introduced a new routine. We called it the Good Morning Tour. The tour even made it to his visual schedule (yes, he calendared his Investment time), which included pictures of his daily routine so he would know what was going to happen and when. Every morning after he woke up, wearing his Avengers pajamas and shark slippers, and with an IV pole in tow, Ari would walk the entire cardiac floor saying good morning to everyone. The nurses, the doctors, other patients, the receptionists, the custodial staff, anyone who happened to be floating in the halls. From start to finish, the tour would take about forty-five minutes.

At one point, Ari told me (Erica) he wanted to go to college in Japan and play baseball there because, you know, that's a good place to prep for the majors. After that, his plan was to come back and play left field for the Red Sox. As he told me, "By then Andrew Benintendi will be ready to retire."

"If you're going to college in Japan, you're going to have to learn Japanese," I told him. So we looked up how to say "Good morning" in Japanese. The casual way of saying it is *ohayo*. On our Good Morning Tour, Ari would *ohayo* everyone, tell them what it meant, and how he'd need to know it when he played baseball with Manny Ramirez in Japan.

I was relieved to see how this new routine completely changed Ari's energy and mood. He was more motivated to do things the rest of the day: to have breakfast, to play, to get out of his room. Despite the daily poking and prodding, and schlepping his IV pole wherever he went, he actually appeared to us to be happier and more engaged with everything. It just took some preplanning with a new morning routine to change Ari's habit from one of staying in bed to one of being the mayor of the eighth floor of Boston Children's Hospital.

We didn't know it at the time but, as our research would later show, the happiest people are 1.9 times more likely to have a morning routine that contributes to getting off to a very productive start each day.

It's true for all of us—so much of what we do every day is driven by our habits. What we eat in the morning, when we shower, where we eat, whether we work out, how we take notes, how we work, how we interact with people, our morning routines, our evening routines. We are habitual creatures.

Still, when a habit gets in the way of reaching your goal, you can make the choice to change it to change your life. And when a goal calls for a new habit, you can choose to create it. In this chapter, you'll learn how.

New Tricks for Old Dogs

I (Erica) have never been one to go to the gym and work out. However, after Lexi was born, while our lives were relatively quiet, I decided it was time to ditch the extra baby weight and signed up for a gym membership. My plan was to exercise before work, so I set my alarm for 5:05 AM. Day one, the alarm went off. I rolled over, picked up my phone, and began scrolling through Facebook. Twenty minutes later, I was still in bed and it was too late to exercise. I told myself I'd do it tomorrow.

The next morning, the alarm went off at 5:05 AM but it was raining out . . . so no exercise that day. The third morning the alarm went off, but Ari and Lexi were up multiple times in the middle of the night, so I hit the snooze button. It's not that I didn't want to exercise, but for better or for worse, my habit was to not exercise.

You have to do things differently, and do different things, if you want different results.

If you want to do something—anything—differently in your life routines, you have to understand habits and how to change them.

In fact, having productive habits is the factor that represents the largest difference between The Extremely Productive and The Rest.

Nearly two-thirds of The XP agree that their work habits contribute *significantly* to their productivity. The Rest?

Only 12 percent. It's also one of the key drivers of productivity.

This is pretty bad news for The Rest. Or, looking at it another way, there's massive room for improvement. (Score one for positive self-talk.)

Too bad you can't teach an old dog new tricks, right?

Wrong! You can change even the most embedded of habits if you know how. Habit change has been a popular self-help topic over the last decade. Still, many pundits overcomplicate habit change, or miss crucial elements that limit the effectiveness of their habit-change advice.

Our own research and client work have led us to believe that the common habit theories are incomplete. We need better and different words to guide us to choose and adopt new behavioral tendencies if we want to get up and hit the gym at 5:05 AM.

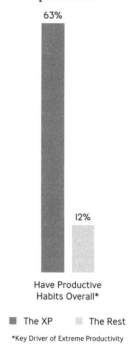

My work habits contribute significantly to being extremely productive.

63%

12%

Have Productive
Habits Overall*

■ The XP   ▦ The Rest

*Key Driver of Extreme Productivity

Thought: The Missing Link in the Habit Loop

Many experts surmise that human behavior follows a habit loop consisting of trigger → response → reward. Incidentally, while we were in the middle of writing this book, we attended a medical seminar where the facilitator handed us a worksheet labeled "The ABCs of Habits: Antecedent → Behavior → Consequence." Same concept, different words. Architect all three, the thinking goes, and you change and build habits.

The trouble is that a major concept is missing from these three-pronged habit models: thought. Habits make thought less noticeable, but thought is there all the same, and it's a huge part of habit formation and change.

We believe that habits are composed of the following four elements, not three:

1. **Trigger:** Something happens that cues a sequence of doing something you tend to do. For example, your phone buzzes in your pocket.
2. **Thought:** The cue triggers a thought, even if it's fast or subconscious. The thought might be, "I should reach into my pocket now to check the message."
3. **Response:** Following the thought, you take action. Hand goes into your pocket, takes the phone. You check the message.
4. **Reward:** This is your gain or payoff. "Oh, great! That report I'm waiting for is here. I'll stop what I'm doing and take a look."

The 4 Elements of Habit

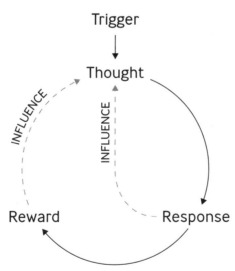

This is many people's habit when a new message alert dings. We allow ourselves to break our concentration for every email, text, or other notification that pops up. Merely receiving a message and looking at it triggers the release of dopamine in your brain. That reward provides even more payoff and reinforces that when the phone buzzes, you look immediately. It's a fairly strong habit: the trigger is disruptive, the response takes little energy, and the reward is powerful, but your behavior is taking away from what you were doing. That's fine if you're watching TV or wasting time, but it's a problem when you're in the middle of Investment time. Still, when the phone in your pocket buzzes, your habit is to look. What do you do?

Change the habit.

Common Work Habits to Change

Here are common habits—both good and bad—that people tell us they would like to change at the workplace.

Unproductive work habits to break

- Checking email first thing in the morning
- Aimless web browsing to start the day (or at any time)
- Accepting too many meetings
- Accepting meetings that aren't essential
- Allowing or inviting coworker interruptions (e.g., keeping your door open)
- Not planning your day/week in advance
- Not calendaring your Investment TIME and GIA each day
- Overpromising
- Procrastination
- Trying to tackle too many priorities
- Leaving essential tasks to the last minute
- Chronic multitasking

Productive work habits to start

- Implementing a morning routine
- Starting immediately on important tasks
- Single-tasking intensely when you need to concentrate
- Working on your GIA first
- Planning and reviewing goals and priorities
- Pruning your priorities to as few as possible
- Planning actions weekly and reviewing actions with an accountability partner
- Reducing clutter in your work environment
- Wearing noise-canceling headphones to block out distractions
- Stashing your phone out of sight and reach

Changing Habits

Before you can change habits, you make choices. You're the choice architect, so to speak. Architects create blueprints for buildings. Choice architects create blueprints for habits.

You don't need a degree to be a choice architect. You do, however, need to:

- Identify the habit you want to change

- Identify *why* you want to change the habit (because, as we know from Habit 1: Recruit Your Drive, knowing and making the *why* explicit is motivating)

- Make a blueprint to change the habit

Once you choose the habit you want to change, you can intervene in several different places around the 4 Elements of Habit. You can change the trigger, thought, or response, and define, increase, or otherwise change what the reward is, as well as whether and how much you want it.

The illustration below shows all the places where you can influence and change habits and the tactics, or hacks, you can use to do it. We cover the hacks in detail in this chapter and throughout the book.

4 Elements of Habit:
Habit Change Tips and Hacks

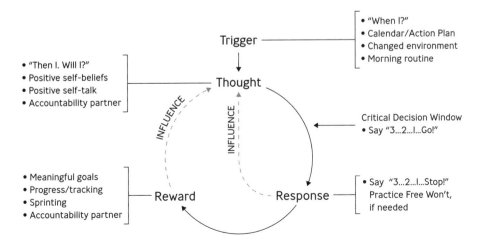

Driving "Automaticity"

You'll notice in the graphic on the previous page there are two dotted lines with the word "influence." Simply put:

- The more often you take action or respond a certain way to a trigger, the easier it is to do it. (For example, every Monday, Wednesday, and Friday at noon going to hot yoga.) At first, any new behavior feels like a slog, both getting started and keeping at it. Do that behavior every day for one hundred days, however, and doing it the one-hundred-first day will be easier and require less energy and less thought.

In this way, **response** influences **thought.**

- The more you feel the reward, the more you appreciate it. If you go to hot yoga every Monday, Wednesday, and Friday at noon and, after years of pain, your back finally feels good, you'll be more intent on going to hot yoga three times a week at noon.

In this way, **reward** influences **thought.**

Both of these phenomena drive a concept the academics call automaticity. Habitual behaviors aren't *actually* automatic, but they can *feel* automatic. When a behavior feels automatic, you think, mostly subconsciously, "I can do this. This is easy." Versus what you thought a month before, which was likely consciously and overtly how difficult it was going to be. It takes a while, more than conventional wisdom says, to develop the feeling of automaticity.

A popularly bandied-about statistic is that it takes twenty-one days to form a habit. That's not quite right. Psychologist Pippa Lally's research at the University College of London suggests it takes much longer for habits to form and new behaviors to start feeling automatic.[1] Lally found it could take up to 254 days, though the average was sixty-six days. The difference lies in three factors: the person, the behavior, and the circumstances. For example, if you've been exercising regularly and it's nice out (circumstances), and you enjoy it (person), running for thirty minutes (the behavior) is much easier to make a habit than it would be if you haven't exercised in years, it's the middle of winter in Saskatoon, and you prefer riding a bike. (That person in Saskatoon might consider forming a different healthy exercise habit.)

In any case, the more consistently you perform the behavior, the easier it is to do the next time. You develop the feeling of automaticity. At that point, once a behavior feels automatic, you can reasonably call it a habit.

The three hacks we share in this chapter will help you Reengineer Your Habits—change existing ones or create new ones—by targeting the trigger, thought, response, and reward stages of the 4 Elements of Habit:

1. Say, "When I, Then I." And Ask, "Will I?"

2. Change your environment

3. Make your morning routine sacred

I. Say, "When I, Then I." And Ask, "Will I?"

Antiepileptic medications fail fairly often, but not because the medications themselves don't work. They fail because patients don't take them on schedule. Psychologist Ian Brown set up a randomized trial to work out why—and what factors might make a difference.[2]

Before his team's intervention, patients only took their medications on schedule 55 percent of the time. Then researchers asked them to make a "When I, Then I" statement, such as "When it's eight o'clock in the morning, and I've finished brushing my teeth, then I will take my prescribed medication."

Those who made the statement increased their medication compliance to 79 percent.

This is trigger-thought-response planning. Here's another example: "When I feel my phone buzz in my pocket (trigger), then I will turn off that alert (thought-response) before doing anything else." Execute on this sequence and you not only change your response but also remove the trigger in the future. You become the choice architect, making the plan and taking away power from your phone and whoever and whatever else is driving distraction from the other side.

By thinking about what you will do differently in advance, you introduce conflict in your habit routine. This is what you want! You used to check the alert because of automaticity. Now you've driven a cognitive wedge between the trigger and the old response. This evokes a completely new, highly conscious thought: "An alert now means turn off the alert, not check the message."*

Thought Is the Cognitive Wedge

Where other habit change methods fall short is when they say, "You have a habit. Once the trigger happens, your response is automatic." That's not right. Remember from page 6 that the dictionary defines a habit as "a settled tendency or usual manner of behavior; an acquired mode of behavior that has become nearly or completely involuntary."

We don't completely agree. It's not completely involuntary. It's only *nearly* involuntary.

That sliver of difference means everything.

Thought and choice are there—they're just idling. If you want to change the habit, you must rev up from that idle to introduce conflict in the form of thought. Instead of reacting the old way (almost) without thinking, you introduce conflict. The conflict acts as a cognitive wedge in the behavior. You prompt a decision where before it felt like there was none: Do what you have typically done

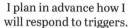

I plan in advance how I will respond to triggers.

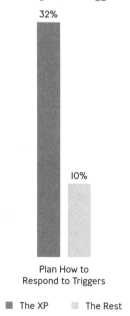

32%

10%

Plan How to
Respond to Triggers

■ The XP   ▧ The Rest

---

* What if it's the school, your child, or the doctor? Make choices for when you leave your phone or alerts on. Many people find they can turn off their phone for an hour here or there and allow themselves some solitude. Or, allow only certain contacts to alert you, even when your phone is in dark mode. Or, turn off 95 percent of alerts, but not all. The point is if you question the behavior, you can organize your response deliberately.

in the past, *or* do something else that you've architected in advance to achieve a new kind of reward?

This is what The XP do. They are 3.2 times more likely than The Rest to plan in advance how they will respond to triggers that impact their productivity.

Plan "When I, Then I" statements for the habits you want to change, and you will drive that cognitive wedge.

Let's say you want to break the habit of starting your day on emails and correspondence that sidetrack you. Then 9 AM rolls around and you don't—you go right into the in-box rabbit hole.

I (Erica) can sometimes fall into this habit, and when I do, I almost always feel behind. Just recently I caught myself doing this, and asked myself what change would help. The answer? Starting with my GIA. I told myself, "When I finish my morning routine, then I will get started with my GIA, not correspondence."

It was exceptionally challenging the first few days to resist the temptation to check email, Slack, and other messaging. But I did, and my productivity soared. It worked, all because of the "When I, Then I" statement.

It's not foolproof, though. If "When I, Then I" doesn't work, consider changing from a statement to a question. You can strengthen your resolve by asking, "Will I?" on top of saying "When I, Then I." Instead of saying, "I will," change it to asking, "Will I?" This has been shown to increase accountability.[3] People who tell themselves to do something don't do it as often as those who ask themselves if they will. Tomorrow morning, if you ask, "Will I begin working on Investment activities when I finish my morning routine today?" and tell yourself, "Yes," you might just find you're more likely to do it.

2. Change Your Environment

Our environments matter deeply to us: what we see, what we hear, what we touch, taste, smell. Take a moment to think about the physical space where you spend your workdays. Does it make you feel energized and focused, or does it feel like you're walking the hallways of a cardiac intensive care unit?

Our environments affect our behavior in two significant ways:

1. When we're in a particular place, we tend to do (or not do) specific things.
2. How the environment is designed drives us to do some things and not others.

I (Mike) don't like to write at the office. Don't get me wrong, it's a nice office. It's bright and light, energetic and modern. But when I'm there, my brain is in grow-the-company mode: client results management, product development, marketing, staffing, sales, global expansion. These are significant Investment areas for me, but they're not writing.

When I want to write, I go someplace else. My favorite place is overlooking the lake where we live. It's a place I love to be. When I'm there, my brain knows what it's meant to do: write. Nothing else, just write.

Like monkeys catching sight of a banana, our brains grab at any opportunity for distraction. All those books on your bookshelf. The way your office chair cuts into your back. The smell of leftovers heating in the microwave. Any of these things can take you off task quicker than you can say, "Squirrel!" Especially if your office is open format, it can seem impossible to block out the chatter.

As you might have guessed, The XP are tuned in to their environments, designing them for maximum personal productivity. More than half of The XP organize their work environments to maximize their productivity, while fewer than one in five of The Rest do.

Take a page out of The XP playbook and tap in to the environmental factors contributing to your motivation. There are a bunch of ways to change your environment. Some of them may be in your control, others not. Control the ones you can.

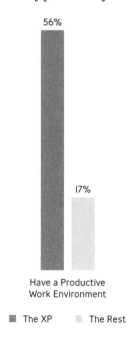

I organize my work environment to maximize my productivity.

56%

17%

Have a Productive Work Environment

■ The XP   ▦ The Rest

Fifteen Tactics for a Highly Productive Work Environment

1. Declutter your desk: Remove all the pens, paper clips, and random pieces of paper. (Do it late in the day, so you're not distracted from your GIA first thing in the morning.)

2. Move your bookshelf: Get it out of your line of sight when you're at your desk.

3. Create a view: Put up a calming piece of art to use as a concentration point. (Or a privacy screen.)

4. Wipe your whiteboard clear: Erase those old notes and lists.

5. Shut the door: If your office has a door, close it.

6. Get a room: If you don't have a private office, reserve a meeting room or set up your base somewhere free of distractions.

7. Light the way: Add overhead lights or a lamp to your workspace to improve your mental cognition and alertness.

8. Make it bright: Choose bright, cool lighting, rather than warm and dim, to maximize productivity in most tasks.

9. Keep quiet: If you're in a loud workspace, wear noise-canceling headphones to reduce ambient sounds from conversations, printers, phones, the landscaping crew, and so on.

10. Turn it off: If you're working at home, turn off the TV, the dishwasher, or the washing machine.

11. Add scents: Run an aromatherapy diffuser with a scented essential oil you find appealing. Research has shown odors you respond to positively can boost your alertness and productivity. Try peppermint, lemon, or cinnamon—all have properties that contribute to a productive environment—but it's most important just to find one you like.

12. Green your space: Having a plant in your workspace—and there's one for every type of environment—can improve productivity and job satisfaction, according to psychologists.

13. Maintain an even temperature: Keeping the thermostat at a setting optimal for everyone is impossible, yet being too hot or cold will harm productivity. If you can't adjust the thermostat, dress in layers so you can adjust your own comfort level.

14. Use multiple monitors: If you work on a computer, these can boost efficiency and productivity, according to multiple research studies.

15. Make it ergonomic: Interacting with your work setting and equipment in a way that is physically suitable and safe for the human body—ergonomic seating, height-adjustable work surfaces, and adjustable monitors—will increase your comfort and productivity.

3. Make Your Morning Routine Sacred

Some days we wake up ready to attack work and conquer the world, feeling like nothing can hold us back from achieving our goals.

If only we could feel like this more often.

Getting started, focusing, not being distracted, feeling positive . . . sometimes these are just hard to seize. How likely are you to be highly motivated on days when your mojo is a no-go? Not very.

A consistent morning routine can make all the difference, even when you start the day off on the wrong foot. Each morning, I (Erica) choose a podcast or audiobook to match my mindset. Self-help, motivational, parenting, grief, finance, business strategy, marketing—I pick something from my library that provides what I need that morning. Then on my thirty-minute commute, I get my head in the space I need it to be for that day. It's a habit that has also helped me transform my Mandatory time of commuting into Investment time and Treasured time. (More on this in Habit 4: Obsess over TIME.) I listen to books or podcasts most days, but not all the time. Sometimes what I need is to drive in silence, periodically count my breaths, and allow my brain thirty minutes of low gear. Again, it depends on what I need in that moment.

It's a keystone habit of the most productive people to have a consistent morning routine that starts the day off right. More than half of the XP have a morning routine that gets them off to a productive start each day, as opposed to just one in four of the Rest.

Many people have told us our 5-Step Extreme Productivity Morning Routine (see page 79) has been the productivity hack that has made all the difference for them.

Morning Routine and Energy

With the right morning routine, you can focus on the quality of your energy, even turning it around if it's not good when you first get going. Think of the way Ari's energy was reinvigorated when he started each day with the Good Morning Tour versus starting the day with screen time.

> When it comes to energy, there are two parts to consider: quality and sustainability. Quality comes first. If you don't have good-quality energy, it's tough to sustain energy at all.
>
> The XP are 3.5 times more likely to sustain energy for long periods. It's a key driver of Extreme Productivity. Improving the quality of your energy, exercising, taking Treasured time, practicing mindfulness, having meaningful goals, and getting enough sleep all tend to help people sustain their energy.

5-Step Extreme Productivity Morning Routine

The Extreme Productivity Morning Routine goes like this:

STEP 1: **Read your objectives.** The crux of effective action planning is to have quarterly, monthly, and weekly objectives and to tie your Investment activities to achieving those objectives. Many people write short-term objectives and then forget them. If you reread them, you won't. The best practice is to have them right above your action plan or to-do list, so you are forced to look at them every day. This will help keep you focused on what's most important.

STEP 2: **Ask, "How's my mindset?"** Check in with yourself. If you're feeling down, low, sick, tired, unmotivated, or in a bad mood, it's going to affect your motivation. Bad days tend to follow bad moods. Practice positive self-talk if needed. Take a walk, vent to a friend, journal, listen to a podcast. Do something—anything—to turn it around.

STEP 3: **Ask, "Will I?" for critical tasks.** You know what you need to do. It's right there on your action plan. But sometimes people don't do what they tell themselves to do. If you ask yourself if you _will_ do it, there's a significantly higher chance you will.

STEP 4: **Ask, "How will I be better than yesterday?"** Give yourself one piece of advice that will help you be better than yesterday. Taking into account the compounding effect, if you're 1 percent better each day, it only takes seventy-two days for you to be 100 percent improved.

STEP 5: **Start with your Greatest Impact Activity.** Identify your GIA for the day and begin immediately on that. Do not check email. Do not listen to that voice mail. Start with your GIA. The XP are four times more likely than The Rest to begin work every day on the activity that will contribute most to their overall success. (We understand that some people must check messaging in the morning. If you do, question deeply what needs a response. It's the questioning of email behavior, then challenging yourself to change what you can, that has saved many people an hour, or three, a day.)

These five steps may sound like common sense, but common sense is not commonly practiced. Want to have a great day? Follow the Extreme Productivity Morning Routine consistently.

Stack the Hack

No single habit or hack will drive your Productivity Quotient to the maximum score, 180. But each one you implement in your life will nudge you up the scale, as they nudge you toward changing your habits.

Imagine the odds of completing your GIA, even if it's a new habit for you, if you stack up just a few of the hacks inside the 9 Habits of Extreme Productivity.

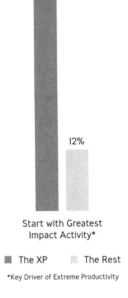

I begin work every day on the activity that will contribute most to my overall success.

48%

12%

Start with Greatest
Impact Activity*

■ The XP   ▨ The Rest

*Key Driver of Extreme Productivity

Odds You'll Complete Your GIA on Any Given Day

Odds	Hacks Used	Total Time Needed to Employ Hacks
Virtually assured		

Put a stopwatch, sprint, and eliminate possible distractions as you work on your GIA

Say 3 . . . 2 . . . I . . . Go! on your GIA right after your morning routine

Calendar your GIA

Ask, "Will I do my GIA first unless there's an absolute emergency?" and you answer with an honest "Yes." (Note: can be part of morning routine)

~5 minutes

Say, "When I get to work, then I will start my GIA" (Note: part of morning routine)

Identify your GIA the previous day

Decide starting with your GIA is a habit you want to change, and blueprint the change with the strategies in this graphic

If you do nothing

Not likely

Odds are good, no?

And you can do this for *any habit you want to change*—bad ones you want to stop and productive ones you want to begin—even if you're waking up in a hospital room each morning.

✳   ✳   ✳

Have we persuaded you yet to Reengineer Your Habits? The choice is yours, of course. But we hope you'll use the TIME for Action steps at the end of this chapter to begin creating your own Habit Change Blueprint and practicing the 5-Step Extreme Productivity Morning Routine so you will personally experience just how powerful—and simple—they really are.

TIME FOR ACTION

- **Use the Habit Change Blueprint:** Choose which habits you will change one by one and how. Go to: MyProductivityCode.com/booktools to download the Habit Change Blueprint worksheet. Add a single habit or a handful in the "Habits I Want to Change or Develop" column. Then, on the right, fill in the "Why Am I Doing This" column for each habit. Hold off on the "How I Plan to Change or Develop This Habit" for now. We'll get back to that soon.
- **Use the 5-Step Extreme Productivity Morning Routine:** Go to MyProductivityCode.com/booktools to download a meeting invite for 7:30 AM every weekday that includes the Extreme Productivity Morning Routine.

This wraps up The Productivity Code Key #1: Manufacture Motivation, which sets you up to achieve your goals. Are you beginning to see how you can get into the mindset of continually defining what is important to you? And, importantly, how it's in your power to Recruit Your Drive, Ignite Your Proactivity, and Reengineer Your Habits to activate and harness your motivation? In the next section, you'll discover how you can become the master of your time so you can achieve your goals with Key #2: Control Your TIME. We'll see you there.

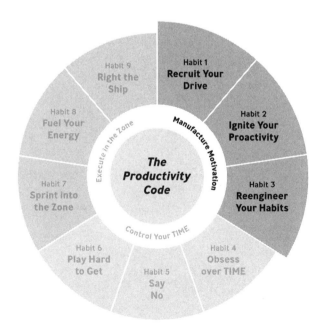

CONTROL YOUR TIME

Consider the following:

- The average adult spends four hours per day watching TV but under-estimates their viewing time by one full hour per day.[1]

- The typical knowledge worker spends seventeen hours, or a third of their workweek, processing emails. Thirty percent of said emails are not important.[2]

- Overall, people spend:
  - 5.5 days per year, 132 hours total, deciding what to eat[3]
  - 250 hours per year, or 41 minutes per day, on Facebook[4]
  - 171 minutes per day checking their smartphones[5]

We could go on, but we'll close the statistics here with our own productivity research: most people spend an average of 4.3 hours per workday on Empty (wasted) and Mandatory (could be delegated or simply not done) activities. That's about *half of every workday down the productivity drain.*

Mandatory/Empty Time Analysis
Current # of Hours and Potential to Decrease
HOURS SPENT PER WORKDAY

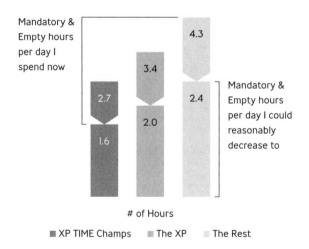

Mandatory & Empty hours per day I spend now

4.3

3.4

2.7

2.4

2.0

1.6

Mandatory & Empty hours per day I could reasonably decrease to

# of Hours

■ XP TIME Champs   ▓ The XP   ▒ The Rest

Productivity has long been seen primarily as a time-management challenge. Learn certain hacks and organize your to-do list the right way, and you'll get more done. This is true to an extent, but there's so much more. With the right mindset and tools, you can completely redefine how you spend your time:

- Slash wasted time.

- Maximize your Investment time.

- Complete your Greatest Impact Activities every day.

- Ruthlessly defend and control your time so nobody steals it.

- Become impossible to distract.

- Get in the zone and concentrate.

- Become unstoppable every hour.

- And feel better when you find Treasured time for yourself ~~not~~ today.

We've already covered the first key, Manufacture Motivation. You need to be psyched up and able to get started. You need to know what you want and why. These are preconditions for spending your time productively. Once you know what your goals and priorities are, you can align your days and organize your time to get there.

In this second key, Control Your TIME, we'll help you see where your time goes now, choose what to do and what not to do, and be the master of your own time destiny.

OBSESS OVER TIME

THE MAP

It's being here now that's important. There's
no past and there's no future. Time is a very
misleading thing. All there is ever, is the now.
We can gain experience from the past, but
we can't relive it; and we can hope for the
future, but we don't know if there is one.

—George Harrison

Often after our Good Morning Tour and breakfast, Ari would go back to the hospital room and watch expanded game summaries on NHL.com with Zayde. Each summary runs about twenty minutes with highlights and analysis on various games played the night before. Ari would watch all of them, maybe two hours' worth of hockey.

One morning I (Mike) was itching to get some important work done, but Zayde had a cold and couldn't come. While Ari was consumed in CHCU (critical hockey catch-up), I was distracted, trying to focus on work in the back of his room, feeling a bit annoyed that I was stuck in the hospital for hundreds of "not todays" waiting for a heart.

This morning as Ari watched, he started mimicking the hand signals that all the referees used. He'd say the penalty, then do the signal. I was torn, trying to get work done, feeling annoyed, and also sitting in the presence of this magical kid who, seriously, at five years old, was trying to figure out how all the hockey penalties worked and the proper way for referees to signal them. And I was there, in attendance but not present.

What was I thinking? How could I miss this?

I put the work away and pulled up an online sheet of all the hockey hand signals. Together, we started memorizing them. Hand pass, tripping, interference—and goal scored, of course. GOAL!

Lesson learned in productivity and life. We have to make choices. When the morning started, I was making the wrong one. I was trying to get some work Investment time in while feeling bitter that nobody else could do the "babysitting" that morning while I had work piling up.

I'm grateful I made the choice to change my mindset that morning. Ari and I spent the rest of the day together. We learned the hand signals, played hockey in the elevator bank, enjoyed his favorite board game (*NFL Rush Zone*), and sampled all the soups in the cafeteria. I deeply Treasured that time.

The next morning, March 3, 2017, we got the news: Ari's heart transplant would happen n̶o̶t̶ today.

It's Your TIME

Obsessing over time can help you fit more of the important stuff in your life. Time doesn't literally expand, but it feels like it does when you are mindful of where you spend it. We love vlogger Meir Kay's inspirational video on YouTube.[1] The notion is that we can easily fill our "jar"—the time we have available—with sand, the small stuff: chores, shopping, screen bingeing, and such. But if we put the big rocks into our jar first— the important pursuits that matter most, like family, relationships, and health—we find that we can still fit the sand and water (the lesser pieces) around them as we wish.

Before we can fill the jar with big rocks, though, we have to empty out the old sand. We have to *make* time.

But it's not easy. For us, it was going to take more than turning off alerts and working in chunks of twenty undistracted minutes. We had completely lost control of our time. We needed the hacks, but we needed more.

We needed to *obsess over time*.

A few years back, I (Mike) began gaining weight, my waistbands were tight, and I didn't feel well. I needed to change how I ate, starting with the Atkins Diet, which became a now decade-long low-carb journey. It's not recommended you ease into it when starting. Rather, you go into Atkins boot camp for two weeks. They call it the "Induction Phase": for fourteen days, you follow very exact and specific rules to "transform your body into a fat-burning machine" before you throttle back out of turbo on the fifteenth day.

First order of business for me, and part of the appeal of Atkins, was to focus on my heart and mind as well as my piehole, and make sure I completely committed to the change.

I had to obsess, even if just for a short period of time, to make the change meaningful and durable. With Atkins, it was straightforward: I could just drop my old eating habits and follow their low-carb rules. They told me what to eat. I saluted and enjoyed the bacon and Brussels sprouts.

It's not quite the same with your time. While you do need to obsess, you also need to make hard choices. If you do, however, you'll find it's worth it. A thousandfold.

In the first chapter of this book, we quoted Annie Dillard in *The Writing Life*: "How we spend our days is, of course, how we spend our lives." She continued: "What we do with this hour, and that one, is what we are doing. A schedule defends from chaos and whim. It is a net for catching days. It is a scaffolding on which a worker can stand and labor with both hands at sections of time. A schedule is a mock-up of reason and order—willed, faked, and so brought into being; it is a peace and a haven set into the wreck of time; it is a lifeboat on which you find yourself, decades later, still living."[2]

If we want to build a schedule to defend from chaos and whim, if we want a net to catch our days, if we want to stand and labor with both hands at sections of time, we need to make big changes.

TIME is the map that allows you to make those changes. It points you in the right direction. It tells you where to go, where to avoid, for each day, hour, and minute. It guides you to the right places and away from the wrong ones.

Indeed, we need to obsess in order to take this level of control over our time and days.

Where does obsessing over time start? With making the choice to do it. Are you willing to spend a week to make obsessing over time your top priority? If so, then welcome to your time induction. We'll show you how to:

1. Take T, Increase I, Minimize M, Eliminate E

2. Put your GIA first

3. Track your time and make choices for how you want to spend it

I. Take T, Increase I, Minimize M, Eliminate E

As we said in the "New Mindset About TIME" chapter, most time management systems focus too much on *seiryoku-zenyo* to get things done, but not *ikigai*, or reason for being. The latter is the mindset you want to have as you pull out the TIME map to manage how you spend your days.

We found that when we looked at time as a series of levels with Treasured topping the list, it changed our lives. Later, when we began teaching these ideas, it changed the lives of many others.

How you define activities within the TIME framework is deeply personal. It's also dynamic—it changes depending on where you are and what you need in the moment.

Level	Description	Action
Level 4: Treasured	Time you hold dear	Take some now, maximize for future
Level 3: Investment	Time that generates outsized return	Increase: prioritize, calendar, maximize
Level 2: Mandatory	Time you feel you must spend	Minimize/outsource
Level 1: Empty	Time you waste	Eliminate/minimize

Take T: Treasured time

This is time you hold dear doing the things you love. *Ikigai.* This is where we all want to be. Common examples include:

- Quality time with loved ones
- Vacation with friends and family
- Alone time
- Sports and games
- Work
- Hobbies
- Community service
- Your favorite TV show

With Treasured time, as with all categories, it's different strokes for different folks. One of the most common issues we help people work through is getting beyond what they have been *told by others to believe* they should treasure, and, instead, to identify what they, themselves, deep down actually treasure.

Let's start with work. Some people find time at work to be a chore. If that's you, when you saw it on this list, you might have thought, "Work? Really?" Other people find deep fulfillment at work. If this is you, be proud of that. Own it. Wear it like a badge of honor. Don't let anyone take away the purpose and sense of wholeness you find in work.

Another common area pregnant with emotion for some people is family. Many people have been *told by others* they should treasure time with family. Some people can't stand certain branches of their families, but they feel a deep sense of shame for *not* spending time with them. If certain types of family time are not Treasured time for you, you don't owe it to anybody to say that it is.

You get the idea: different strokes. The only strokes you need to figure out are your own.

What fills your cup? What do you love doing? Who do you enjoy spending time with? These are your treasured activities.

Whatever Treasured time looks like for you, if you spend the other categories of your time wisely, you'll find yourself with more time available to treasure. The XP, in fact, are twice as likely as The Rest to say, "I regularly devote the right amount of time for me to do activities I treasure."

Our research confirms it: the number-one key behavioral driver to maximizing happiness is taking Treasured time. That says it all. As we explained in "A New Mindset About TIME," not waiting until later to take Treasured time helped us to restore our energy and keep us going when times got hard.

Increase I: Investment Time

This is the time spent on your highest-priority activities, those activities that give you the highest return on your time and greatest success. You get an outsized return on your Investment time because it pays dividends when you gain skills and knowledge, accumulate experience, and drive priority initiatives forward.

What your Investment time looks like will differ based on your goals. What is it you want? Your Investment time is spent on those activities that will put you on a trajectory to reach your desired destination. As I (Mike) mentioned back in Habit 1: Recruit Your Drive, my big-picture goal is to be a full-time philanthropist. In addition, I have concrete goals, my three-year and annual goals, that will bridge me to my big-picture goal. For me, my Investment time will be devoted to things like tripling the size of my business over the next three years, which ultimately will help me with my big-picture goal.

For some people, Investment time is about achieving career and financial success. For others, it has nothing to do with those things—it may be all about personal growth and development, health and well-being, or something else entirely. For still others, it could be driven by a mix of personal and professional goals. And, of course, for some, the main goal is finding enough financial stability so you can turn your attention to more fulfilling goals.

I (Erica) have struggled with anxiety for most of my life and post-traumatic stress disorder (PTSD) after Ari died. Among my Investment activities is a regular practice of yoga nidra (restorative yoga sleep, often with guided meditation), which has been shown to reduce stress and anxiety for military veterans suffering from PTSD, to achieve my health and well-being goals.[3] For my longer-term goal of growing a success-ful business, I regularly devote Investment time to things like strategic planning, reading business books, and talking to other business leaders.

How can you use your time today to achieve your longer-term goals? You need to align your mid- and short-term priorities and spend your hours and days deliberately to help you get there.

As our research reveals, maximizing Investment time is the number-three key driver of Extreme Productivity. The XP report devoting 46 percent *more* Investment time per day than The Rest.

The key to achieving your goals: increase Investment time.

Minimize M: Mandatory Time

This is time spent doing things you feel you need to do, even if, in real-ity, you don't. Commuting to work, shaving, mowing the lawn, paying bills, filling out expense reports, proofreading your proposals, print-ing and binding presentation material. All are possible examples of Mandatory time.

You can minimize Mandatory time by converting it into Invest-ment or Treasured time. For example, at one point before we went on heart watch and Ari was still at home, I (Mike) found myself with about a thirty-minute daily commute to and from the office. I arrived at the office only to begin my workday with back-to-back phone calls. I turned things around when I converted the commute from Mandatory to Investment time, scheduling phone calls to happen in both the morning and evening commute. Boom! Upward of five hours a week Mandatory time minimized and Investment time gained.

Another way to minimize Mandatory time is by choosing to delegate Mandatory activities. For example, you can hire a landscaper to mow the lawn, have your groceries delivered, drop your laundry at a fluff-and-fold, or outsource the proofreading of your proposals.

Finally, you can reduce Mandatory time by questioning whether an activity needs to be done at all. Or done by you. Or maybe somewhere in between, like, "Can I attend that hour-long meeting for just the ten minutes you need me?"

Minimizing and outsourcing Mandatory time can make you happier, too, as we learn in a *New York Times* article titled "Want to Be Happy? Buy More Takeout and Hire a Maid, Study Suggests."[4] Negotiation expert Ashley Whillans surveyed several thousand people, asking them about well-being and time-saving purchases, such as ordering take-out food, taking a cab, hiring household help, or paying someone to run an errand. Participants who made these kinds of purchases reported greater life satisfaction than those who did not.

Is this just a strategy for the rich? Not at all. People benefited from buying time regardless of where they fell on the income spectrum.

So don't rule this out as an option.

In fact, our own productivity research confirms the relationship between happiness and spending less time on Mandatory and Empty activities: the median time that the happiest people spent on Mandatory and Empty activities was three hours per day compared to four hours for everyone else. Lest you think that's not a big difference, going from four hours to three hours is a 25 percent reduction. Think of it another way: How would you feel if your income went up 25 percent overnight? Twenty-five percent is a lot.

The key to Mandatory time is minimizing it or converting it into Treasured or Investment time.

Mandatory-Time Discussions Cut to the Quick

Before moving on, we want to acknowledge that this can also be a sensitive area. Helping people assess and change their Mandatory time is one of the most emotional things we do in our workshops and coaching. A woman (we'll call her Sara) attending one of our workshops with her colleagues bristled at the following language in the Extreme Productivity Assessment:

Consider the following non-work activities, and indicate your level of agreement with whether or not you spend significant time each day on corresponding to the statement appearing below on the list:

- *Household work (e.g., cooking, cleaning, laundry, home maintenance, yard work not for fun or quality time, but of necessity)*
- *Shopping/errands (not for fun, but of necessity)*
- *Caregiving (not for fun or quality time, but of necessity)*

She challenged John Doerr, who was leading the workshop, by saying, "I disagree!" at the very beginning of the session, before he even got started. John asked her to share what was on her mind. She read aloud the statements from the assessment and said, "I read some of your articles and I disagree. These aren't Mandatory activities. These are the things I do to make a home for my husband and three children. These are not just valuable, they're a *part of my values*. Where do you get off telling me or anyone else to 'outsource' or 'minimize' these?"

She was visibly upset. He certainly had to be careful here, or she and her colleagues would close their minds for the next two days of the workshop.

John acknowledged the importance of the question and asked if he could ask her a few questions before sharing his thoughts. She said sure, so he asked, "What is it that you do on the work side of things, Sara?"

"I'm a key account manager. I work twenty-five hours a week right now, and work to maintain and grow about twenty accounts."

"And what about the rest of the time?"

Sara replied, "I focus on family mostly. I have three kids—ages four, eight, and nine—they pretty much demand all my attention! And I like it. When the four-year-old gets to school soon, and the other two are a little older, I'll probably come back to work full time."

"I've had young kids, too. I know the feeling!" John said. "Do you have childcare while you're at work?"

"Yes, we have a nanny three days a week."

"Does the nanny ever call in sick?"

"Sometimes. Here and there."

"What happens then?"

"I take the day off and watch the kids. Or my husband does," Sara replied. "We take turns."

"That's great. Does he have a flexible schedule?"

"He's an attorney. He recently started his own practice, so he's flexible."

John continued his questions. "If the nanny calls in sick, are you glad she did, or would you have preferred to work that day?"

"Well, I like having a day with the kids, once I get over the frustration of missing work, but my plan and preference would have been work on that day."

"Got it. Do your kids do activities?"

"Sure, the older two do soccer three days a week. The youngest has music and dance and a playgroup."

"Do you drive them every time to every activity?"

"No, thank goodness. We carpool and split it up, so I don't have to drive every day."

"Why don't you drive every day?"

"Because I have to work! And I have housework and yard work to do, too."

"Got it. What do you do for housework?"

"Same as everyone else, I guess. I'm lucky, now I have someone do the deeper cleaning every other week, but I still do the laundry, the neatening, the food shopping, and everything else that keeps the house going."

They were getting to the heart of the matter. "Do you love all that?" John asked.

"No, not really," Sara conceded, "but somebody has to do it for me to provide the home I value having."

John then addressed the group, "I don't want to know anyone's individual compensation, but is it reasonable to assume the comp range for the whole account team is in the upper five figures or even the low six figures, if they hit their goals?"

Heads nodded and folks responded, "Yes."

"Okay," he continued. "Sara, I agree with you, but if you had someone else to make sure the fridge was stocked, the laundry was done, had backup child care you paid a premium for that was available on days the nanny calls in sick . . . if you drove even less carpool yet still attended the games and activities you wanted to, left the yard work to someone else . . . if you had all of this, do you think you'd be able to spend even better time with your kids, and more time driving your professional success?"

"Sure, having a fairy godmother would be a dream. But that would be crazy expensive."

"How much might it cost for help around the house?"

"It's expensive around here. Maybe twenty dollars an hour."

"Okay. How many hours would you need to take a huge load off you and your husband?"

"Maybe fifteen a week."

"So that would be $300 a week, times 52 weeks is $15,600 a year or $1,300 a month?"

She replied, "So says the math, sure."

"Could you make twice as much as that, and put yourself a few years closer to a promotion, if you had that time? And could your husband bill a few more hours and find a few more clients a year, too?"

"I think so," Sara agreed. Meanwhile, everyone else in the room was furiously taking notes.

"So is it fair to say that you can live by your values *and* create the home environment that you need, but sometimes laundry, yard work, and even childcare are done 'of necessity' and not because you really wanted to do it at that specific time and for that amount of time?"

"Okay, yes. For sure, yes," she responded.

"Then it's not about values, it's about change," John said. "It's about making a plan for what's ideal for you, seeing if we can make the Investment case for change, deciding what we do and do not want to do with clear eyes, and working to make change happen. If so, that's what we're all about to do here in this workshop over the next two days."

"Sounds like a plan," Sara said with a smile, "but I'd like to point out that you're not being very good at time management. We're now starting ten minutes late because you let this discussion hijack your agenda. We better get started."

"This discussion *is* our agenda," he responded. "Thank you for getting us started off right."

Granted, some people don't have the resources that Sara does. People have different income levels, different and very real demands on their time, and different life circumstances. We realize it's some people's job to photocopy and organize other people's days. But most people, we've learned, can find more time to invest in themselves and work their way to the next level, whatever that next level is for them.

Thus, one thing is true about everyone. Their "I can't" statements about changing how they spend their time frequently break down upon analysis. It's not that they can't, because, in fact, they can.

We typically only need to zoom in and challenge people's assumptions so they can zoom out, see the big picture, and come to understand how it can all be different.

Eliminate E: Empty Time

This is precisely as it sounds: time spent, nothing gained. At least with Mandatory Time, if you need to spend thirty minutes to get a haircut, your hair gets cut. If you're flipping through Facebook, watching You-Tube videos, or reading *Us Weekly*, to the extent you don't treasure these activities, you are probably just letting time pass.

Now, you may, indeed, treasure this time. If that's the case, great. And from time to time, we all need brain rest. Going into low-gear mode and wandering aimlessly, whether through a magazine, social media, or the cable channels isn't necessarily bad—we do those things, too. But most people would prefer to decrease the time they spend watching TV, playing games on the internet, scrolling through Facebook, or puttering around the house aimlessly.[5] And most of us could benefit from reallocating a good chunk of Empty time to other uses. *The key to Empty time is to eliminate as much of it as you can.*

Be Mindful in How You Spend Your TIME

Keep in mind that time is dynamic. Maybe you treasure the first twenty minutes watching cute cat videos on YouTube. But forty-five minutes later, did you need to watch the tenth one? Did it give you as much joy as the first one? Let's say you Treasure a New England Patriots game on TV. If you DVR it, you could zap an hour of commercials and perhaps even enjoy that time more. You eliminate an hour of Empty and leave two hours of Treasured. It's a fine line where Treasured time turns to Empty. The most important thing is to be mindful of your time and to check in with yourself regularly, asking, "Why am I spending my time doing this right now?" Once you get in the habit of being mindful of your time and checking yourself, you'll waste much less of it.

Extremely productive people accumulate Treasured and Investment time, and avoid dwelling in the Mandatory and Empty time zones. Yet even the most productive of us struggle with this; more than a third of The XP admit they spend a significant amount of time during a typical workday on Mandatory and Empty activities, compared to nearly half of The Rest.

Sometimes it's not about minimizing Mandatory activities but switching them around. I (Erica) used to have the habit of cleaning up immediately every night after dinner. I spent the day at work; I came home; I made dinner; I tidied up the toys; I did the dishes; I cleaned the kitchen. Then I'd rush through putting the kids to bed so I could have some downtime. After Ari died, I questioned everything. What the hell was I doing, worrying about the house and cleaning up during the precious hour I have each night with my children?

When I went through the TIME exercise, I realized that for me, I treasure time with my kids before bed. So I changed the habit. I decided I was no longer going to do dishes straight after dinner. Instead, I decided to use this time to play, read books, watch a show, and cuddle with them. I stopped rushing through bedtime. I showed up. I was present. I enjoyed it. (And, luckily, Mike loves doing dishes . . . Mandatory time minimized right there, folks!)

Getting the balance right matters. In the pursuit of financial freedom, some people spend the vast majority of their waking hours in Investment time. That's precisely what I (Mike) did for many years: I worked and worked and worked some more, so I could make enough money to achieve financial freedom. I knew that at some future point, I wouldn't have to work anymore, which is what many people want in their "retirement."

The downside is that when I got too caught up in pursuing my future, I ceased to be present with my family and friends. I needed to make changes. I did, and I still work on finding the right balance today.

Obsessing over time is a big-picture, global-way-of-thinking pursuit. It's also tactical, like planning out where you want your time to go on any given day. To that end, in our next hack, we get very specific about one thing you should do every day as a part of your obsession over time.

2. Put Your GIA First

During each day, you expend energy. Energy is a renewable resource, but as you're using it, you lose it. If you spend two hours plowing through email, taking care of Mandatory items, or putting out fires, your tank is no longer full.

What should you do? Put your Greatest Impact Activity (GIA) first. When you work on your GIA first, you start with a full tank.

Throughout this book we stress the power of starting your day with your GIA. But now we'll get into *why* this hack works.

The body of research suggesting that energy, memory, concentration, and analytical skills are better in the morning for most people is indisputable. For instance, based on a study of two million students in Los Angeles County, researchers found math and English GPAs are higher when students take those classes in the morning versus the afternoon.[6] Other studies show task completion accuracy and speed are better in the morning.[7] Alertness is better in the morning, too (though with a burst in the evening).[8] Doctors diagnose better, and get better surgical results, in the morning,* and people's logic is better then, too.[9]

So if you have something important to do, odds are you want to do it first thing in the morning. The XP do just this. Almost half of The XP put their GIA first—but just a little more than one in ten of The Rest do.

While morning is better for most people's energy and concentration, for some people it's better in the afternoon, evenings, or late at night. If this is you, then put your GIA at that other time.

That is, if you think you will definitely get to it and not *push it off for another day.*

Ever have something on your to-do list for a given day that you didn't get to? Us, too. All the time. As a colleague of ours used to say, "I was planning on doing that today, but the alligators got me." In reality, what happens to many of us is that even when we have the best of intentions, we get to our desks and get overwhelmed, derailed with distractions and seemingly urgent needs for our time.

Don't let this happen to your Greatest Impact Activity. Put your GIA first. (And be prepared to exercise Habit 5: Say No, and Habit 6: Play Hard to Get, because once you start your GIA, the alligators will undoubtedly be coming for you.)

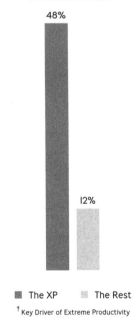

I begin work every day on the activity that will contribute most to my overall success.[†]

48%

12%

■ The XP   ▨ The Rest

[†] Key Driver of Extreme Productivity

---

* Doctors and medical professionals: We're sure you do a solid job in the afternoons and take steps to make sure quality is high throughout the day. Don't shoot the messengers of these study results, please.

3. Track Your TIME

If you are like most people, changing your Mandatory and Empty time habits will be challenging. Allocating more time to Investment and Treasured activities and rearranging your days to work on the right activities at the right times takes great focus and furious intent.

Let's say for argument's sake you're ready to change how you spend your time. You won't know what's possible until you learn where your time *actually* goes. If you want to take control of your time, you first have to understand your time habits.

You may be doing this already if you started the exercise we shared in "A New Mindset About Time": keeping a time log. But if you're like many people, including The XP, you're likely to skip over that activity and not actually stop to do it. (While only 30 percent of the XP track their time, that's still five times more than The Rest, a tiny 6 percent of whom keep time logs.) We get it. Keeping a time log sounds mundane. Who wants to spend time recording what they do all day? Talk about boring.

What's not boring is what you'll see, and how you'll feel, after you log your minutes meticulously for a few days. The reality is it doesn't take that long, it's Investment time, and it works.

The benefits of tracking time not only include learning where your time goes but *feeling* the effects of tracking itself. Try completely wasting time (when you don't want to be, like at work) with a stopwatch ticking off the seconds you waste. You'll feel quite the pull of getting back to something more productive. This is called the Hawthorne Effect: a phenomenon where human subjects of an experiment change their behavior simply because they are being studied. You can see the evidence of the Hawthorne Effect in a Kaiser Permanente weight loss study of 1,700 people that found "Those who kept daily food records lost twice as much weight as those who kept no records."[10]

For two days—just two days—track your time. As you do, try to resist switching back to something productive when you find yourself unfocused. As difficult as it might be, don't fix your time choice just yet. Track where your time *would have gone on any normal, non-tracked day.* Neutralize the Hawthorne Effect by focusing on the fact that this initial two-day time tracking is not intended to change your behavior yet. It is intended to record your baseline. Keep a time log now for just two days as you currently spend your time. Change how you spend it later.

There's no doubt: if you want to optimize your time, you have to know where you're spending it. Know where your time goes, and you will find more of it.

Four Tips for TIME Tracking

Here are four tips we've found helpful with time tracking:

1. Set TIME and activity goals. Know what you want to accomplish on a given day, then define activities that will get you there. Let's say you're in sales and you need to fill your pipeline. Your objective today is to generate one meeting with a potential buyer. You can set your GIA goal as "spend at least four hours obsessively prospecting with no distractions."

Focus on activity over outcomes. You can't necessarily control the outcome, which in this case, is how many meetings you set. But you can control the number of hours spent prospecting.

2. Track activity and TIME level. When tracking, always note your activity (e.g., fixing tech problems) and your TIME level (which would be Mandatory). If you're using our time tracking worksheet, you'll see columns for these. Time tracking software and apps will also allow you to do this easily. By tracking both the activity and the TIME level, you will see what you're spending your time on. Now you can make conscious decisions on how to minimize Mandatory and Empty TIME and maximize Investment and Treasured TIME. In the words of Peter Drucker, "What gets measured gets managed."[II]

Peter Drucker, it seems, knew what he was talking about.

3. Use technology and timers best suited to you. Absolutely use timers. As you begin a task, start the timer and note the activity. When you switch activities, note when you switch and what you switch to, and restart your stopwatch. Count up using a stopwatch, whether it be on a watch, your desktop, an online stopwatch, or stopwatch in software like Toggl, RescueTime, Everhour, TimeCamp, TSheets, or MyHours. Don't use your phone because the act of looking at the stopwatch feature could lead you to distract yourself with email or messages when you otherwise would not have.

If time-tracking software isn't your thing, you can use a simple stopwatch and track your time in Excel, Word, a physical notebook, or a note-taking technology like Notes on your phone (but beware the potential for distraction), Evernote, or OneNote.

The method you use doesn't matter; what matters is that you are tracking your activities and TIME categories.

4. Track in periodic, obsessed daily chunks. It's impractical to track your time meticulously every single day. Start with a two-day tracking experiment.

Also, don't ballpark your time tracking. Recording estimates at the end of the day—"three hours prospecting, two hours meetings, one-and-a-half hours meals and breaks, two hours TV"—is anywhere from a little to extremely inaccurate. People tend to grossly overestimate the time they spend doing anything at work when looking back on activities.* For example, according to a United States Bureau of Labor Statistics study, people who reported that they worked seventy-five hours a week tended to provide actual time logs that reflected working twenty-five fewer hours per week than they estimated.[12] In other words, they remembered having spent 50 percent more time working than they actually did.†

It bears repeating: don't ballpark-estimate. Record *the actual minutes.*

Your obsessed tracking days should be the workdays or non-workdays for which you want to (1) understand where your time goes and (2) focus on changing your time habits.

As you track your time, keep the following in mind:

- **Be honest.** People often lie to themselves when they track time. Don't like that you got drawn into reading news articles for one and a half hours in the morning at work? Track it now; change it later.

- **You can enjoy something without it being Treasured TIME.** Some people enjoy aimless social media scrolling, getting ready to go out for forty-five minutes when twenty-five would do, or reading a magazine. When they're honest with themselves, however, most people trying to drive their careers forward would like to spend less time on these kinds of activities.

- **Don't target zero Empty or Mandatory TIME.** You can't get to zero, and you don't want to. Sure, you can convert Empty TIME like commuting into Investment TIME if you listen to business books or podcasts. Human brains, however, need some downtime. Also, if you target zero Mandatory time, you'll tend to get angry when you have to do something that you don't want to. Accept that it happened, do what you must if you must, and make a plan to reduce it in the future.

---

* This is estimating "looking back" at time. People are largely awful at estimating "looking forward," as well. It's called the planning fallacy and it's well studied. However you slice it, people are bad at estimating time.
† Go figure. People overestimate the amount of time they work and underestimate the time they spend watching TV.

The first step to finding more time is simply this: start tracking. Don't wait for the perfect moment, app, or activity. The sooner you figure out where your time is going, the sooner you can start maximizing time spent on what's truly important to you.

* * *

You can start using the TIME framework and making changes immediately by following the three TIME for Action steps listed at the end of this chapter. Go ahead, we'll wait. In the next chapter, "Habit 5: Say No," you'll learn how one small word can help you find more time.

TIME FOR ACTION

- **Start with Your GIA:** Open up your calendar right now. Block off one hour first thing in the morning for your GIA. When you get to work tomorrow, begin with your GIA. Do not open email, do not respond to your coworker, do not pass Go, do not collect $200. Start with your GIA. How does it feel?

- **Begin Tracking TIME:** Start with a two-day obsessed-time tracking induction. If you haven't done so already, go to MyProductivityCode .com/booktools and download our TIME tracking sheet.

- **Your TIME Table:** Go to MyProductivityCode.com/booktools and download the TIME Table worksheet. Take some time right now to consider the Treasured time you want more of, the Investment time that would turn the dial most for you, the Mandatory time you could minimize or outsource, and the Empty time that you could eliminate.

HABIT 5:

SAY NO

THE BOUNDARY

Daring to set boundaries is about having the courage to love ourselves, even when we risk disappointing others.

—Dr. Brené Brown

When Ari was in the hospital waiting for his heart, I (Erica) would drive back and forth from home an hour each way, every day. I'd get up, spend the first part of the morning with Lexi and Eli, jump in the car around 9:30 AM, and walk into Ari's hospital room by 10:30 AM. I'd spend time with Ari and Zayde while Mike was in and out trying to get work done. I would stay through dinner with Mike and Ari, and leave at 6:30 PM, getting home just in time to tuck Lexi in bed, feed Eli, and put him down as well. Since Eli was still breastfeeding, I was pumping every three hours and waking up with him through the night.

I barely had time each night to do my nails and toes, go out with the girls, go night skiing, and play in my evening canasta league. (Yeah, right. If I so much as got a shower in, it felt like an achievement tantamount to climbing Mount Everest.)

As I arrived at the hospital each morning, I was greeted by Ari with a big hug and sad voice, "Mom, I missed you. When are you going to spend the night?"

When I'd get home each night, I was greeted by three-year-old Lexi asking, "Mom, can you stay home with me tomowwow. Are we all ever going to be together as a family again?"

With cries of, "Can't you stay longer? Stay here with me," I had my heart ripped out of my chest on the bookends of every day, while in the middle of the day I held my son in my arms through IV poke after IV poke, test after test, and procedure after procedure.

I held it together with the kids (mostly). But in my red Pathfinder on the Mass Pike driving to and from the hospital, I let myself cry.

After two months, I had nothing left. Nothing.

So many people had been reaching out to ask what they could do to help us. I usually said no. I could handle it. I could power through. Until I couldn't.

I began to realize I had been saying no to the wrong things. By saying no to help, I was saying no to time with Lexi, Eli, and Ari. I was saying no to finding the strength I needed for myself so I could give my family what *they* needed. I had to make some tough choices and set some boundaries; otherwise, I was afraid I would implode. I had to say no to my pride in order to say yes to myself and find the strength to somehow keep going.

One day the Ethan M. Lindberg Foundation reached out to see if they could help. This was the same foundation we supported by hosting a charity golf tournament to raise money so they could rent a second apartment for families trying to survive long-term stays at the hospital. When we decided to run the tournament, we never thought we would be the ones living at the hospital indefinitely.

With the Foundation's assistance, we decided to take an apartment near the hospital. That way, we could be close to Ari while having a place to go to escape the craziness of the hospital and as a respite from hours spent on the highway.

Yes and no. Yes and no.

By making different decisions on what I said yes to, and what I said no to, I began to redefine my life. Literally.

Changing my yeses and my nos meant hard decisions and sacrifices.

By choosing to spend solid days at the hospital, I had to say no to tucking Lexi and Eli into bed each night. I had to say no to breastfeeding, even though I wanted to continue. I had to say no to waking up to Lexi climbing in my bed and cuddling with me each morning.

It broke my heart to say no to them, but I had to.

Saying no isn't just about cutting out the easy things. Sometimes it means making hard decisions. It's about doing what you must so you can be who you need to be, do what you need to do, and be accountable to yourself for your life and the choices you make.

The Courage to Say No

Not being able to say no is a surefire way to be exceptionally busy but make little actual progress. Not being able to say no is gut-wrenching when you know what your purpose is, you've identified your "Why" and your goals, and still you are pulled so thin you feel like a gerbil on a wheel, running and running, getting nowhere.

When I had all the time in the world, I could say yes to much more. I learned I had the courage and fortitude to say no while we battled for Ari's life.

When crisis gave me no choice, I learned to say no when I needed to so I could say yes to who I needed to be. Now that that crisis was over, I was not going back. When we eventually reemerged to life and living, I learned I could genuinely commit to the activities that aligned with my values and my purpose and say no to anything that didn't.

The word no eventually set me free, and it can for you, too. I see so many places where other people say yes, just like I used to, to things that don't serve them. Seemingly little things at home and at work, like:

- agreeing to make cookies for the bake sale when you already have a too-busy week.
- joining a meeting a colleague asks you to attend because they'd value your opinion at the end.
- completing the satisfaction survey from the health insurance company about your recent doctor visit.
- agreeing to take over part of a problem a coworker is stuck on.
- taking on a new client that you know won't be a good fit for one reason or another.
- showing a colleague how to use the company's new project-planning software in the middle of your workday, even though there's an online tutorial.
- taking on the volunteer coordinator role for your college alumni association because they asked.
- soliciting donations in person from local merchants for the library's annual gala fundraiser (ten items valued at $100 or more each, please).
- meeting friends for drinks at the airport because they have a one-hour layover, despite the fact that it will take you three hours, one way, in traffic to get there.
- signing up for a hip-hop class because all your friends are doing it and you have FOMO (real-life example).

Anything on this list can drain your time and your ability to take the Investment actions you need to achieve your goals. It's hard to do the thing you know you should when other things and people try to pull you away.

Don't let them. Say no.

You might read this list and think, "I'm a good team player. I should help my colleague." "I should take that meeting with a potential client even if I don't think they are likely to be a good fit." "I should help out with the bake sale."

But are you sure? Sure you shouldn't say no? What would happen if you stopped "shoulding" all over yourself?

Why Is It So Hard to Say No?

No is the only word that can tame your greedy inner chimp who thinks any opportunity to do anything is a banana worth chasing. That's the metaphor psychologist Steve Peters uses for the limbic system, which is the impulsive part of the brain.[1] Your inner chimp is fixated on sex, food, and danger, driven toward the first two and fleeing the third. When information reaches the brain, the chimp gets first dibs. *Yes* is the chimp's first answer to anything mildly attractive, and *no* is a distant second.

While your inner chimp says yes, your brain has no built-in counter-primate to say no. In fact, people's resistance to saying no is quite strong. At Cornell University, Vanessa Bohns set up an experiment to see whether participants would agree to do something unethical—in this case, deface a library book. Over 60 percent of people went along with it. "They would make comments like, 'I don't want to get in trouble' or 'This seems wrong,' but they would still do it," Bohns said. "You can feel uncomfortable about what you're being asked to do but still wind up going along with it because it's even more uncomfortable to say no."[2]

In previous chapters, we covered how to set goals and build action plans, to find your why and your purpose, and organize to fulfill them. To Control Your TIME, you must learn what to say yes to, or you won't know what to do. It stands to reason that to create boundaries and Control Your TIME, you also must learn to say no.

Brené Brown is often credited with saying, "We wear busyness as a badge of honor. We'd be afraid of what people would say if we weren't busy." We want to be the helpful one, the indispensable one, the capable one. In our enthusiasm to do it all, however, we get distracted by too many passing bananas.

It comes down to this: if you don't take control of your time, someone else will.

Or, more to the point, a whole lot of people will derail you, day by lost day, piece by insidious piece.

Saying no is about boundaries. It's looking at what's really important to you (look back to your goals in Habit 1: Recruit Your Drive), then aligning your time to those things (Habit 4: Obsess over TIME), and setting boundaries around them (right here in Habit 5: Say No).

What should you say no to? Anything that does not align with your goals. It's that simple.

If leading in your community is one of your goals and the bake sale is an important fundraiser to do that, then bake the damn cookies. If it's not, then don't. The cookie police aren't coming for you. Perhaps there's a less time-consuming way for you to support the fundraiser, like making a donation.

When you surround your goals with solid boundaries in this way, it makes what you say yes to that much more meaningful . . . impactful. Many times, however, people say yes when they should say no—even when they have clarity on their goals and actions—because they have issues with assertiveness.

Guess who is good at saying no at the right time? Yes, The XP. Even though it's a low-frequency behavior across the board (few respondents regularly say no), it's one of the most significant gaps between The XP and The Rest.

Take a close look at the list on the next page of low-frequency behaviors from our productivity research.

As you look at the list, notice that nine of these twelve behaviors are related thematically to both Habit 5: Say No, and Habit 6: Play Hard to Get (more on Habit 6 in the next chapter).

We know these things aren't easy to do, not even for the most productive people. Still, The XP are dramatically more likely to do them than The Rest. You have to learn to say no when your priorities and needs will be derailed if you don't. Sometimes, this will mean conflict with others' priorities and needs. When this happens, it's in your interest to just say "so be it" and set a very high bar for diverting from what's most important to you.

Saying no will be easier for some people than others. Some people are highly assertive naturally, but most aren't. In fact, 58 percent of people have a need to be liked, and thus have greater difficulty saying no.[3] If reluctance to say no is a deep-seated attribute for you, you might need extra practice, support, or coaching to learn how and break the banana-chasing pattern.

Low-Frequency Behaviors by Percent Difference
% Very Much Like Me

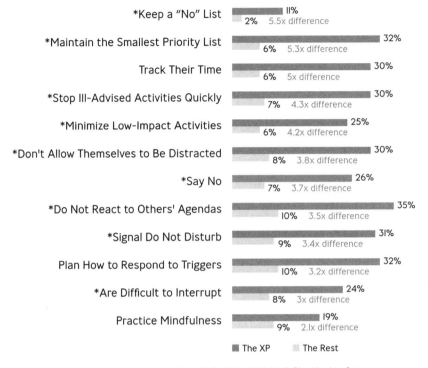

*Keep a "No" List — 11% / 2% — 5.5x difference

*Maintain the Smallest Priority List — 32% / 6% — 5.3x difference

Track Their Time — 30% / 6% — 5x difference

*Stop Ill-Advised Activities Quickly — 30% / 7% — 4.3x difference

*Minimize Low-Impact Activities — 25% / 6% — 4.2x difference

*Don't Allow Themselves to Be Distracted — 30% / 8% — 3.8x difference

*Say No — 26% / 7% — 3.7x difference

*Do Not React to Others' Agendas — 35% / 10% — 3.5x difference

*Signal Do Not Disturb — 31% / 9% — 3.4x difference

Plan How to Respond to Triggers — 32% / 10% — 3.2x difference

*Are Difficult to Interrupt — 24% / 8% — 3x difference

Practice Mindfulness — 19% / 9% — 2.1x difference

■ The XP   ▨ The Rest

*Themes corresponding to Habit 5: Say No and Habit 6: Play Hard to Get

Regardless of your psychological starting point for saying no, here are three hacks for setting the bar high for a yes, learning to say no, and—if you have to say no—doing it tactfully:

1. Keep a to-don't list

2. Do less: if it's not gung ho, it's no

3. Practice saying no

I. Keep a To-Don't List

Success and saying no seem to go together.

Billionaire and Berkshire Hathaway CEO Warren Buffett claims that "really successful people say no to almost everything."[4] Most days, Apple founder Steve Jobs would ask then head of design Jony Ive, "How many times did you say no today?"[5] One of our favorite business quotes is from Michael Porter: "The essence of strategy is choosing what not to do." And then there's David Maister's seminal article, "Strategy Means Saying 'No.'"[6]

One of the characteristic behaviors of The XP is maintaining an active no list, so they know which activities to avoid. Compared to The Rest, they are 5.5 times more likely to do this.

Most of us struggle even when saying no to ourselves. Roy Baumeister and John Tierney, authors of *Willpower*, report that one person typically has at least 150 different tasks to be done at any one time, and that an executive's to-do list for Monday alone could take more than a week to finish.[7]

Be brutal with your priority list. If you have thirty-two priorities, you have none. Get a colleague or coach to help you be resolute and say no to the lower-level priorities. You don't have to lose them altogether. That's mentally taxing. Instead, create a to-don't list, which will help maintain the boundaries you've established.

We all have to-do lists. We all need to-don't lists. Items on your to-don't list can be temporary or permanent. You can think of your to-don't list as a parking lot for ideas in different categories. Some might be categorical nos (never drive into the city at 4 PM on a Friday). Some nos might be no unless something changes (your friends' flight changes from Friday to Saturday due to weather . . . "Great, I'll see you at the airport!"). Perhaps an idea sounded good, but after you vetted it, you figured out it isn't worth it ("Yes! I'd love to see you . . . uh . . . a three-plus hour drive one-way to the airport in traffic . . . I can't at that time").

Other nos might not be at the top of your priority list right now. It may not be no forever. It's no, for now. For example, a client offers you her VIP pass to attend the major industry conference with its all-star speaker agenda and you really want to attend, but this year it overlaps with a series of client visits you've scheduled on the other side of the country. You could rearrange the client meetings and possibly make it to the conference on the final day. But, no, your priority right now is these marquee clients, so your focus is on them, and not the conference, for now.

When it's time for a new priority, with your handy to-don't list, you have a menu of ideas to spark your next move. Your next top priority might just be one you said no to previously. Or it might be something new. In any case, by keeping a to-don't list, you can know at a glance what you're not going to do or focus on now.

Here's what a to-don't list might look like:

My "To-Don't" List

Possible priorities or actions that are good, but not great right now, or great but not priorities right now.

- Focusing on deals under $25K unless they are strategic accounts
- Focusing on accounts that can't be at least $250K
- Joining meetings when asked unless I'm really needed or it helps me meet my goals
- Web surfing during the workday
- Producing a podcast
- Hiring a senior seller in the UK

Your to-don't list might also include more general items like these:

- Don't say yes to requests that will divert serious time from my priorities. If I say yes, I have to make the case that this is *more important than my own priorities*.

- Don't say yes to meeting requests blindly. Make sure I can get something out of the meeting, or I will offer something genuinely critical, and that attending it is *more important than my own priorities*.

- Don't say yes to more than one hour's worth of community activities, like cookies for the bake sale, per week.

- Don't accept meetings between 8 AM and 1 PM, or on Tuesdays, as it will interrupt my concentration.

- Minimize meeting time. If the meeting is an hour, say no to any time I don't need to be there. Find out my critical time (which could be ten minutes).

- Need to leave forty-five minutes early to cook dinner? Get takeout. Save thirty-five minutes. (That's a lot easier these days with so many affordable and healthy choices offered in most communities.)

- Don't add a new priority until I accomplish another or retire one and put it aside.

- Don't accept new clients with less than $X potential in annual revenue or margin.

2. Do Less: If It's Not Gung Ho, It's No

For seven years in our business, we invested in growing three distinct service areas. Truth was, though, we didn't have the bandwidth to scale all three to world-class standards. We could be pretty good at all three, but no better. And we were only gung ho on one of them: sales training.

Just a few years earlier, our firm had been featured on the Inc. 5000, *Inc.* magazine's list of the fastest-growing companies in the country. And yet after this one revelation, we renamed our company and started almost from scratch.

Scary? Sure.

Yet with this clear focus, a willingness to invest, and a productivity mindset, we rocketed to the top. Several years later, we were on *Training Industry*'s list of the top twenty sales-training firms in the world. (As a reference point, there are around eight hundred companies that offer sales training in the United States alone.)

When we asked ourselves what we were gung ho on, and answered with clarity, the whole world opened up to us.

For your Investment activities, if you're not wholly enthusiastic about doing something and the return it offers, say no. Don't do it.

Also, even if you're gung ho about more than one priority, trying to do too many can kill them all. As research by psychologists Robert Emmons and Laura King shows, having too many conflicting goals makes us do less to achieve them—and ruminate and worry more.[8] It's a lose-lose proposition.

Most people have too many concurrent priorities. As outlined in the article "The Art of Strategy Is About Knowing When to Say No," Brian Halligan, founder and CEO of HubSpot, aspired to expand their operations into Europe.[9] However, he knew he couldn't do it well until he finished changing the company's go-to-market focus. It pained him to say no to Europe (for now) and put it on hold, but he did. A year later, he put Europe back in motion and succeeded.

If you have simultaneous priorities, ask yourself, are they all getting done to your satisfaction? Do you have too many goals, too many objectives, too many projects going at once?

If this at all feels like you, be brutal about paring down the list. You don't have to delete the priority; you can move it to your to-don't list under the heading "No for Now."

Then you can focus on the top priorities, the few that will get you the greatest return. The ones that are right for this moment. With each of your priorities, ask yourself if you're gung ho about it. Remember, if it's not gung ho, it's no. This is the best test for deciding whether a priority should remain a priority. And if you have more than a handful of gung-ho priorities, you still need to prioritize. Then move as many as you can to the "No for Now" list.

Do less. If it's not gung ho, it's no.

Solid advice for all of us.

3. Practice Saying No

What if you're not naturally assertive? If saying no is a real challenge for you? If, despite your best intentions and with your to-don't list in hand, you still say yes when you should say no? As we mentioned earlier, you're not alone. Happily, though, with time and effort, you can learn to set boundaries.

Something that can help all of us who legitimately struggle here is to practice saying no. As therapist Darlene Lancer, author of *How to Speak Your Mind: Become Assertive and Set Limits*, writes, "Once you get practice setting boundaries, you feel empowered and suffer less anxiety, resentment, and guilt. Generally, you receive more respect from others and your relationships improve."[10]

Here are six ways you can practice saying no:

1. Low-stake scenarios: Practice saying no in small, unimportant situations, such as not giving your email address to a retail store clerk when they ask.

2. Try this at home: Stand in front of a mirror. Stand tall, smile, and say in a pleasant voice, "No, I can't do that right now."

3. Take time to breathe: Stop and breathe for a few seconds before saying yes to anything so you can give yourself a moment to assess your own needs.

4. Write it down: How do you want the situation to play out? Write what you'll say, such as, "Thanks for thinking of me, but I'm sorry I have to decline."

5. Follow your gut: Look down and ask your gut if it wants to say yes. If it's telling you to say no, listen to it.

6. Fallout analysis: How bad will it be if you say no? Take a moment to consider whether this is truly a make-or-break moment. Usually, if you say no, nothing bad happens.

You may also find that working with a trusted coach or accountability partner can help you overcome this challenge by exploring options and practicing your "say no" responses. Don't be discouraged if it takes some effort. It's worth it—you're worth it.

A few years back, one of my (Erica's) friends said about me, "Erica always says yes. When she's invited places, she goes." I thought about that comment for some time. I do indeed say yes to as many invitations as I can because personal relationships and friendships are a priority for me. Being with the people I love is my Treasured time: time that helps me to recharge and fills me up again. So I'm good with saying yes—when it counts.

The big point about saying no? It's difficult. It's emotional. But it's necessary if you want to focus on your priorities and not those of other people.

✳   ✳   ✳

Okay, time to take a deep breath . . . and time for action. Check out the TIME for Action steps on the next page to do a TIME Tracking Review and Create Your To-Don't List. No matter where you are on the continuum of setting boundaries, these two steps will get you moving in the right direction. In the next chapter, we'll dig into Habit 6: Play Hard to Get.

TIME FOR ACTION

- **TIME Tracking Review:** If you've followed our process, soon you should have a few days' worth of data on how you spend your days. Review the list and be brutally honest about activities on it that you can say no to. Highlight them. Write them down. Practice how you will say no. When faced with the situation again, say no.

- **Create Your To-Don't List:** Wherever you keep your to-do list, add a to-don't section. Personally, we use Evernote and OneNote. You might use one of these, Excel, a Word doc, or a for-real notebook. It doesn't matter where you keep your list, just that you keep one. And remember. It's not no forever. It's no for now.

PLAY HARD TO GET

THE SHIELD

The fox who keeps to one den is the
easiest caught by the terriers.

—Frank W. Abagnale, *Catch Me If You Can*

Once when Lexi had just turned three, she asked what Erica and I (Mike) were making for dinner. "Chicken and Brussels sprouts," I replied.

"I don't like Brussels sprouts," she groaned. "They make me want to hurl. I want something else."

"Well, dear," I said, "let me give you some options. With your chicken you can have Brussels sprouts or Brussels sprouts. But if you want, I can make you some Brussels sprouts. Unless that doesn't work for you, I can see if I can rustle up some Brussels sprouts. In any case, if you don't want them, you don't have to eat them."

Fast-forward about a year, we were living full time in the hospital with Ari. Across the hall from room 8224 there was a small, low-traffic family lounge. While Zayde would sit in the room with Ari, I had to stay close if I wanted to catch the doctors for rounds. Erica and I felt like our voices needed to be heard daily on Ari's care plan, so we did not like to miss rounds. As I typically had morning duty, I had to be either in Ari's room or that lounge until rounds came and went.

I had to work, but (as you know) I couldn't work in his room. I'd like to say the family lounge was my office of preference, but it was more like my office of Brussels sprouts. The family lounge was all I was going to get. If I wanted to be able to work and still be steps away from Ari if he needed me, there were no other options on the office location menu. I had no choice but to swallow it and stomach it. Every day. No matter how much I whined.

Though Erica will, of course, corroborate that I never whine. Much. (Turnabout is fair play, Lexi. Fair play indeed.)

After Zayde got to the hospital, I had at best a forty-five-minute window to get work done. I'd try to concentrate, but no sooner would I sit down than a new hospital battle would start. People would come in and say, "Good morning," or, "Hey, do you know where the coffee is?" Most of them had the "my daughter/nephew/grandson/cousin is going through hell and so am I" look on their faces. And mostly they were itchy to chat.

Would their desire to interact overcome the obviously-absorbed-elsewhere impression I so painstakingly tried to paint on my face? Actually, it wasn't a battle, it was more like a night of poker. Every five minutes, with each new lounge visitor, I was dealt a new hand to win or lose.

Usually, their hands beat mine, and we chatted. I didn't mind the chats, but when it came to work, my frustration level rose, and my disposition sank.

I absolutely understood their yen to chat. I felt the same at times myself. Sometimes I needed to let off steam and talk to someone else who got it. But while the Brussels Sprout Lounge was a break room for everyone else, it was my only option for work. I needed a solution.

One day at the "office," I was listening to a conference call. I wasn't an active participant in this one, so I was just silently sitting with earbuds in. I was only half listening to the call and half responding to emails (and doing neither well, as I hadn't learned the one-task-at-a-time lesson yet) when I noticed something fascinating: people came and went, but nobody asked me where the coffee was.

Hypothesis to test!

The next day, I got noise-canceling headphones. I'm talking *Episode IV* Princess Leia double-bun "see, I'm wearing headphones"–style headphones. I'd mount them up and turn them on so everyone could see the little green power light. But I didn't play music. I didn't want to listen to anything. I only wanted everyone to get the hint, silent and clear, "This guy is not present for chat. He is not the droid you are looking for. Move along."

Nobody asked me where the coffee was ever again. Headphones on, I had disappeared in plain sight.

Suddenly, the Force was with me.

Hooked on Distraction

Ever hear of Nir Eyal? He's the author of *Hooked: How to Build Habit-Forming Products*.[1] Most haven't heard of him. You know who has? Everyone at every technology, gaming, and social media company trying to get you addicted to their products.

Two decades ago, when I started working, part of my job was selling. Prospecting. It was just me, a phone on my desk, and a ticking clock. Every once in a while, I could hear a side conversation or one of my colleagues on the phone. But mostly it was quiet. Much as I wanted to distract myself, the only noise or interruption was that clock ticking away all day.

Nowadays we all have email, texting, Facebook, LinkedIn, Snap-chat, Instagram, multiple phones, YouTube, and everything we could ever read, including up-to-the-minute news, always available morning and night on our desks and in our pockets. As if simply being aware it's there is not enough, to remind us of it, we distract ourselves and every-one else at all hours with constant beeping, buzzing, dinging, whirring, and chirping.

They have us hooked. Deloitte found in a 2018 study that people col-lectively check their smartphones upward of eight billion times per day.[2] Across all age groups, people checked their phones forty-seven times a day in 2017, up from thirty-three times in 2014, for two hours and fifty-one minutes (that's 171 minutes a day!).[3]

No question, we are living in a world of ever-increasing distraction. As reported in the *New York Times*, people are distracted on average every eleven minutes.[4]

The effects on our productivity of this relatively very recent change are mind-blowing:

- Researchers discovered that interruptions make you twenty per-cent dumber.[5]
- Even three-second distractions double workplace errors.[6]
- When people get disrupted, it takes on average twenty-three min-utes and fifteen seconds to get back to task.[7]
- Twenty-seven percent of time disruptions result in more than two hours diverted from the previous task.[8]
- After only twenty minutes of interrupted performance, people reported significantly higher stress, frustration, workload, effort, and pressure.[9]

Indeed, distraction is bad and getting worse. (Thanks, Nir.) Not a few of us, not some of us, but most of us have phone, computer, media, and general habits that allow us to be distracted constantly. We don't think much about constant interruption and rapid task switching, but it's kill-ing our productivity.[10]

Perhaps you're the exception. They do exist. They're called The XP and they're nearly four times more likely to say, "I do not allow myself to be distracted by people or technology when I'm trying to concentrate."

*Don't Allow Themselves to Be Distracted

30%

8%   3.8x difference

■ The XP   The Rest

*Themes corresponding to Habit 5: Say No and Habit 6: Play Hard to Get

And it's no accident. They're deliberately making it difficult for people to interrupt them when they're concentrating by playing hard to get.

Playing hard to get is the shield they wield against the never-ending barrage of attention-seeking shrapnel that rips The Rest apart. It protects The XPs' ability to concentrate, keeping their focus safe in the midst of ever-increasing daily pandemonium.

The shield provided by playing hard to get doesn't just allow for concentration, it opens the door to peace. When you play hard to get, a sanctuary will open for contemplation, mindfulness, and uninterrupted calm. A little quietude goes a long way to improve your attitude.

Our advice here is simple, powerful, and effective, yet it's difficult to do, sometimes physically and often emotionally: play hard to get, and you'll become impossible to distract.

Here are three hacks we've found make the difference:

1. Be free from the shackles of alerts

2. Signal "do not disturb"

3. Be someplace else

I. Be Free from the Shackles of Alerts

When email first arrived on the scene, alerts were helpful. Our email would ding, and we'd know to look. Who remembered, after all, that we even had email? It was new. In the beginning, alerts were just a small and infrequent distraction. "You've got mail" was fun for a while.

Getting an email alert was like eating one chocolate chip cookie when we otherwise ate healthily. In fact, when Blackberry introduced push notifications in 2003, it was done to minimize how much we looked at our phone. We didn't need to look at all. We'd get an alert when an email came in. And when it did ... cookie! Take a look.

Now we are fed a steady diet of cookies around the clock—7.4 trillion push notifications per year through Apple's servers alone.[11]

Like many things addictive and pernicious, alerts felt good at first, but ultimately and insidiously, they became shackles.

The only way to be free of the shackles of alerts is to turn them off. Close and log out of applications that distract you. Disable push alerts. Do these things, and you give yourself a fighting chance. We have all our alerts turned off except meeting notices, so we don't forget to be in the right place.

When you turn off notifications, it's going to feel strange. Like you're missing a friend who used to be there all the time. A friend you depended on. You may find yourself incessantly reaching into your pocket to check to see if anything is there since your buzzes, badges, and dings didn't go off.

No joke, it's withdrawal. The addictive nature of alerts has been studied and proven regularly over the past few years. Alerts cause releases of dopamine. Dopamine makes you feel pleasure. But the latest research shows that dopamine causes what's called "seeking behavior." Dopamine makes us want, desire, seek out, and search. Behavioral psychologist Susan Weinschenk, who specializes in user experience, says, "With the internet, Twitter, and texting, you now have almost instant gratification of your desire to seek. Want to talk to someone right away? Send a text and they respond in a few seconds. Want to look up some information? Just type your request into Google. Want to see what your colleagues are up to? Go to LinkedIn."[12] Dopamine is also stimulated by unpredictability. You don't know precisely when emails, tweets, and texts will show up, nor from whom they will come. When they do come . . . dopamine. Your phone is like a slot machine in your pocket.

So just leave the phone in the other room, right? If only it were that easy. Author Catherine Steiner-Adair conducted over one thousand interviews for her book *The Big Disconnect: Protecting Childhood and Family Relationships in the Digital Age*, and found many people shared experiences that showed symptoms of psychological dependency.[13] For instance, many of her subjects said they couldn't leave the house or even go to the bathroom without their phones. Separation from their phones caused significant anxiety.

If you're ready to remove the shackles, expect withdrawal. It won't be easy, but it's worth it. Our lives changed for the better when we shut off phone alerts. We now use the silent mode on our phones, and nothing barks out at us. No dings, no sounds, no pop-ups on our computers.

Today, we can't stand alerts. One of us will be trying to read on a Kindle app on the iPad, when the *Washington Post* pops up to announce that the Emmy nominations are out. Ugh. Now, every time an alert comes up it's like playing a game of whack-a-mole: it comes up and it gets turned off, again and again. Now we're at the point where unintended alerts are infrequent at best.

Badges, too. They had to go. We learned to check emails when we wanted, not when the little red number went up. It was freeing and it felt great to take control of how we interacted with the media around us.

Try Turning Off Alerts for a Day, If You Can

If you're thinking, "I can't do this," you're not alone. When researchers at Carnegie Mellon University tried to recruit thirty people for an experiment where their smartphone notifications would be turned off for seven days, they couldn't find anyone who would participate.[14] Crazy, right?

But they did get thirty people to do it for *one* day. These thirty people reported mostly that they enjoyed the experience, felt less distracted, and were more productive on their day without notifications. The one-day experiment motivated two-thirds of the participants to change their phone notifications on an ongoing basis after the first day. Two years later, 43 percent of the participants had different alert settings, and some continued to keep most or all of their alerts off.

Are you willing to try it for a day? If yes, how about getting started now?* You might be surprised at how different you feel. (Well, at first expect withdrawal, but it'll get better.)

When you turn off alerts, you are effectively posting your first "do not disturb" sign on your time. However, turning off alerts doesn't stop people from trying to interrupt you incessantly, both online and off.

2. Signal "Do Not Disturb"

Most of us signal "disturb me" without even realizing it. We try to reply to emails and messages right away, ostensibly telling everyone, "I'm

---

* As for how to turn off alerts, it all depends on the device. You'll have to turn them off one by one. Our best advice is to search online for how to turn something off, and then follow the instructions. Get technical help if you run into snags.

here for you, right now." We answer our phones. Our doors are open, signaling, "Come and talk to me."

The XP signal "do not disturb" better than most. Almost one in three of The XP make a habit of signaling "do not disturb." The Rest? Less than one in ten do it.

*Signal Do Not Disturb   9%   3.4x difference   31%

■ The XP   ▨ The Rest

*Themes corresponding to Habit 5: Say No and Habit 6: Play Hard to Get

If it's time to concentrate, change your signal to "do not disturb." Close your door. Do like Mike did in the hospital lounge and put the Princess Leia buns headphones on even if you're not listening to anything. You can even put up an actual sign that says, "On a deadline. Come in if it's truly urgent. If not, please check back later."

You can turn on your email out-of-office assistant while you're in the office. Everyone knows that sometimes you won't be around. The out-of-office hall monitor won't come by to see where you actually are. Need to concentrate for a day? Turn it on. Set your message to say "I'm not available today and not regularly checking email. Back on Wednesday. If you need help, contact my colleague at . . ."

Do the same on messaging services like Slack (either by pausing notifications or setting up regular "do not disturb" hours), Skype (set your status to "do not disturb"), and any other apps and platforms that demand your attention through the course of a typical day.

Seven Great Interruption Minimizers

Along with the hacks outlined in this chapter, here are additional tactics to become impossible to distract specifically for those of you who work in offices.

I. **Take an office cruise:** Preempt later interruptions from colleagues by doing a lap around the office. If checking in with your teammates is important, this will help you get some conversations out of the way. (While doing this, make it clear that you're checking in because you won't be available for a set period of time.)

2. **Get to the office early or work late:** Adjust your workday to make the most of the hours when fewer people are in the office. They may be the most productive hours of your day.
3. **Schedule meetings:** If a coworker stops by to talk about a non-urgent matter, invite them to come back at a designated time or set up a meeting. If it's urgent, it's urgent, but it won't take long before people get used to scheduling time with you when it isn't.
4. **Designate meeting days:** If meetings are important for you, pick a day for mostly meetings. That way you get into the rhythm of going from meeting to meeting, but not out of rhythm if you are trying to concentrate, then going back to a meeting, then back to concentrating, and so on.
5. **Chat over food:** Invite colleagues to join you for breakfast, lunch, coffee break, or dinner. It gives you a respite from your desk and gets some of the ad hoc conversations out of the way.
6. **Don't try to concentrate during "office rush hour":** Note the time of day your colleagues are most likely to seek you out. Plan your less concentration-intensive work for that time to reduce the impact of interruptions.
7. **Talk to your kids:** We often work at home. Our kids don't really care why we're there, they're just glad we are! One day we talked to them about us being at work. "If we're in the office, we're working, but if we're out, let's hang out!" Even at ages three and six, they got it (for the most part) and played along, happy to have breaks and lunch with us when we came out.

3. Be Someplace Else

If you're in a spot in the office (or home, or wherever) where people interrupt you, and you need to concentrate, don't be there. If they can't find you, they won't distract you.

If what you need for work are your phone and your computer, you're in luck. You can bring them anywhere you want and work. If you don't want people to find you, be someplace else. This, of course, requires buy-in from a boss for many people, but "someplace else" can be a quiet spot in the office where you normally aren't, or home, if that's allowed. Explain what you need and what it will let you accomplish and many bosses will help find a solution.

When I (Erica) needed to work from the hospital, I couldn't work with Mike in the family lounge. Working next to each other, we'd end up spending that time catching up, talking about the treatment plan for Ari, sharing what's new with Lexi and Eli, and working out the logistical plan for the next few days. After all, on most days we were like ships passing in the night, so when we were together, we talked.

I also needed a quiet area to work, which is hard to find in a hospital with literally thousands of people in and out each day.

I asked the folks at the Center for Families if they knew of any options for quiet workspace. Come to find out they had four small conference rooms that could be booked. I started working there. No one could find me and when I shut the door to the conference room, I also shut out all the distractions and noise.

Some people make up little excuses why they can't work someplace else, such as, "I use a second computer screen. I'm so much more productive with it." Perhaps, but you're less productive when people bother you if they know where to find you. If you really need it, get a portable second screen that fits in your laptop bag. The point is, if you want to work someplace else to concentrate, you probably can.

The Dual Benefit of Being Someplace Else

As we noted when we talked about *changing your environment* in Habit 3: Reengineer Your Habits, being someplace else not only helps you become impossible to distract, it can also feed creative energy and help you get specific types of work done. Certainly, creativity sometimes thrives with collaboration, but it also thrives in solitude.

Great Minds on Solitude

"The mind is sharper and keener in seclusion and uninterrupted solitude . . . Originality thrives in seclusion free of outside influences beating upon us to cripple the creative mind. Be alone—that is the secret of invention: be alone, that is when ideas are born."—inventor Nikola Tesla

"Solitude, whether endured or embraced, is a necessary gateway to original thought."—poet Jane Hirshfield

"Without great solitude no serious work is possible."—artist Pablo Picasso

"It is only in solitude that I ever find my own core."—author and aviator Anne Morrow Lindbergh

"You need not leave your room. Remain sitting at your table and listen. You need not even listen, simply wait, just learn to become quiet, and still, and solitary. The world will freely offer itself to you to be unmasked. It has no choice; it will roll in ecstasy at your feet."—writer Franz Kafka

There are countless stories of people across disciplines—from writers to business leaders to academics—who change their locations to improve their productivity.

Simon Winchester, the author of *The Professor and the Madman*, sometimes works in New York City, but when it's time to write, he goes to Sandisfield, Massachusetts, home of cows, chickens, forests, and crickets. While there, he lives in an 1800s-era farmhouse and churns out work.[15]

Being someplace else changes your creative fortunes because it breaks the distractions from your other work routines and changes your frame of mind. And when you're someplace else, the do not disturb signal is as strong as it gets.

You don't need to use these three hacks all the time (well, yes, keep your alerts off all the time), but practice these Playing Hard to Get strategies and gift yourself the shield to focus, concentrate, and get done what you want to get done.

It is not easy. Even though The XP are better than The Rest at playing hard to get, they still have a lot of room to improve; across the board, all respondents in our research scored the lowest in Habits 5 and 6, Say No and Play Hard to Get. The benefits, however, are undeniable.

Play hard to get and you'll be impossible to distract.

✳ ✳ ✳

We have two simple things—one easy and one more challenging—for you to do in this chapter's TIME for Action steps. Do these and you'll be raising your own shield, playing hard to get, in no time.

> ### TIME FOR ACTION
>
> - **Turn off your alerts** on your phone and computer: Try it for just one day and see how it feels.
> - **Invest in noise-canceling headphones:** It's an investment you will not regret. When you put them on, you, too, can disappear in plain sight.

This concludes The Productivity Code's Key #2: Control Your TIME. By Obsessing over Time, Saying No, and Playing Hard to Get, not only do you find where your time goes, but you also begin to make choices—sometimes tough ones—about what to do and what not to do. Ultimately, you put yourself on the path to becoming the master of your own time destiny. You can feel good about this: you're saying yes to yourself, your goals, your purpose. You're taking control of your time.

In the next section, Key #3: Execute in the Zone, we give you the most effective system we know for becoming unstoppable: getting, and staying, in the zone.

EXECUTE IN THE ZONE

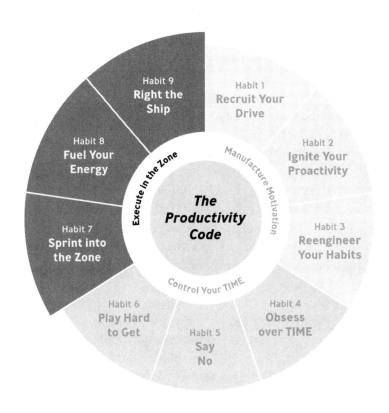

Take a moment to think about a time you had amazing, completely-dialed-in, extremely productive focus. Perhaps your extended family—thirty of them—were headed to your house in an hour, and you transformed into a veritable Iron Chef. Maybe you put off writing that semester-defining paper until the day before it was due. Then you sat down, cracked your knuckles, and banged out an A+ masterpiece in twelve hours; the only thing you completely forgot to do was eat. There was that time on the mountain, skiing faster than ever, yet feeling an odd sense that everything had slowed down. You saw individual snow-flakes fall and heard the clacking chatter of the ice as if you could liter-ally feel the unique contours of each piece as it cracked under your edge. Everything clicked as you attacked the mountain like Lindsey Vonn in a furious rage.

You nailed the deadline, you made the leap, you produced 10X. Everything came into focus as you operated on a whole new level.

You were in the zone.

Steven Kotler, author of *The Rise of Superman*, describes the zone, or flow, as "an optimal state of consciousness, a state where you feel your best and perform your best." The zone "naturally catapults you to a level you're not naturally in," says Harvard Medical School psychiatrist Ned Hallowell. "Everything you do, you do better in flow, from baking a chocolate cake to planning a vacation to solving a differential equation to writing a business plan to playing tennis to making love. Flow is the doorway to the 'more' most of us seek."[1]

When you can get in the zone *at will*, you become unstoppable.

In Key 1: Manufacture Motivation, you find your why, build determi-nation, prepare to act, and get ready to change your habits.

In Key 2: Control Your TIME, you plan rigorously to spend time on some activities over others, take action to protect your time, and become impossible to distract.

None of this, however, will save you from yourself if you can't concentrate.

Research—both our own and by many others—confirms that most people, even with no external distractions poking at them, are rapid media switchers, rapid task switchers, and generally have difficulty shutting down their inner critic, who lobbies them incessantly to block their respective mojos. All of these are barriers to getting in the zone, stopping you from becoming unstoppable.

What we've done here, in Key 3: Execute in the Zone, is provide the most effective approach we know for helping people *get in the zone at will*, stay there, and fuel their energy all around. Also, while getting and staying in the zone, and during all habit change commitments, people lose their way. They fall off the wagon. Habits 7: Sprint into the Zone, 8: Fuel Your Energy, and 9: Right the Ship address all of these stumbling blocks.

If you want to become unstoppable, keep reading.

HABIT 7:

SPRINT INTO THE ZONE

THE ZONE

Oh, I'm sorry, did I break your concentration?

—Jules Winnfield

After hospital rounds, I (Mike) would leave the Brussels Sprout Lounge (a.k.a. the eighth-floor family break room) as, headphones or not, one can only stomach so many helpings of Brussels sprouts. Typically, I'd head down to the Boston Children's Hospital Center for Families, right off the main lobby of the hospital. As the primary children's hospital in a major city, the lobby commotion itself is not unlike a New York City street. The Center for Families tended to be a little frantic (think Fifth Avenue Starbucks during rush hour, except wafting in the air was Purell, not cappuccino). Because it was less quiet and less intimate than the eighth-floor lounge, people were much less likely to single me out to chat.

Erica and Zayde would take Ari down for lunch around noon and we'd eat right there. Ari would test out all the soup samples I'd dared to pilfer from Au Bon Pain that day, and we'd look at the huge mural of a world map on the wall, talking about where his favorite athletes lived, like David Ortiz from the Dominican Republic, Xander Bogaerts from Aruba, and Rory McIlroy from Ireland. Family lunch was a priority for me and I allowed it to take precedence over work whenever it happened. After we finished, Ari would go back upstairs, I'd grab a large black Pike at the actual Starbucks, and sit back down to work.

If Ari was not doing well, I typically didn't even try to work unless I needed a distraction from the pain. But in the early afternoons, he was mostly playing golf or baseball upstairs with the physical therapy team, talking to the steady stream of social workers, nurses, and doctors that came to see him, or Skyping into his preschool classroom.

These were the days I could work. I'd select in advance my Greatest Impact Activity and shield out all the distractions. Headphones on but silent, I was still invisible. No rounds, no visitors, no nothing-gonna-break-my-stride. And yet, somehow I couldn't find it. I could not concentrate.

The problem was I hadn't yet attempted to best the most insidious perpetrator of distraction destruction, the master of mental pandemonium, Dominus Concentratus Interruptus, Captain Squirrelchaser himself: me. Here's what would happen.

1:22 PM. Ari, Erica, and Zayde head upstairs to play hockey in Ari's rink (the service elevator bank on the eighth floor). I say goodbye and put on the Princess Leias.

1:35. Even though I said I wouldn't check my email before I started working, I still do. And my texts. And my messages. I don't even respond,

I just read and make mental notes of responses I need to make. Thirteen minutes lost. I pull up my to-do list.

1:36. Because I have my action plan for the week set up, I see my GIA and dive in. Messaging off, email off, no alerts; I'm ready to concentrate.

1:38. I open my email, see two unimportant messages to delete. Delete. Back to work.

1:38:30. Well, I might as well check Facebook and texts. I didn't even think about reaching for my phone to look; I just did it, like a reflex. Anyway, no new messages, but I scan the new Facebook stories for a minute.

1:41. Scanning stories becomes watching one video: a sales tip posted by a pundit I like. It's not a cute kitten video, so I give myself a pass to watch while working.

1:44. Pundit done. Nothing new; I get to work. Progress.

1:55. Whew, I'm cruising, getting a lot of work done and drinking hot coffee like it's streaming down an ice luge at a fraternity party. Then—bathroom break. Don't ever get old, folks.

2:01. Back to work and back at it. And not even going to check messaging first!

2:02. Well, checked messaging on the walk to the bathroom. One email needs a reply by end of day. Better get to it, or it'll scratch at my concentration like a burlap necktie.

2:21. Reply sent! And two other quickie replies to emails that came in while I was replying to the not-quickie. How productive. Back to work.

Even with no distractions intruding from the outside—no alerts, no phone calls, no walk-ins—I somehow worked for an hour, but only concentrated on my chosen topic for the eleven minutes between 1:44 and 1:55.

To be clear, that's sixty minutes of "work" . . . but only eleven minutes of focus.

Now, you might think, "He was at the hospital. It's not easy to concentrate here." If you did, you'd be making an excuse for me that, at this time (a) wasn't quite true, and (b) more to the point, this isn't unlike what an after-lunch hour might have looked like if Ari were home doing well and I was at the office. This isn't how I worked at the hospital. This is *just how I worked.*

Based on what I now know, I could have gotten **21.82 times more work done** in that hour. While this might appear to be a calculation error, and admittedly I'll never be a math Jedi no matter how much training I get, I mean it: 21.82 times. (More details later.) Even using straight subtraction, I worked eleven minutes on my GIA and could have worked forty-nine more.

Let's say completing my GIA should take me a solid two hours. Assuming I took ten minutes each hour for restroom and leg stretch, that's two hours and twenty minutes, or 140 minutes to complete if my focus was locked in.

However, to get 120 minutes of concentration done on my GIA at 11 minutes an hour, I would need 10.9 hours. This might have been okay(ish) when I was spending eight or ten hours at the office, but not now. Not if I wanted to keep my work life together and meet payroll each month. At the hospital, my work window on good days averaged two or three hours max. So I did what any modern business wiz with an MBA would do: I researched how to concentrate at work, and tried one of the methods I had found (timeboxing; more on this later).

Boom! Off to the races. Completely locked in. The work flowed like freestyle rhymes from Eminem. Except it was me. Within minutes I was the baddest rapper in the history of rap itself.

I was in the zone.

Get in the Zone

Mihaly Csikszentmihalyi has developed the most well-known, fully-fleshed-out theory of the zone in his book *Flow: The Psychology of Optimal Experience*.[1] As the subtitle suggests, the zone is about much more than being productive, because when you find yourself in it, you'll feel more confident, engaged, and happy. It's why Executing in the Zone fits so well with The Productivity Code: it adds becoming happier to the process of accomplishing more.

The zone itself is the mental state where a person performing an activity is fully immersed in a feeling of energized focus, full involvement, and enjoyment in the process of the activity. When you're in the zone:

- Time feels suspended—you don't notice it passing, and yet it's flying!
- You feel extreme focus.
- You achieve exceptional clarity of goals, actions, and rewards.

- You're not just happy; you feel euphoric by focusing on and working on the task.
- The task feels increasingly effortless.
- You feel in control and confident the activity is doable.
- You feel rewarded merely by the fact of engaging in the activity.[2]

If you want to maximize the amount you accomplish per work hour, get in the zone.

Getting into the zone is one of The XPs' most powerful and effective strategies. Not only is it a key driver of extreme productivity, but it is also one of the most significant differences between The XP and The Rest. Forty-nine percent of The XP make it a regular practice, versus only nineteen percent of The Rest. Not only are The XP 2.6 times more likely to get into the zone, they're 3.8 times more likely to concentrate for long periods of time and 2.6 times more likely to devote their undivided attention to the activity at hand.

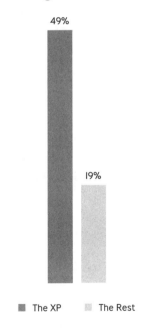

I can get into the Zone.

While the zone is a commonly understood phenomenon to athletes, musicians, and artists, it's discussed a little less often in the worlds of work, education, and home, or indeed anywhere else where focus is beneficial (e.g., cooking, remodeling a bathroom, even reading). However, getting in the zone is just as available to any of us as it is to artists, musicians, and athletes. Csikszentmihalyi himself reported the zone is described in "essentially the same words by old women from Korea, by adults in Thailand and India, by teenagers in Tokyo, by Navajo shepherds, by farmers in the Italian Alps, and by workers on the assembly line in Chicago."[3]

Once you realize what being in the zone can do for you, you'll have quite the itch to get in it, because when you're in the zone, if you work for an hour, you don't just work an hour: you work an amazing hour.

We'd been in the zone before, notably when practicing kata in karate or when throwing our fellow jujitsu-mates. (We both have black belts in karate and jujitsu.) When we were in the dojo, we didn't key in on how we found the zone, but, in retrospect, it's now clear. In the dojo the zone happened to us: we showed up and conditions in the dojo guided us to get there. But we didn't consciously seek it.

As I (Mike) mentioned, I got into the zone for the first time *intentionally* at the Center for Families after I found out about timeboxing. According to Matthias Orgler on Medium, "Timeboxing is a very simple technique to manage time and become more productive. The idea is to allocate a certain amount of time to an activity in advance and then complete the activity within that time frame."[4] The idea behind timeboxing is fairly straightforward: it's a concentration aid.

I tried one of the popular approaches, which essentially consisted of putting a twenty-five-minute timer on. About fifteen minutes in I was completely in the zone. Then, as our daughter, Lexi, would say when she notices she's missing a Halloween candy from her pumpkin pail, "Big problem, Houston."

The timer went off and slammed me right out of the zone. I shook it off soon enough and tried the timer again later. Bam, happened again—as if awoken from a 10× productivity dream, I was yanked right back to Earth. This system might have worked for other people, but it didn't work for me.

In fact, none of the other systems I found worked for me. They either had fatal flaws like this one, or they were too complicated or unrealistic to apply. So we developed our own system for timeboxing, called TIME Sprinting.

Here are the three guidelines for TIME Sprinting:

1. **Sprint:** Work obsessively on one planned task only for twenty to ninety minutes with a visual stopwatch on, counting up. If you reach ninety minutes, take a break.

2. **Relay:** Perform four TIME Sprints in a row with up to six-minute breaks in between. Each four-sprint-in-a-row sequence is a relay.

3. **Block distraction by keeping a distraction capture list:** If you feel a distraction, don't switch tasks. Keep a notepad handy and write down the distraction. Return to sprinting on your chosen task.

This is all you need to TIME Sprint. You can stop here and try it. The hacks that follow in this chapter build on these three guidelines.

I. Establish a Daily Routine of Obsessed, Planned Sprints

This is your gateway to the zone. A sprint is simply twenty to ninety minutes of obsessed focus on one planned activity with a stopwatch on. As simple as TIME Sprinting is, it's incredibly powerful. If you can shut out all other activities for at least twenty minutes, you give yourself a good chance of getting, and staying, in the zone.

Here's what to do. Work obsessively on one planned task only for twenty to ninety minutes with a visual stopwatch on, counting up. If you reach ninety minutes, take a break. This is where our timeboxing system diverges from many others. Most timeboxing systems instruct you to put on a timer (not a stopwatch) for anywhere from twenty-five to seventy-five minutes and start focusing. The problem with timers, however, is that they go off, thus breaking your concentration. It may seem like a small change to use a stopwatch versus a timer, but it feels significantly different.

When you're using a stopwatch, you might glance over at it and see that only five minutes have gone by. This is your signal to keep focusing. You still have fifteen minutes before you allow yourself to pour that coffee, check your messaging, open a browser, or do anything except obsess over your selected task.

Next thing you know, you're flying through work and you look again at the stopwatch, now reading eighteen minutes. Two to go. But you're next glance at the stopwatch? Thirty-four minutes! At that point, if the work is flowing, you can keep going until the ninety-minute mark. Or take a break. Your choice.

The suggestion that you stop at ninety minutes is based on the cyclical rhythm of human rest and wakefulness. Your attention and focus will naturally decline at this point. Called the basic rest-activity cycle by noted physiologist and sleep researcher Nathaniel Kleitman, it's present as we move through the stages of sleep, as well as when we're awake and move from higher to lower levels of alertness and focus.

If you've been seated or stationary, the end of a sprint is a good point to take a walk, hydrate or take a meal break, or otherwise refresh yourself. If you're changing the world as you reach the ninety-minute mark, by all means, keep going. But ninety minutes is generally a good time to take a break whether you feel like taking it or not.

Sprint

Twenty to ninety minutes of obsessed focus on one planned activity.

Four Conditions to Get in the Zone

We once spent a day with sales industry legend Neil Rackham going over a set of research data that became the basis for our book *Insight Selling*. Neil said at the time he was sent a book a day to review, with requests for writing forewords and providing endorsements.

When we asked him why he chose us to meet with, he said that our research was much more rigorous than others, while our recommendations based on the findings were clear and easy to follow. He went on to say, "A great conceptual model simplifies reality but retains validity. It seems you figured that one out." Kind words.

There are a number of conceptual models out there that seek to describe the process for getting in the zone, yet the ones we've seen complicate it to such an extent that they are impractical for everyday use. The takeaway is we haven't seen the need for anything beyond the following four eminently controllable and practical factors to help you find the zone.

1. **Task clarity**
2. **Strong consequences**
3. **Zone-conducive environment**
4. **Complete focus**

If you follow the 9 Habits of The Productivity Code, each of these will already be in place for you.

Task clarity happens by planning actions weekly, calendaring your investment time, starting with your GIA, and perhaps a bit curiously, keeping a no list. **Strong consequences** will happen long term through the goal-setting exercises as you choose your new reality, and short term by tracking progress weekly with an accountability partner. You'll establish strong consequences through having a commitment contract (which we'll cover in Habit 9: Right the Ship) and planning your rewards as you Reengineer Your Habits (and hopefully not because you fear the loss of health insurance as we did). A **zone-conducive environment** will happen when you change your environment to suit your productivity needs, including being someplace else and signaling do not disturb if either will help you avoid distraction or better tackle a particular task.

As for **complete focus**, choosing one activity and putting a stopwatch on is half of it. The other half is quieting the crazy person in your head, your inner voice, who tells you every few seconds to switch tasks. This is where sprinting guideline number three (keeping a distraction capture list) helps by having a notepad and pen handy to write down possible distractions. More on this and why it works coming up.

2. Do Four Successive Sprints in a Relay

Think of a relay as interval training for productivity. Just like a runner or a swimmer, you're building up stamina by doing four sprints in a row.

Let's say you're sprinting and you reach the twenty-six-minute mark. You want a glass of water and feel like you should stretch your legs. In our experience, if you only take this break for six minutes or less, you will likely be able to resume your task and be back in the zone within minutes. In fact, researchers have found that taking short breaks from your main task helps you stay focused on that task, while skipping those breaks results in decreased performance.[5]

Maximize Your Productive Work Time Units

In a ten-year McKinsey study, executives reported being approximately five times more productive when they achieved flow.[6] In the example on page 137, we mentioned that Mike got about eleven minutes of work done on his GIA in one hour. These minutes were *not* in the zone because he didn't allow for enough time to get there.

Now let's say he sprinted for the full sixty minutes, and it took him fifteen minutes to get in the zone. That means the latter forty-five minutes of the hour he could have been five times more productive. Thus, let us introduce the concept of *productive time units*. One minute not in the zone focused on an investment activity is still productive. Think of that one minute as equaling one unit. If you're in the zone getting five times as much work done each minute, then one zone minute equals five productive time units.

Here's the math on Mike's productivity with a solid hour in the zone (the After example) compared to eleven minutes worked on his GIA (the Before example) but not in the zone.

Hour Worked

Before	After
Minutes worked on GIA: 11	Minutes worked on GIA not in zone: 15
Minutes in zone: 0	Minutes in zone: 45
Wasted minutes: 49	Zone multiplier: 5
	Minute equivalents from zone time: 225 (45 minutes x 5)
Productive work time units: 11	Productive work time units: **240**

240 / 11 = 21.82 times more productive with one solid hour in the zone

Once you've done four sprints in a row with a maximum six-minute break in between sprints, take at least a fifteen-minute break. Peretz Lavie, who researched ultradian rhythms (biological cycles occurring within twenty-four hours), identified twenty-minute "troughs," periods of drowsiness in between the cycles when we naturally feel more alert and productive.[7] A minimum fifteen minutes between relays gives your mind what amounts to a catnap: a brief refueling so you can dive back in and continue to be productive.

Note that this fifteen-minute break should be a break—not an excuse to check your email. That's like calling shoveling the driveway in a snowstorm a break just after you've cleared the roof. Clear your email after your breaks, or later as its own sprint-and-relay process.

During the course of any normal workday, plan for a maximum of four relays. You need white space so you can turn TIME Sprinting into a week-after-week, month-after-month marathon. Try to do it too much every day and you'll find it difficult to maintain as a habit. Plus, you need time to allow your mind to wander outside of the full concentration of a sprint.

Along with time to let the mind wander, most of us have other activities to complete—from meetings to classes to phone calls to meals to correspondence—that don't lend themselves to TIME Sprinting. However, TIME Sprinting using relays is ideal for longer projects that require ongoing concentration. In fact, most of this book was written using successive sprints and relays on writing days. Whether your projects include preparing next year's budget, writing a business strategy, painting a watercolor, planning the annual family vacation, or anything else that would benefit from you being in the zone, relays can help you get there.

3. Block Distraction:
Keep a Distraction Capture List

In the first few weeks of adopting TIME Sprinting as a habit, we both found that we would choose an activity, put a stopwatch on, and start in. Often, three to four minutes later, we'd find ourselves opening a web browser, checking email, or picking up our phones by reflex for no reason. Three minutes! We found ourselves having to practice "free won't" (which we'll cover in Habit 9: Right the Ship) to stay focused on the sprint.

We had no idea we were media and task switching so much until that stopwatch went on. But we were. Our productivity was suffering immensely because of it. After a few days in a row of sprinting and adding one new hack, which we'll get to shortly, the nervous "check messages" tic subsided, and we also noticed something amazing: our inner critics, who typically chattered away incessantly, hushed up several minutes into each sprint.

When we introduced sprinting to other people, here's the kind of thing they would report as they approached, but didn't get into, the zone.

I'm fourteen minutes into a TIME Sprint on a Wednesday. I'm cruising along, but then remember my first soccer league game is on Saturday. Problem: I don't have cleats. Meant to get them last weekend. Now it's Wednesday, I can still get them delivered by Friday if I order them today. Made a mental note not to forget. Then, I try to get back to sprinting, but after a few minutes lost focus and ended up switching tasks to buy cleats.

Buy cleats. Look up yesterday's sports scores. Check your favorite news site. Check the current temperature. Figure out dinner. Email the electric company to fix the error on the bill. Check your bank balance because you have to pay bills. Pay your bills. Check two days after you paid bills to see if the bills got paid. Text your significant other to say hello.

This inner critic in your head never stops telling you to do things right now *that will take you away from what you've already told yourself to do right now.* Inner critics are devious, multiskilled little jerks. As we outlined in Habit 2: Ignite Your Proactivity, they sabotage you with negative self-talk, but also masterfully divert you from what you literally already told yourself to do (or not to do) at any given moment.

Unless you're more Zen than anyone we've ever met, your inner critic will invade your brain and attempt a hijack no matter how hard you are trying to concentrate. Here are two powerful yet simple ways to shut down these voices of your inner critic:

- Write down task-switch-inducing distractions as they come to mind.
- Get in the zone.

No kidding. That's it! These hacks work amazingly well.

To the latter point, consider the work of Charles Limb. He used functional magnetic resonance imaging (MRI) scans to study the brain activity of rappers and musicians who achieved a state of flow. The part of the brain that controls impulses and is responsible for self-monitoring is called the dorsolateral prefrontal cortex. Think of this region as a lovely top-floor apartment where your inner critic lives, distracting and second-guessing you through the intercom like your own personal Statler and Waldorf. But Limb found that "when the dorsolateral prefrontal cortex goes quiet, those guesses are cut off at the source. The result is liberation. We act without hesitation."[8]

In other words, if you want to shut down your inner critic, feel great, and reach your potential, then Execute in the Zone.

If you want to enter the zone as you're approaching it but not yet there, write down any distracting thoughts as they emerge and tell yourself to stay on task. These will help you stay focused on your preselected activity. This is what I should have done that day in the hospital when I felt the unanswered email would scratch at my concentration like a burlap necktie. Writing down "Reply to Fred's email" would have removed the pea under my mental mattress.

If you let distracting thoughts build up or simply try to remember them, they will tax your ability to concentrate, acting like a mental magnet to pull your attention away from your chosen TIME Sprint single-task, and toward the squirrels, until you attend to them.

Few mental distractions are urgent items. Perhaps you do need to get cleats before the end of the day. The challenge here is not getting cleats today; it's the mental itch that trying to remember will produce.

All you need to do is keep a list handy, either physical with a pen and paper, or on your computer, to write down the distraction. Writing it down is close to 100 percent effective for scratching the mental itches of must-remember items that stockpile as you try to concentrate. Further, once you get in the zone, your inner critic will calm down quite a bit because of all that dorsolateral prefrontal jazz.

When you're done sprinting and relaying and you've taken a break, you can review your distraction capture list and do anything you choose. Take five minutes and order the cleats. Often you'll find yourself saying, "Uh, do I really need to look up the temperature in Boca right now?" What seemed so compelling an hour ago suddenly doesn't need action at all.

✳   ✳   ✳

Ready to use the three rules to get into the zone? Complete the activities in TIME for Action below. You'll try out sprints, relays, and capturing and containing distractions, then reflect on your own TIME Sprint experience. In the next chapter, you'll see how you can maintain the momentum with Habit 8: Fuel Your Energy.

TIME FOR ACTION

- Try out a sprint. Remember to follow these three guidelines:
  1. **Sprint**
  2. **Relay** (four TIME Sprints in a row with up to six-minute breaks in between)
  3. **Block distraction with a distraction capture list**
- Reflect on your TIME Sprint experience.
  - How many minutes in were you before you were tempted to task-switch (open a browser, check email, check your phone)? If it was only a few minutes, don't fret. That's common in the beginning. Keep sprinting.
  - How did it feel?
  - Did you achieve flow? (Note: It might take a few days of ongoing effort to get there. Don't quit.)
  - What were you able to achieve while in flow?
- For more information, visit MyProductivityCode.com/booktools and download TIME Sprinting FAQs.

HABIT 8:

FUEL YOUR ENERGY

THE FUEL

It's 106 miles to Chicago, we got a full tank of gas, half a pack of cigarettes, it's dark, and we're wearing sunglasses.
Hit it!

—Elwood and Jake Blues

One summer afternoon, I (Erica) found myself in the backyard with Lexi and Eli. Lexi was chatting with two of her girlfriends, soaking in the sun, waiting for the boat to come back so she could take it out for a girl cruise. Eli was out on a paddleboard. He hasn't yet gotten into sports and may just never, but he's a big outdoorsman, and loves being on the water.

Me? I was sitting and enjoying homemade lemonade, one of Ari's favorite treats, that the kids made earlier in the day. It was eighty-two degrees and sunny with a light breeze and white, wispy clouds, the kind where you see alligators and continents and dogfights between X-wings and TIE fighters, all depending on how you look at them. Midafternoon is always a great time in our backyard as the sun dips behind the trees, giving us just a bit of shade on our beach.

I sat. I sipped. I breathed. I soaked in a moment, feeling entirely present yet outside of time itself. I closed my eyes and felt the sun on my skin. As an old beach lady, the feel of the hot sun on my (nowadays well-sunblocked, slightly more wrinkly than it used to be) skin still felt exhilarating.

My eyes blinked open when I heard the boat motoring back to the dock. Mike hopped out and secured the boat ropes on the cleats as a wiry, blond, short-but-not-too-short fifteen-year-old boy hopped off with his wakeboard under his arm.

It was Ari. Fifteen-year-old Ari, hair half dry in the sun and wind after a run out on his board. He walked toward me, scars fading on his chest and belly, smile as mischievous and cheerful as ever, eyes as penetrating. They met mine.

And then I woke. I had drifted during a guided meditation.

And I was full of grief, again exhausted. Full-body exhausted, the kind where your mind is overloaded, you can't move a finger, you can barely roll over—exhausted.

Grief takes everything out of you, to the point where you wonder if there's anything left to live for. After Ari died, there were days, weeks, months where it certainly didn't feel like there was. Yet, in that moment, something felt different.

Two months after Ari died, my dear friend Jessica Lindberg, founder of the Ethan M. Lindberg Foundation, reached out to me. She told me about Restoring a Mother's Heart, a retreat she was hosting for mothers who had lost children to chronic illness. Jessica invited me to attend.

I had been scared to join. I didn't know if I was ready. I didn't know if I could open myself up and talk about all of the pain, hurt, anger, depression, guilt, and other emotions I felt.

But I said yes.

Before I left, I was telling a friend about it. She said, "I hope it brings you some peace." It wasn't the first time someone had said this to me. When I went to Cape Cod or the beach in Maine, people would always say, "I hope you feel peace there." I hated that. How am I supposed to feel at peace after my son had just died? What is peaceful about that?

The retreat involved a lot of yoga and meditation. We talked about the connection between our bodies, minds, and spirits. To experience healing, all of these need to connect. For me, each had broken into countless scattered shards. I was terrified to put them back together. I was terrified that healing meant that I had to let go of Ari somehow.

So ... no, peace is not what I wanted. And yet, wanted or not, invited or not, peace stopped in for a brief visit during a Tara Mohr–inspired meditation.* I was at our house, on the beach, with now ten-years-older Lexi and Eli, and Ari pulled up after a ride on the boat.

This was the first moment since Ari died when I felt anything save despair. This was the moment I realized life could still go on. The grief was back, but I felt ineffably different. Changed.

Through the hard work we did over the course of the retreat, I learned that peace didn't mean moving on without Ari. Moving on is not the right sentiment as it implies a leaving behind. I was not leaving behind, I was journeying on *with*. My relationship with Ari endured.

I moved on from moving on and began to move forward. *With* peace. *With* Ari. The peace I felt was just a glimpse, but ephemeral as it was, it *happened*. This meant something of great consequence: peace was, in fact, available to me. This time was simultaneously an end, a beginning, and a continuation of chapters in my life. Perhaps most importantly, it was the sign I needed to tell me that my life journey would, indeed, now begin again.

---

* The Inner Mentor Visualization from Tara Mohr's book, *Playing Big*.

Energy renewed, I left the retreat. While it had been only four months since Ari died, a weight had lifted. Purpose returned. Love returned. It was time to spread that love with others.

The first time I had ever practiced yoga or meditated was at this retreat. Since then I've made it a point to do both regularly. It was not clear at all to me before, but it has never been anything but undeniably clear since: most of us need to take care of our minds, our bodies, and our spirits—all of them together—to fuel our energy.

Your Path to Sustainable Energy

Our approach to productivity isn't just about making sure you have fuel in the tank so you can give more to your workday. It goes way beyond that. We want you to have enough energy to give yourself whatever it is you desire. To tap in to a source of sustainable energy that allows you to achieve your purpose.

When you want to do something, energy is either there or not at the start, and either grows, remains constant, or depletes as you go. In this chapter, we share with you the keys to ensuring your energy is generally as high as it can be, and holds for as long as possible when you want it to be there for you.

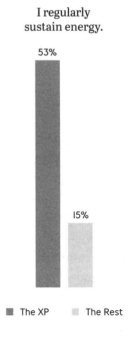

I regularly sustain energy.

53%

15%

The XP   The Rest

Energy so you can get started and power through, so you can produce. Be in the game. Be effective.

Energy—and the stamina to sustain it over long periods—is the fuel that drives productivity. If you don't have the energy to get started with something, or the energy to stick with it, don't expect to be productive.

It's no surprise, then, that our research reveals energy is a key driver of productivity.

Not only that, there is a stunning gap between The XP and The Rest in their agreement with the statement *I regularly sustain energy for long periods of time*. More than half of The XP agree that's very much like them, compared to just 15 percent of The Rest.

Energy is also a key driver of top performance, job satisfaction, and happiness. What is especially notable when it comes to happiness is that the ability to sustain energy for long periods is second only to devoting time to Treasured activities as a key driver of happiness. Your path to sustainable energy puts you on a path not only to extreme productivity, but also to well-being and happiness.

While there's a vast body of research and inquiry into this topic, we tend to think of it simply. The best way to maximize energy is to focus on your mind, body, and spirit as if they were three legs of a stool. We'll cover each in turn in this chapter. Before we do, however, two points are worth noting.

First, everyone is different. What you need to do to drive your energy, or work on your personal energy challenges, might be very different than what someone else might need. Improving your energy may also be something you want or need to do with a medical or other professional.

Second, finding, building, and enhancing energy is the source of much academic and spiritual study, and many professionals make it their life mission to help athletes, performers, and others improve their energy. We acknowledge and appreciate the deep expertise and disparate energy philosophies out there in the world.

Meanwhile, after experiencing our fair share of life and energy challenges, and trying quite a few strategies to fuel our fires, we've found the following points have helped us and others tremendously.

The Energy Triad

Why are some people so much better at regularly sustaining energy for long periods? We've been seeking the answer to this question for years. Simple though it might seem, it has indeed boiled down for us—after years of searching, reading, researching, coaching, and living—to the connection of mind, body, and spirit.

The XP Energy Triad

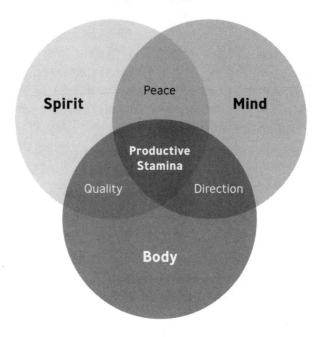

When your mind is in the right place, you have clarity: you know what you should and shouldn't do (based on your choices, not other people's), your inner voice is playing the role of mentor—not critic—and the overall noise level is at least periodically quiet and kept to a reasonably low hum.

When your body is properly tuned, you can act, move, and do as you need.

When your spiritual energy is good, you feel connected, a oneness with the universe.

Then there are the connections.

Spirit + Mind = Peace: You feel oneness, rightness of being. And you have clarity.

Mind + Body = Energy Direction: If you know what you're supposed to do and can focus on that, and your body is willing and able to comply, you can almost feel the inevitability of action moving in a specific direction.

Body + Spirit = Energy Quality: If you feel good spiritually, and your body is ready to act, there's a buoyancy about the movement.

However, you need all three to achieve **productive stamina**. It's easiest to understand why when you see what happens when one of the legs of the energy triad stool is missing.

The XP Energy Triad

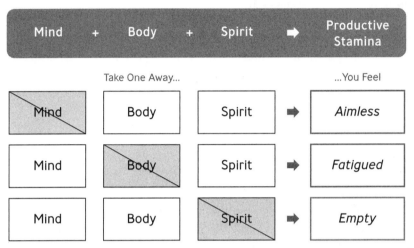

Take away mind and you don't have clarity. If you aren't supervising your inner critic well enough, she can spin you around in circles. Without clarity in your mind, you become aimless.

Take away body and you are physically tired. Fatigued. You might feel well connected to the universe and know what you want to do, but your get-up-and-go musta got-up-and-went. Note that your mind can get tired, too. We'll cover how to battle mental fatigue, as well as physical.

Take away spirit and you might know what you want to do, while your body might be ready to act, but at best you move around like an empty shell. At worst it's so debilitating that you can't bring yourself to act at all. Like how we felt when we lost Ari.

Here is what has resonated with us, and for those we've worked with, to affect all three.

1. **Mind:** Concentrate early in the day, minimize decisions, and practice positive self-talk and mindfulness.
2. **Body:** Eat well, sleep well, and take care of your body.
3. **Spirit:** Feel connected. Take Treasured TIME, find your spiritual path.

I. Mind: Concentrate Early in the Day, Minimize Decisions, Practice Positive Self-Talk and Mindfulness

One day a judge in Israel led a series of parole hearings, including three similar cases of fraud and assault.

At 8:50 AM the judge heard the first case involving an Arab-Israeli serving a thirty-month sentence for fraud.

At 3:10 PM the judge heard the second case, one of a Jewish-Israeli serving a sixteen-month sentence for assault.

At 4:25 PM the judge heard case number three, featuring an Arab-Israeli serving a thirty-month sentence for fraud.

One prisoner received parole. Two didn't. Can you guess which one did? Was it the specifics of their crime and repentance that got them parole? No. Was it their ethnicity or gender? No.

It was the time of day that their case was heard. Morning cases were granted parole about 70 percent of the time. Cases that appeared late in the day were granted parole less than 10 percent of the time. In fact, after a review of 1,100 parole board decisions, this pattern held true day in and day out.[1]

Early in the day, at least for most people, energy is highest. Typically, you're rested in the morning—after you've slept and before you've made a lot of decisions that tax your mind and deplete your energy. If you need to concentrate, do it in the morning when both your physical and mental fuel tanks are full.

Minimize Decisions

Ever wonder why, after three hours of registering for wedding gifts, by the time you are done, you don't care a bit what you put on the list—you just want to get out of there? Why are you most vulnerable to buying snack food at the end of a marathon supermarket shop? Why is tackling mentally taxing projects at night so much harder—at least for most people—when you've had to make decisions all day? It's because of mental fatigue.

For each decision you make, you pay a biological price. Decisions tax the brain. They make you mentally tired. When you're mentally fatigued, one of two things are likely to happen: you either avoid doing anything at all, or you make impulsive decisions. (Regarding the latter, anyone who's tried hard to eat well during the day and made it until 8 PM, then, seemingly without thinking, broke into the potato chips—you know what we mean.) The solution may sound simple, but it is the most effective: make fewer decisions. Barack Obama only wore blue or gray suits, so he wouldn't have to think about it. Einstein wore only white shirts. The only shirt Turtleneck Superstar CEO Baby wears is . . . you guessed it.

Planning Helps Fuel Energy

In Habit I: Recruit Your Drive, you build your big-picture plan, then plan your week. Doing both these things helps conserve and fuel your energy. When you know your *why*, you fuel your spiritual energy. When you know what your plan for the week is, you don't need to stress over the decision of what to do next—you've already preplanned it and you have confidence that what you are doing will help you reach your goals.

This is why we suggest you create your weekly action plan once a week in advance and calendar your Investment activities, and why you should tackle your Greatest Impact Activities early in the day before you've made too many decisions. Spending two hours clearing out emails and taking care of small things leads to mental fatigue. Adopt a consistent morning routine. Don't make breakfast a decision; have the same meal most days. Anything you can do to minimize your decision burden will maximize your mental energy.

Use Positive Self-Talk

If you are feeling down, negative, or otherwise not in a good emotional state, it's nearly impossible to be energetic and engaged in a task.

As we shared in Habit 2: Ignite Your Proactivity, your inner voice—be it in critic or mentor mode—is talking at you at a rate of up to 1,000 words per minute. We are constantly telling ourselves stories about what's going on around us, what's happening to us, and what happened to us in the past.

In *Becoming*, Michelle Obama reveals the story she's told herself about her childhood: "I grew up with a disabled dad in a too-small house with not much money in a starting-to-fail neighborhood, and I also grew up surrounded by love and music in a diverse city in a country where an education can take you far. I had nothing or I had everything. It depends on which way you want to tell it."[2]

You get to choose the story you tell yourself. For the best mental energy, make it a positive one. Choose love, music, education. Choose knowing you have everything you need, or taking positive steps to get there, versus focusing on what you don't have or can't change right now.

Step 2 in the 5-Step Extreme Productivity Morning Routine in Habit 3 is to ask yourself, "How's my mindset?" The way to ensure you have a bad day is to start with a bad attitude. If you don't feel your mental energy is in the right place, take a walk to clear your head, practice positive self-talk, meditate, breathe deeply, say "3 . . . 2 . . . 1 . . . Stop!", distract yourself with a book, or talk to a close friend.

Once you start working, sprint and relay. When you get in the zone, you can temporarily shut off your inner critic. This is why getting in the zone often yields five times more productivity than a typical minute. TIME Sprinting is a *harnessing of mental energy.*

Find your path to feeling better emotionally—you'll find your energy stores are full more often and easier to replenish after you draw from the well.

Practice Mindfulness

Mindfulness—being aware and present in the moment—is a great way to fight anxiety and increase energy. A growing body of research supports this, along with its productivity and happiness benefits. In fact, in our global research study, we found The XP are more than twice as likely to practice mindfulness than The Rest. And the happiest respondents are almost three times more likely than everyone else to do so.

There is an actual neurobiological reason why mindfulness works—it can literally change your brain. Studies by Harvard neuroscientist Dr. Sara Lazar have shown that mindfulness and meditation change the brain structure, increasing gray matter in the frontal cortex (the control center of the brain, responsible for memory and decision making) and the hippocampus (which assists learning and the regulation of memories and emotions), and reducing the size of the amygdala (the "fight or flight" center of the brain), which eases stress.

In one of Lazar's studies, participants who had never meditated were put through an eight-week program, meditating thirty to forty minutes per day. Their brain scans pre- and post-program revealed the aforementioned dramatic brain changes.[3]

In our own lives, we have found the Headspace app useful for improving mindfulness, and we enjoyed Dan Harris's book *Meditation for Fidgety Skeptics*—being both fidgety (ahem . . . Mike) and skeptical (ahem . . . Erica).[4] We've also used diaphragmatic breathing—deep abdominal breathing, which activates the parasympathetic nervous system—to reduce our stress and anxiety, and maintain our energy levels.

2. Body: Eat Well, Sleep Well, and Take Care of Your Body

Let's assume you've been working to adopt the 9 Habits of The Productivity Code. You've recruited your drive. You're feeling proactive, and you've replaced unproductive habits with productive ones. You're obsessing over TIME, and consistently eliminating distractions as you focus on Investment activities. This is all great, but if you don't sleep well at night, or are tired during the day for whatever reason, it's unlikely you'll get much done. Sure, you might be able to trudge through at times, but if you're feeling depleted physically, extreme productivity is unlikely.

Now, let's imagine you do sleep well, and subsequently have a productive morning. Then at lunch, you go for the unlimited pasta feast. Before you tackle your orgy of rigatoni, you have three pieces of bread. Then you down the pasta. Then go for cupcakes and ice cream.

For most people, this lunch would be on the big side. Probably big enough that it's not realistic for many of us to even think about approaching it. But it serves to make a point: if you ate this mother lode of carbs and sugar, after a brief high you'd probably crash harder than Jake and Elwood through Toys "R" Us.

Even if most people dialed it back to simply a big pizza or pasta lunch, they still would have trouble concentrating or feeling like they could get much done, and not necessarily connect it to the carb fest they had two hours earlier. The point is, just as sleep and exercise matter, the food you put in your body matters both directly and immediately, and over the long term.

There is, of course, no shortage of experts who will have different systems to help you eat well, sleep well, and exercise to maximize your energy. Eating programs such as low carb, keto, paleo, plant-based, Mediterranean, and more. Exercise programs like high-intensity training, cardio, weight resistance, strength training, barre, and so on. For me (Mike), the Atkins system has worked well in terms of diet, and my exercise routine includes cycling, golf, and hot yoga. But what works for me is of no consequence: you need to do you.

Find a system that works for you and you'll improve your ability to become extremely productive and feel a whole lot better. In fact, our research confirms that not only are The XP two times more likely than The Rest to be active and physically fit, but those qualities are also key drivers of happiness—with the happiest people 1.7 times more likely to possess them.

3. Spirit: Take Treasured TIME, Find Your Spiritual Path

Golf always reminds me (Mike) of my grandfather, my Zayde. When I was seven years old, we'd pitch around the field behind the McCarthy School in West Peabody, Massachusetts. I can still remember the welt on my head from that time he nailed me with a fifty-yard sand wedge shot. Ouch! Still, I stuck with the game.

We'd go out when I was eleven and hack around on the Middleton par 3. I wasn't very good, but good enough to stay on the course. By twelve, I was caddying at Salem Country Club, at fourteen working in the bag room, and by sixteen parking cars and shining shoes.

And I played. A lot.

By the time I got to college, my playing dropped off. After college, I didn't want to spend all my money on the links, so golf took a back seat to the rest of life. Then, when Erica and I got together, both working with no kids, we started to play. Then Ari came along, and once more golf went on hold.

Until, that is, Ari fell in love with golf. He was a golf maniac. Loved watching Top 10 golf videos from The Golf Channel on YouTube. Top 10 Lucky Bounces was his favorite, with Hale Irwin from 1984 taking the top spot.*

Every Saturday when Ari was three and four, he'd wait at the door at 10 AM, ready to head to the course. We'd spend all day there: two hours chipping and putting, an hour at the range, lunch in the clubhouse watching golf, and then out to play holes.

Erica would call me around 3:30 PM with a, "Where are you?" Typically, we'd be on the twelfth hole or so.

The weekend before Ari went into Boston Children's for his transplant consult, he had his choice of activities. What did he want to do? Play golf. We got in ten holes at Wedgewood Pines in ninety-degree weather before he said, "Okay, I'm done."

That was the last time he really played.

After Ari died, I couldn't do anything. I tried playing golf, but it was too painful.

About a year later, I was sitting with my ninety-nine-year-old Bubbie (Zayde's wife) at a nursing home. Her health was failing. She knew she was dying, but still had her faculties. I asked her to take care of Ari when she got to the other side. "Bubbie, I had a vision that Ari and Zayde were out playing golf at the Middleton Par 3 and came to your house in West Peabody, expecting tuna sandwiches and half-sour pickles." We both cried. She said when she got there, she'd be ready with the tuna and have golf going on the TV.

A few months after she died, I started playing golf again. I'm not playing for Ari; I'm playing for myself. But when I'm out there, I feel Ari and Zayde with me on every shot.

Finding spiritual energy is an incredibly personal journey. I didn't know when, or even if, I'd find my spiritual energy again. I didn't know that after twenty-five years I'd be hooked on golf once more, and for the first time in a decade find myself invested in something just for the fun of it. But it happened.

---

* Years later, Ari ended up spending half an hour with a gracious Hale Irwin at the US Senior Open.

Far be it from us, however, to wax philosophical about how you should find your spiritual energy. It's too big a topic, and too personal a journey, to treat here with the respect it deserves. We'll leave it simply that the following six practical actions have helped us dig our way out of very deep spiritual holes, get our footing, and find some tranquility and fulfillment in the storm of our lives:

- **Take Treasured TIME.** The mental health benefits of leisure activities include lower levels of depression and improved physical and psychological status.[5] Our XP research shows taking Treasured TIME is a key driver of happiness *and* that The XP take Treasured TIME more than twice as often as The Rest.

- **Find meaning in your time.** Set goals that, should you achieve them, really mean something to you. If you have a specific life destination, and truly want to arrive there, energy will find you. If this is something you'd like to do, revisit Habit 1.

- **Go outside to feel alive.** Being outside in nature makes people feel more alive, according to a series of studies published in the *Journal of Environmental Psychology*. "Nature is fuel for the soul," says Richard Ryan, lead author and a professor of psychology at the University of Rochester. "Often when we feel depleted we reach for a cup of coffee, but research suggests a better way to get energized is to connect with nature."[6] Just twenty minutes outdoors is often enough.

- **Breathe.** Relaxed breathing techniques are an excellent way to reduce stress and anxiety.

- **Try yoga.** Researchers at Boston University School of Medicine used spectroscopic MRI to compare brain activity in participants who did one hour of yoga versus participants who instead read for an hour. The yoga practitioners showed an increase in GABA, a brain neurotransmitter that helps to control fear and anxiety responses.[7]

- **Find your personal spiritual path.** Whatever the journey is for you, if you can find and connect with your spirituality, you can find peace, focus, and the foundation for ongoing sustained energy.

You've set your goals, feel motivated to tackle them, identified exactly what to do, and tuned out distractions. If you've done all these things, you have a great start on being extremely productive. But if your fuel tank is empty, all of this is for naught. You must fuel your energy. To do so, focus on your body, mind, and spirit.

* * *

How is your energy? Take some time right now to assess it. How do you feel in your body, mind, and spirit? Follow the TIME for Action suggestions below to better understand how you can fuel your energy. The time spent focusing on your body, mind, and spirit will yield rewards of well-being and happiness along with productivity.

TIME FOR ACTION

Take a short inventory of your energy. How do you feel in your body, mind, and spirit? What are some specific actions you can take to help improve any areas you feel are lacking? Work these into your weekly Action Plan.

RIGHT THE SHIP

THE COMEBACK

You are braver than you believe, stronger than
you seem, and smarter than you think.

—A. A. Milne

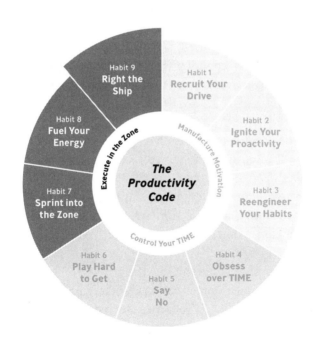

When Ari was first diagnosed with congestive heart failure in July 2016, I (Mike) started drinking more. Until this point I wasn't a heavy drinker, but now the frequency and amount were ticking up.* I needed to stay up to give Ari his 11 PM meds. I was tired and bored, but I had to stay awake. I would drink to have something to do, drink to escape, drink to help me fall asleep when I was done with Ari's meds.

Still, I found myself often unable to fall asleep, or waking up in the middle of the night and not able to fall back asleep. Four months later, I was essentially living full time in the hospital with Ari. I had a hard time sleeping even in a quiet, comfortable bed at home. Trying to sleep at the hospital for any stretch of time, with any kind of regularity, was never going to happen, scotch quotient notwithstanding.

After Ari fell asleep, I'd go out, have a few beers, and watch the Celtics. Then I'd go back to the hospital—I'd fall asleep, but I wouldn't be able to stay asleep. I'd often find myself walking the corridors at three o'clock in the morning, sometimes due to the nightly commotion of beeps, voices, doors, and code alarms, or, all too often, because Ari had needed me medically, to read him Harry Potter at 2 AM, or hold a barf bucket because his overnight potassium supplements that flowed in through his g-tube roiled his stomach.

This went on, as we know, for the better part of a year.

Then he came home for one month. I don't even remember if I slept then.

After Ari died, everything got worse, sleep included. All in, for two years or so, I don't remember ever sleeping more than two to four hours in a night. For the longest time, my tank wasn't just empty, it was sucked dry of even one drop of fuel.

About a year later, while I might not have been conscious of it, I must have had Andy Dufresne somewhere deep in my psyche telling me, "I guess it comes down to a simple choice really. Get busy livin', or get busy dyin'."

It was time for me get my shit together.

I stopped drinking. I started riding my bike, going to physically challenging hot yoga, and playing golf. And started dropping some weight, eventually twenty-five pounds.

---

* I didn't drink that often, but when I did, I became another person. And that person drank a ton.

Within a week off the sauce I slept for ten hours one night. Then eight the next. And I've slept seven to eight hours almost every night since.

Thinking back to Habit 8: Fuel Your Energy, I don't think I could have done this if my spiritual energy, flat on its back, beaten and bloodied on the mat for two years, hadn't somehow miraculously started to show signs of life. I don't think my spiritual energy would have continued to bounce back if I hadn't started taking care of my body. I don't think my mental and spiritual energy would have bounced back if I'd done aerobics instead of yoga.

It all worked together.

But, even now—with the eating and exercising—I have these mini daily hiccups where I veer off track. (Not with drinking. Definitely with ice cream and missing bike rides.)

The Best-Laid Plans

For all of us, even the best-laid plans go awry. You can know what to do, you can set up your time and day so you are prepared to get the right things done, and you can have the energy to tackle your priorities. Still, sometimes you just don't. At least I don't. I end up procrastinating, wading through low-impact activities, allowing myself to get distracted, not TIME Sprinting when I should be concentrating.

Changing habits and being productive isn't easy. We all get derailed and lose focus sometimes. As we mentioned earlier, even The XP go off course, but they are 5.3 times more likely than The Rest to recover quickly. They describe it like this: "If I find myself doing an activity or continuing with a habit I want to stop, I usually stop quickly once I realize I should."

Expect that your path to building good habits will involve one step forward and two steps back—sometimes. If you try

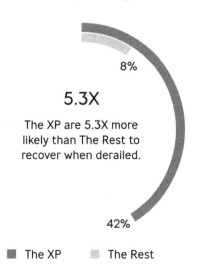

8%

5.3X

The XP are 5.3X more likely than The Rest to recover when derailed.

42%

■ The XP   ▨ The Rest

to do something important, make some progress, and then fall off the wagon, you will fall into a specific category of those we studied: humans.

You don't need to have super willpower to change, to make a comeback. What you do need is a strategy to follow when you veer off course. We've found the following three hacks highly successful for righting the ship when we find ourselves not doing what we know we should, whether it's work-related or not:

1. Practice free won't

2. Make micro change

3. Make a commitment contract

I. Practice Free Won't

Deeply ingrained habits—like what we do when we wake up, our phone-checking routines, how we act when we meet someone—happen *almost* without thought. As we noted in Habit 3: Reengineer Your Habits, the thought is there, but it can be so fast that we start the behavior without consciously seeming to initiate it. Does the behavior, then, just happen? Is there nothing we can do about it?

No, it doesn't just happen.

Yes, there is something we can all do about it. One thing in particular works remarkably well: Practice "free won't."

In the late 1970s and early 1980s, neurologist Benjamin Libet conducted a series of experiments to see whether conscious thought initiates physical behavior.[1] He asked participants to carry out a simple task—such as pushing a button whenever they felt like it—and to make a note of the time when they were first aware of the urge to act. While they did this, the participants were hooked up to an EEG machine monitoring the electrical activity in their brains. Libet found that brain activity that would drive the physical action occurred nearly 300 milliseconds *before* the subjects reported the urge to act.

That the buildup of energy to act came before the conscious decision to act suggests that action is driven by unconscious thought, not conscious thought. It's not surprising, then, that many of the habit scientists suggest that a trigger, not conscious thought, drives a response.

Many interpreted Libet's results to mean that we may not truly even have free will.[2]

Libet himself, however, didn't see it that way. He pointed out that during the 500 milliseconds leading up to an action, the conscious mind could choose to reject that action. While the subconscious would dictate the impulses, the conscious mind could still act to suppress or veto them.

Focus on Now with Free Won't

As we know from Habit 8: Fuel Your Energy, decision making is mentally exhausting. So is maintaining any kind of willpower. The challenge with willpower is that you often have something going on in the background like, "I have seven more hours where I must do X, focus on Y, or avoid Z." This is like setting up your willpower as a dam, with continued willpower effort building up as a great force to break it. When it comes to willpower, if it keeps on raining, the levee is going to break.

The most powerful way to combat this is not to focus on the next seven hours, but to focus on now. This is the power of saying "3 . . . 2 . . . 1 . . . Go!" and "3 . . . 2 . . . 1 . . . Stop!" Don't worry about the next five hours of work where you need to concentrate. Just concentrate right now. If you're distracted, say "3 . . . 2 . . . 1 . . . Stop!" and put a timer on to help you stay focused on the task.

When we first started practicing mindfulness, we were worried that we'd never be able to calm the distracting voices in our heads. It turns out (a) this is a very common worry and (b) we can practice mindfulness even if the voice keeps coming back. If you're practicing mindfulness and your thoughts are distracting you, the idea isn't to say to yourself, "I keep having thoughts. I can't do mindfulness." Instead, the idea is to recognize, label, and observe, and focus on now, saying something more like, "That's just a thought. Okay then, back to it, breathe . . ."

Let's say you're distracted. You tell yourself, "3 . . . 2 . . . 1 . . . Stop!" Last time you tried to concentrate, you only made it five minutes before your mind wandered. That's okay. Say "3 . . . 2 . . . 1 . . . Stop!" again and start over. Don't worry if you only made it five minutes. Don't worry that you might not make it five minutes again. Just focus on now.

In other words, we may have no "free will," but we certainly have "free won't."[3] Regardless of what type of brain activity causes us to initiate certain behaviors, *conscious thought can conclusively cause us to stop that behavior.*[4]

In Habit 2: Ignite Your Productivity, we outlined how saying "3 ... 2 ... 1 ... Go!" can help you get started on an activity. If you want to stop an activity, it works in reverse.

Say "3 ... 2 ... 1 ... Stop!" Practice free won't.

When Ari was in the hospital and I (Erica) was splitting my time between the three children, I made a conscious decision to be present and engaged when I was with each of them. I changed my mindset about my time with the kids from Mandatory time, where I had to take care of them, to Treasured time, where I could enjoy them and play with them. I remember making this switch in my mind, writing in my Productivity Code Planner, and then I'd show up at the hospital, start playing hockey with Ari, and before I knew it I was pulling my phone out of my back pocket to check Facebook. I'd instinctively open my email to make sure I didn't miss anything. I'd begin responding to text messages.

I didn't want to be doing these things. I didn't plan to do them. They just happened. So I told myself, "3 ... 2 ... 1 ... Stop!" and I put my phone away. A few minutes later I'd be reaching for it again. "3 ... 2 ... 1 ... Stop!" It was a simple trick that made all the difference.

Start browsing on your favorite news site during a TIME Sprint? "3 ... 2 ... 1 ... Stop!"

Start eating potato chips at 9 PM after a day with a long bike ride and healthy eating (ahem, Mike)? "3 ... 2 ... 1 ... Stop!"

Start reading text messages while you're concentrating? "3 ... 2 ... 1 ... Stop!"

Excessive TV? Drinking too much coffee? Task switching? Starting your workday with something other your Greatest Impact Activity? Doing something better delegated to someone else?

Veto these activities. Say "3 ... 2 ... 1 ... Stop!" Practice free won't.

2. Make Micro Change

Which of the following two choices do you think is more difficult?

Option 1: Save $1 today

Option 2: Save $700,000

When given these options at presentations, over 90 percent of people raise their hands that option two is more difficult. However, in effect, if you can do option one on an ongoing basis, you achieve number two without any extra effort at all.

If you save one dollar a day and put it in an exchange-traded fund tracking an index like the S&P 500, which has an average fifty-year return from 1965 to 2014 of 11.23 percent, you'd save $698,450 in that time frame.[5] The effect of small actions, over time, can have very big consequences.

In a similar vein, it's easier to do something small, then build up to something big. Getting started on anything takes activation energy, as we discussed in Habit 2. If you know you're getting started on something difficult, it takes that much more activation energy. Thus, if you're having trouble getting started or staying with something you want to do, set progressively smaller and smaller goals until you can stick with them.

We've talked to people who are straight-out daunted by the idea of focusing for at least twenty minutes, so they don't start a TIME Sprint. Where twenty minutes might seem like a lot, five minutes seldom does. If you're having trouble getting into difficult tasks, make the task smaller. Here you can shrink the sprint to just five minutes and lower the activation-energy bar significantly.

Eventually you will build stamina. Five minutes might seem small, but then you can go seven. Then ten. Then twenty is no big deal.

For many people, going through the goal-setting exercise and defining their big-picture goals is daunting. They've never thought about it and don't know where to begin. Start with your one-year goal and build out your quarterly priorities from there. Once you have one goal figured out, others will follow.

And the progress feels good. As Teresa Amabile and Steven Kramer explain in *The Progress Principle*, one of the most motivating factors for anyone—and what often constitutes their best days at work—is when they feel like they are making progress toward a goal.[6] Amabile and Kramer analyzed nearly 12,000 questionnaires and diary entries provided by 238 employees across seven companies. "Even when progress happens in small steps, a person's sense of steady forward movement toward an important goal can make all the difference between a great day and a terrible one," they wrote.

Indeed, it's fairly easy to break larger tasks down into smaller tasks, and then to get them done. Once you do, you'll like how you feel.

And once you know this, it makes sense why doing this is so effective. It feels good.

Stanford's BJ Fogg has made a study of habit formation.[7] He believes change is built best when focusing on tiny habits.* Flossing your teeth is an example Fogg uses, recommending that you start with flossing just one tooth. You can use a "when I/then I" statement to trigger you: "When I finish brushing my teeth, then I'll floss one tooth." Seems so easy and small, it should take practically no energy to do it.

Then, reward yourself. "You declare victory," Fogg says. "Like I am so awesome, I just flossed one tooth. And I know it sounds ridiculous. But I believe that when you reinforce yourself like that, your brain will say "yeah, awesome, let's do that."

Once the habit is formed, Fogg says you'll find yourself flossing all your teeth.

Breaking down large tasks into smaller ones is a behavior we see The XP demonstrating regularly. When overwhelmed by a large task, The XP break it down into smaller, more approachable tasks.

Make it a micro sprint, and you'll achieve micro change. Tell yourself you're only committing to five minutes of focus. Or five minutes of exercise. Or five minutes of anything that you want to do but are having trouble starting or getting back to.

This strategy works particularly well for me (Mike) to right the ship when I've fallen out of a habit I want to get back to. Bike riding is a big one here. When I got back on my life horse, I got in the habit of riding for about two hours several times a week. If I went a week or so where I didn't ride at all, the idea of riding two hours was fairly daunting. So was riding an hour.

Then my inner critic would start in. "You don't even want to ride. You don't have

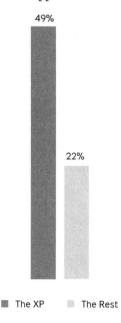

If I'm overwhelmed by a large task, I break it down into smaller tasks that are approachable.

49%

22%

■ The XP   ■ The Rest

---

* Though every time I read "tiny habits," the voice in my head starts singing "Tiny Bubbles" à la Don Ho. Inner critic? Inner voice? Inner karaoke machine!

the time, and you need to get to work anyway. Plus, give yourself a break, the Celtics are on the DVR." Then . . . couch.

But then I gave myself a different break. I told myself to ride for fifteen minutes, then watch the Celtics after. It felt so much easier. I said "3 . . . 2 . . . 1 . . . Go!" to get started, and went for a ride. Sometimes I might go only twenty-five minutes, or I might go for an hour or more. But I went!

This works for yoga, too. Sometimes I want to go, but don't want to go. I'm on the fence. The big difference maker? Signing up for class. I go online and put my name down to attend. In reality, this means almost nothing. I can skip and I'd owe a five-dollar no-show fee that, in effect, I don't think they even charge me. But do I skip? Almost never . . . once I sign up.

Making the task smaller, making micro change, makes quite the difference.

Micro Change Kick-starters

Micro change can be applied to almost anything. Here are some examples:

- Want to start your mornings off right? Tell yourself, "When I get to the office, then I will read just the first Extreme Productivity Morning Routine question."
- Want to get back on track during the day? Stop what you're doing (3 . . . 2 . . . 1 . . .) and read your objectives for this week.
- Want to eat less? At your next meal, leave one bit of food on your plate that you otherwise would have eaten.
- Want to grow a big account? Schedule a meeting with a colleague to discuss it.
- Want to get an A this semester? Commit to studying for five minutes one time.
- Want to listen more? In your next conversation, ask one open-ended question and don't speak until the other person has finished and paused.
- Want to practice mindfulness? Download the Headspace app and listen to the introductory session.
- Want to track your time? Start with your current activity.
- Want to turn off all your notifications? Turn off one.

You get the idea. Regardless of the task, if it feels big, make it small to make it happen. Make micro change.

3. Make a Commitment Contract

"Put your money where your butt is." That's the saucy title of a research paper by Dean Karlan and Jonathan Zinman.[8] They studied whether they could get people to quit smoking by approaching people on the streets in the Philippines with a proposition: we'll give you money and put it in a bank account for you if you quit smoking, but if you smoke within the next six months, you lose the money.

The researchers held the potentially soon-to-be nonsmokers accountable through nicotine-detecting monthly urine tests. It worked surprisingly well. Thirty percent of people who opened the account and committed to not smoking with money on the line and accountability checks quit smoking. Contrast that with the fact that of the 70 percent of smokers who want to quit smoking, about half try in any given year, but only 6 percent succeed.

Based on these results, the researchers surmised that across a variety of areas, people who sign an ironclad commitment contract would be more likely to stick to them than if they just say or even write that they are going to do something.

Karlan and Zinman have now studied over 400,000 commitment contracts with over $35 million on the line. According to them, when a referee (that is, an accountability partner you report to every week) is used in the commitment contract, the average success rate is 61 percent for goals related to money and finance. For those wanting to lose weight, the success rate is a not-too-shabby 47 percent. When the goal involves using both a referee and a financial stake, the success rate for financial resolutions is 87 percent (and a healthy 73 percent for weight loss). Overall, they've found that those who make a commitment contract with a referee increased their chances of success up to 200 percent. Putting money at stake increased the chances of success by up to 300 percent. That's triple the likelihood you'll succeed.

In the previous section on micro change, we noted that to get yourself to attend yoga, signing up in advance increases the odds of going. Not only is that a micro action, it's a micro commitment contract. There's something very powerful about committing to something in writing and putting any amount of money on the line.

I (Mike) raised the ante and gave it a try with my own money. Losing weight has been a challenge for me. I fluctuate up and down ten pounds, but I want to stay down twenty. Until last year I hadn't been able to see it through. To right the ship that was sinking due to my outsized waistline, I made a commitment contract: if I didn't make my weight goal every week, I had to send money—get this—to *an organization I despise.* (Yes, I designated the money to go to an *anti-charity*, which for me upped my resolve to not fail even more.) So the math was:

Written contact + money on the line + an accountability partner + emotional investment of potentially funding an organization that is anathema to my values.

I lost the weight and am now where I was just after my senior year of high school. And the bad guys at the anti-charity didn't get a dime from me.

If you're serious about doing what you've committed yourself to do, you can set yourself up to see similar improvements. You can make a commitment contract late in a process like I did when dieting alone wasn't working, or you can do it early to prevent commitment failure. In any case, if you want something badly enough, put your money and reputation where your mouth is.

Want to write a book? Sprint and relay every day at least once? Do your homework every day? Practice golf four times a week? Get a business plan written in six weeks?

Make a commitment contract. Put something at stake. Have an accountability partner. (If you don't already have one, take a look back at Habit 1.) A commitment will give you the incentives (or disincentives) that bring to life the change you want.

The secret to long-term Extreme Productivity is not to be perfect all the time (no one is, after all), but to get back at it quickly when you fall into unproductive habits and patterns.

* * *

Extreme Productivity is *not* about perfection. It is about being able to right your ship when it's listing to port or starboard, or capsizing. Use the following TIME for Action suggestion to help you get started on new habits or return to lapsed habits, starting today.

> ### TIME FOR ACTION
>
> - Add one thing to your weekly Action Plan that is a micro change or activity that could lead to a longer-term commitment or habit change.
> - Try making a commitment contract for yourself, putting a little something on the line on Stickk (www.stickk.com).

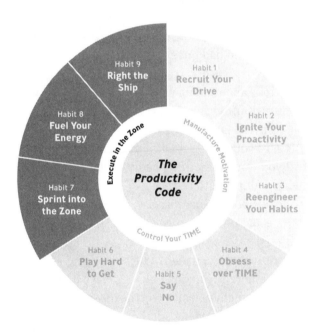

This is it. You've done it! You've made it through the final key, Key 3: Execute in the Zone. You're now equipped with your very own toolkit to Sprint into the Zone, Fuel Your Energy, and Right the Ship. You've cracked The Productivity Code.

Previously, in Key 1: Manufacture Motivation, you learned how to find your *why* and harness your motivation. In Key 2: Control Your TIME, you learned how to find the time to achieve your goals. And now, with Key 3: Execute in the Zone, you know what to do to be able to concentrate, get things done, and become unstoppable.

If you've been completing the TIME for Action activities at the end of each chapter along the way, you've likely already begun incorporating some of The Productivity Code into your life. Or, maybe you've just read straight through without stopping to practice. In either case, you might be thinking, "Where exactly do I go from here?" Not to worry, we're not going to just drop you off here and drive away into the sunset. We want to make sure you have everything you need to fully and completely commit to your extreme productivity journey. At the end of this book, you'll learn how (see Appendix A). And for another thing, well, we've got some loose ends in our story left to wrap up.

EPILOGUE

ERICA

We waited with Ari for his new heart, mostly living at Boston Children's Hospital, for 211 days. On March 3, 2017, when we learned it was finally coming, we figured we'd let Ari tell his friends and family himself. Mike and I knew Ari's heart was on the way in the early morning. We told Ari a few hours later while playing baseball with him on "his baseball field," a large activity room just off the hospital lobby. As we told him, we did our best to catch his reaction on video, then posted it on social media to let our family and friends know it was happening.

Our family, friends, and tens of millions of others around the globe ended up watching that video, including one special-feature story producer from ESPN. He reached out, inquiring if ESPN could create an *E:60* feature documentary about Ari. Ari wanted to do it, but soon after he began to reject his heart. A few weeks later, we thought we'd lost him after his first cardiac arrest. Somehow, after months on life support and a grueling, uncertain recovery, on June 16, 2017, he was ready to come home. By his request, the ESPN crew was right there with us.

Several weeks later the ESPN guys came over to interview and film Mike, Ari, me, and our family for forty-eight continuous hours. My one-on-one interview was on Monday, July 17. The cameras and lighting were set up in our rental house living room for what turned out to be my four-hour interview about Ari. Even at four hours, it was barely enough to scratch the surface of his life.

We talked about everything from his initial diagnosis before he was born six years earlier, to just the week previous when Ari got a surprise visit from Red Sox stars Xander Bogaerts and Christian Vasquez, and how they were, in turn, surprised and mesmerized by our special, magnetic, and captivating little boy.

The interview was an emotional roller coaster as I relived the highest highs—like the night five years earlier when Ari was born and came out screaming, and the afternoon one month before when he walked out of Boston Children's Hospital, new heart beating in his chest. And the lowest lows—like the first time (of so many) we handed him over to the surgeons, not knowing if he'd survive the visit to the OR, and the terrible night Mike called to tell me that Ari's heart had stopped, CPR went for twenty-seven minutes, and they weren't sure if he was going to make it. Yet the interview ended on a high note because Ari was home; he had made it.

During the interview, they asked me, "Erica, how would you describe Ari's heart?"

I paused for a bit and thought, and said, simply, "Unstoppable."

Ari died four days later.

A few weeks later, after Ari's funeral, sitting shiva, and then too many quiet days at the house, while we could still smell him on his clothes we picked up from the floor, while we were still putting away his toys, and while we hadn't yet closed all his books from the last page he had opened them to, we decided to continue. We wanted the world-class storytellers at ESPN to share Ari with the world, one last time, to pay him tribute and honor his life and spirit.

The producers came back a month or so after Ari had left us and interviewed me again.

Nervous, sad, and still in shock, I sat down to talk with Tom Rinaldi.

A few hours in, toward the end of his interview, he asked me, "You told us last month Ari's heart was unstoppable. Now, how would you describe your son's heart?"

Surprised I could even get words out through my tears, I replied, "Larger than life. Because even now that it has stopped, I think it's going to go on and touch so many people."

✳   ✳   ✳

"I need you to help me be strong. I can't do this without you." This is the last thing I whispered to Ari as we removed his breathing tube and turned off the machines that were keeping his war-torn, battered, broken little body alive.

I didn't know if I could write this book. But once I started, I felt Ari with me every step of the way.

Ari was unstoppable and continues to be. Our hope is this book, sharing Ari's story, and a bit of ours, plays a small part in honoring Ari, allowing him to continue to touch people so deeply as he always did. To help them lead bigger, more fulfilled lives. To realize time is precious and fleeting, and to get the most joy, meaning, and laughter out of every moment. To never, ever miss an at-bat, and to swing for the fences while you can. Starting ~~Not~~ Today.

ACKNOWLEDGMENTS

Just as we couldn't have gotten through the last decade without the incredible support of our family, friends, and community, we could not have written this book without assistance from a large number of people in our lives.

Thanks to our amazing colleague and friend Mary Flaherty who led the charge with our productivity research and assessment tool, and then masterfully helped us weave together our deeply personal story with the business topics and research in this book. Her guidance, advice, writing, and editing made this book infinitely better.

Thanks to our colleagues at RAIN Group who, while we lived in the hospital, kept the business going and thriving and who helped refine and share our productivity system with clients. John Doerr, Bob Croston, Jason Murray, Andy Springer, Steve Elefson, Dave Shaby, Gord Smith, Beth McCluskey, Stephanie Whitesell, Kate Olson, Aly Jamison, Ted Hill, Erica Benedick, Grant Heale, Miguel Upegui, Ago Cluytens, Vivek Kumar, Katie Bissonette, Aletha Dalicandro, and the rest of the RAINiac team around the world.

Thank you to Ari's large team of doctors, especially Wayne Tworetzky, Betsy Blume, Ram Emani, Jim Lock, and Audrey Marshall, and to the literally hundreds of nurses and team members at Boston Children's Hospital, for your love of Ari and the amazing work you do every day saving children's lives.

Thanks to the fantastic team at BenBella Books: Matt Holt, editor in chief, Matt Holt Books, for believing in the power of our message and story. Claire Schulz, thanks for helping to make the book more accessible for all readers and shepherding us through the process, and James Fraleigh for catching all the little details. Sarah Avinger, thank you for working through many colors, fonts, and layouts to get to a cover design we love. And the rest of the team who helped to write the description, design the graphics, and spread the word about the book. It takes a village to write and publish a book.

Thank you to Sally Collings for your contributions. To Dan Kline, a man of faith and courage proud and true, for helping us think through the positioning, for your feedback throughout, and for your passion about our project. To Tom Rinaldi for the amazing foreword to ~~Not~~ *Today*.

We could never thank our incredible parents enough, Linda, Marvin, Stan, and Nancy. We are incredibly grateful for everything you've done for us. Your generosity, your support, and your love have gotten us through the long, hard days. Without each of you we would not be here, together, telling our story.

And finally, to our daughter, Lexi, and our son Eli, thank you for keeping us smiling. You inspire us every day.

APPENDIX A:
YOUR PERSONAL 90-DAY
PRODUCTIVITY CODE CHALLENGE

Do or do not. There is no try.

Yoda

As we told you in the Introduction, our intention in sharing our journey and learning is to transform the way you live, to help you become more productive and effective, more satisfied, and happier in your life.

Piece of cake, right?

We wanted to give you a very different lens through which to view productivity. You can shift the paradigm from productivity as working harder, managing your in-box better, and grinding more out, to working on things that fill you up and mean something important to you. Finding more Treasured time for yourself. Filling your tank so you can sustain energy and focus for the long haul and achieve your long-term goals.

The Productivity Code and its 9 Habits are that lens. Assuming you've read everything leading up to this chapter, you're pretty well educated in all it entails. Hopefully you've tested some of the habits and hacks, and they've made a difference for you. Many of those we know who have been introduced to the 9 Habits as you have tell us they feel different simply after reading them.

There is, however, one missing piece we committed to sharing with you: a specific, step-by-step process for how you can start transforming your life immediately. In this appendix, we share the tools you need to make a personal commitment to a 90-Day Productivity Code Challenge.

Change Is Hard

No two ways about it: changing habits and working differently is hard. But if you can start something, you can keep it going. If you can do it ~~not~~ today, you can do it tomorrow. If you do it tomorrow, it'll be easier to do the next day and for ninety days total. Do it for ninety days, and you'll completely change your productivity habits and succeed where it means the most for you.

After taking the Extreme Productivity Assessment, I (Erica) uncovered that Habit 4: Obsess over TIME was a big challenge for me. I was working long hours, getting a lot done, but I wasn't focusing on the right things. For two days I obsessively tracked my time. I then applied the appropriate category to each of my activities. I was shocked at what I found. A good portion of my day was spent on Mandatory activities. It left very little time to focus on my Investment activities and push my priorities forward. I was stretched too thin. I had to learn to say no to other people's priorities so I could focus on my own. I launched a ninety-day challenge to specifically minimize Mandatory time. I questioned everything. Began delegating more. Entirely stopped doing things that weren't adding value.

Before I knew it, obsessing over time started to become routine. As I'd get started on any task, I'd stop and ask myself, "Is this the best use of my time? Could someone else do this?" It applied not only to my work, but to my life. Before Netflix would automatically "play next" I'd ask myself, "Am I going to get as much pleasure out of this next show as I did the first? Is there something else I'd rather be doing right now that would fill me up?"

By the end of the ninety days, my habits around how I spent my time had changed dramatically.

Deciding to begin a ninety-day challenge should be done thoughtfully. We'll start, then, by giving you an overview of why time-based personal challenges work, why some work extraordinarily well, and others not so much. Then we'll go over the 90-Day Productivity Code Challenge and what you need to do to get the most out of it.

Purpose of the 90-Day Productivity Code Challenge

To adopt The Productivity Code's 9 Habits in a systematic way to unleash your productivity.

Making Time-Based Challenges Work

Personal challenges ranging from food to fitness to sports are popular these days. Why? Because, when constructed properly, they work. Here are six factors present in the most successful challenges, including, of course, the 90-Day Productivity Code Challenge. Note that challenges often fall apart when just one of these six factors is missing.

- **Desirable outcome.** The more motivated people are to achieve the outcome, the more likely they are to engage in, and stick to, a time-based challenge. If being more productive and feeling good about it is important to you, then you're starting in the right place.

- **Mindshare.** Believe it or not, some people forget they are doing a challenge. They say, "I'm all in for this," and then they forget. Thus, the challenge itself must build in ongoing touch points to keep the challenge top of mind while it's happening. The full 90-Day Productivity Code Challenge available through MyProductivityCode.com is built to give you regular reminders and productivity boosters—through email, your commitment contract, your accountability partner and check-ins, your morning routine, and online learning—to keep you focused on the challenge itself. Meanwhile, if you want to follow the process and complete a 90-Day Productivity Code Challenge by yourself, you'll find the fundamental outline in this appendix.

- **Simultaneously enjoyable and difficult.** The more difficult the activity, the more rewarding it is when complete. You can say, "That was really hard, and *I got it done!*" At the same time, the more daunting and not-fun a task seems, the more difficult it will be to start and stick with it. For most people, adopting The Productivity

Code is between somewhat and very challenging, but it's rarely super easy.

The Productivity Code Challenge also has enjoyment built into it. Yes, it's daunting to start difficult tasks, but when you TIME Sprint and get into the zone, you'll enjoy the process. At the end of each task and day, you'll feel the satisfaction of having done something difficult of your own choosing that was worthwhile. And you can choose to reward yourself with Treasured time when you start finding more time in your day you didn't even know you could reclaim.

- **Extreme task clarity.** Challenges work when people know exactly what to do, when, and for how long. Ambiguity breeds confusion. Confusion destroys challenges.

The Productivity Code Challenge is built to be very specific. Use the morning routine every day. TIME Sprint when concentrating. Make your weekly task plan very clear and check in once a week with an accountability partner on them. And so on. Just review the Productivity Code Quick Reference Guide and print the Productivity Code Planner to remind yourself what to do: MyProductivityCode.com /booktools. To get going, have a look at the Productivity Code Challenge Quick Start Guide on page 193.

- **Commitment strength.** The more strongly people state their commitment to the challenge, and *how* they state their commitment to the challenge, affects greatly whether they stick with it or not. Thus, we encourage you to make your commitments not just verbal, but written and public (public in the sense of sharing it with an accountability partner and coach). Consider also taking it one step further and make a commitment contract with yourself to stick to your own goals and plan.

- **Accountability partner.** People are more likely to stick with a challenge when they feel they owe keeping their commitment to another person. The Productivity Code Challenge works best when you name an accountability partner and follow the guidelines for weekly check-ins.

How the Productivity Code Challenge Works

Build and follow the Productivity Code Planner so you can adopt the 9 Habits of The Productivity Code. The planner can be found in the online resources that come with ~~Not~~ *Today*. As this appendix continues, we'll walk you through filling out a planner.

Complete the planner and your challenge will be underway. It might be obvious, but the key to becoming extremely productive is to adopt the 9 Habits. The 90-Day Productivity Code Challenge is singularly focused on helping you do that.

You can do this alone, or you can get further support with training, reinforcement, and ongoing email by visiting our website, MyProductivityCode.com. Keeping the Productivity Code Challenge, and concepts behind it, top of mind and reinforcing how they work so you learn them well are a huge part of many people's success. If you participate in the MyProductivityCode.com online training, you can apply all of the learning while receiving reinforcement and feedback.

It's important to note that taking the 90-Day Productivity Code Challenge is, of course, completely optional. When anyone is forced to do the Productivity Code Challenge or any challenge like it, it's easy to sabotage one's own results, not fully commit, and say it didn't work. As we said in Habit 1: Ignite Your Drive, when what you're doing doesn't feel personally meaningful, if you perceive the task as part of someone else's agenda, you don't have psychological ownership over it, and the odds you will attack it with passion, intensity, and consistency are predictably low. But when you *elect* to do it, if your heart's in it, it's very powerful. At the crux of the Challenge is to put your Productivity Code Planner together and get started. Following the planner is all you need to do to get a Productivity Code Challenge underway.

Productivity Code Challenge Components

Let's take a look at how to do this. As a quick recap, there are some areas in the Productivity Code Planner you may have already filled out as you worked through ~~Not~~ *Today*.

Extreme Productivity Planner

Goal Plan

Big Picture Goal—My New Reality

Define the destination of your journey. Big Picture, what do you want?

I want to retire in twelve years at age 55 with enough money in the bank to enjoy my retirement and pay for my two children's college.

The Foundation—Why

Your "why" is the foundation of your goals and will help you stick to them long term. Why have you chosen your Big Picture Goal?

Giving back to my children, being around at 55 when they are still at home in school for several years, and being able to live free of debt or financial worry will allow me to live a great majority of my life focused on giving back and enjoying Treasured time every day.

Three-Year Goals Between: 2018   and: 2021

What do I need to achieve in three years that will put me on the path to achieving my Big Picture Goal?

Financial
- Retirement savings of XXX in three years
- Total compensation of Y

Strategic
- Positioned internally as the go-to expert on the XYZ Technology
- Get promoted to Vice President of Strategic Accounts

Annual Goals Between: 2018   and   2019

List your goals for this year. Write down no more than five (as few as possible). Put your most important priority first.

Goal	Behind	On Track	Ahead
Total compensation of Z, at 120 percent of quota	☐ Behind	☐ On Track	☒ Ahead
Selling my first cross-functional deal at the enterprise level	☐ Behind	☒ On Track	☐ Ahead
Growing three of my accounts to over $500k in revenue each	☒ Behind	☐ On Track	☐ Ahead
Building a plan with leadership to become a VP, and executing on that plan	☐ Behind	☒ On Track	☐ Ahead

Your Big Picture Goal and New Reality are set. (If you haven't set these yet, revisit Habit 1: Recruit Your Drive.) And you know why this is important to you. On your way there, you're thinking three years ahead and know your goals for this year.

You may have a compensation goal for this year, but you may also have career milestones, education, or other achievements you'd like to accomplish in the next twelve months.

The switch from bigger-picture goals to actions happens at the ninety-day mark. Ninety days is far enough away for you to accomplish great strides, but close enough that you know you have to tackle your greatest impact activities to get there.

Thus, you have priorities this quarter with your top priority bolded. (Note this priority is often what becomes the focus of your Productivity Code Challenge One Big Thing statement, which we'll explain in a bit.) You have your objectives this month and this week. And then you have your immediate action plan or to-do list.

Extreme Productivity Planner

Action Plan

Accountability Partner Name: Jim Appleton

Report Progress on (day and time): Fridays at I p.m.

Priorities This Quarter	Objectives This Month
No more than 5. As few as possible. Bold the most important priority.	*As few as possible. Bold the most important objective.*
• **Prospecting: Double my efforts for net new logos** • Account growth: build and execute plans to grow 5 of my I5 most important accounts • Drive 5 new proposals for greater than 6 figures	• Spend 25% of time prospecting • Build and approve 2 account plans • **Focus on my top I5 deals in the pipeline to drive 6-figure proposals** • Avoid small sales to increase time for big ones

Success Metrics:	Success Metrics:
• Pipeline growth from $4.5m to $5.5m • 5 new six-figure opportunities in the pipeline • 5 completed and approved account plans • My SVP approving my career advancement plan	• **I5 proactively set new meetings** • **2 account plans approved**

To Do This Week
Plan actions and calendar Investment activities for next week on (day and time)
• Calendar I5 hours of prospecting and don't get distracted • Hold account plan meeting #I and begin building accounts • Write and present the ACME proposal • Prepare strongly for my 3 most important sales meetings • Build an opportunity plan to win the Smith deal and give the competition no chance

To Do—Core List	
GIA Today:	Prospecting: 4 hours calendared! No distractions.
• Do morning routine every day • ‹To-do list of all items goes here. Look at your to-do list this week and prioritize them in order.›	

Along with your goal and action plan, you know which positive statements you want to make to yourself and habits you want to change; you also have a plan for how to change them, and for how you want to change your time.

You know how you want to avoid distraction, what you want to avoid from your "to-don't" list, and how to maximize your energy. From here, creating your 90-Day Productivity Code Challenge tends to be fairly easy.

Productivity Code 2-Week Quick Start Guide

For those of you who want exact guidelines to implement a Productivity Code Challenge, do it like this:

Week I: Getting Started

1. Build your Productivity Code Planner. If you already have your goals and action plan set, jump to page 194 and only fill out the pages on the 90-Day Productivity Code Challenge.
2. Print the 9 Habits of the Productivity Code Quick Reference Guide at MyProductivityCode.com/booktools and post it on a wall where you can always see it.
3. Select an accountability partner.
4. Review your Productivity Code Planner with them; make sure you are truly committed.
5. Calendar fifteen minutes to plan your weekly actions, such as Friday at 2 PM; set this as a recurring meeting with yourself for three months.
6. Send your weekly action plan at this time to your accountability partner.
7. At the same time, calendar your GIA and other Investment activities for the next week.
8. At the end of each week, use this time to grade yourself on your previous week and send your weekly action plan for the next week to your accountability partner.
9. Commit to sprinting and relaying when you need to concentrate. Put a stopwatch on! Follow the sprinting guidelines in Habit 7: Sprint into the Zone. It's life changing.

Week 2: Practice Habit Change

- Review the Week I Quick Start Guide and stick with Week I activities.
- Say "3 . . . 2 . . . 1 . . . Go!" to get started on your activities.
- Say "3 . . . 2 . . . 1 . . . Stop!" to stop anything you want to stop.
- Pick one habit to change this week. Only one. Use the Productivity Code Planner as your guide to select a habit and make a plan to change it. Ideas:

- Talk to yourself all week; change negative to positive self-talk
- Cut one hour of Empty or Mandatory time and redirect that time purposefully
- Do the XP Morning Routine every morning
- TIME Sprint without fail when you need to concentrate*
- Download a mindfulness app and try it once a day for ten minutes
- Change one eating habit
- Pick one exercise to do or add to your routine
- Track your time for two full days in real time

Week 3 and beyond: Repeat Week 2 Habit Change

---

* Yes, this was in week 1, but some people find it difficult. When you do, make micro change. Pick one thing and don't let go until you change the habit.

Start Your Productivity Code Challenge

First, decide if it's a good time to engage in a challenge. If you're getting married or having a baby in a week, it's better to wait. If it is a good time, check the box to accept the challenge and adopt The Productivity Code's 9 Habits.

Extreme Productivity Planner: Extreme Productivity Challenge

Instructions:

- Read the form and decide whether or not to accept the 90-Day XP Challenge. This is 100% voluntary.
- If you choose to accept:
  - Find an accountability partner; calendar weekly accountability check-ins **now**
  - Define your One Big Thing
  - Create a commitment contract

☐ **Yes**, I accept the 90-Day Extreme Productivity Challenge and am 100% committed to execution

☐ **Yes**, I will make a commitment contract with myself in 30-day increments to follow my XPC plan

I will also adopt the following key XP principles as I work . . .

Recruit My Drive
- ☒ Choose my New Reality: build goal plan and review quarterly
- ☒ Plan actions weekly
- ☒ Track progress weekly with a partner

Obsess over TIME
- ☒ Take T, Increase I, Minimize M, Eliminate E
- ☒ Put my GIA first
- ☒ Track my TIME

Sprint into the Zone
- ☒ Establish a daily routine of obsessed, planned sprints
- ☐ Relay: Do four successive sprints
- ☒ Keep a distraction capture list

Ignite My Proactivity
- ☒ Calendar Investment TIME
- ☒ Talk to myself
- ☐ Say "3...2...1...Go!"

Say No
- ☒ Shrink my priority set: if it's not gung ho, it's no
- ☐ Practice saying no
- ☐ Keep a to-don't list

Fuel My Energy
- ☐ Mind: Practice positive self-talk and mindfulness
- ☒ Body: Eat/sleep for energy, be active
- ☐ Spirit: Take Treasured TIME

Reengineer My Habits
- ☐ Say "When I, Then I. Will I?"
- ☐ Change my environment
- ☒ Make my morning routine sacred

Play Hard to Get
- ☐ Be free from the shackles of alerts
- ☒ Signal "do not disturb"
- ☐ Be someplace else

Right the Ship
- ☐ Say "3...2...1...Stop!"
- ☐ Make micro change
- ☒ Sign a commitment contract

One Big Thing for 90 Days
See Quarterly Priorities for ideas. Make result both specific and measurable.
What is your One Big Thing?
Double my prospecting time from 1 day (8 hrs a week) to 2 days (16 hrs a week) and *concentrate fully when executing.*
Targeted Result
More than double my pipeline from $1.2m to $2.5m

Signature _____ Date _____

Second, define your One Big Thing. This is the one thing that, should you focus on it day in and day out over the challenge period, will drive your overall success.

To figure out what your One Big Thing is, scan your priority list for the quarter and month and ask yourself what objective is difficult and most important. Then state what you want to do about it (your Targeted Result).

For example, say you want to improve customer service email response time. You know response times are incredibly important and that across the board, teams are taking too long and inquiries are falling through the cracks. In your Productivity Code Planner you'd put:

- One Big Thing for 90 Days: Roll out new process for email response.
- Targeted Result: Reduce email response time from four hours on average to one hour.

Whatever you choose, make sure you have an accountability partner and a day and time for weekly check-ins on progress.

Third, decide if you're willing to make a commitment contract with yourself to hold yourself accountable. Commitment contracts are wildly successful in helping people be accountable *to the commitments they make to themselves.* If you aren't willing to sign a contract with yourself and put some teeth into it, then you have to ask yourself if you are really 100 percent committed to execution. Meanwhile, we often recommend people set up their commitment contracts on Stickk.com (no affiliation; we just like the site). As we covered in Habit 9: Right the Ship, Yale economists found that those who make a commitment contract with a referee (another name for an accountability partner) increase the chances of keeping their commitments by 200 percent. And putting money at stake increases chances of success by up to 300 percent. This is how you can triple your likelihood of sticking to your commitments.

Follow your commitment contract for thirty days three times. Why thirty days three times, you ask? Well, you can do anything for thirty days, but do it only for thirty days and it'll be fleeting. It takes ninety days plus or minus to make living by The Productivity Code a habit. And that's what you want . . . new skills and habits so you can maximize your productivity and success ~~not~~ today.

TIME FOR ACTION

- If you're feeling ready, accept the 90-Day Productivity Code Challenge to adopt The Productivity Code's 9 Habits.
- Fill out the one-page form and pick something bold for your One Big Thing.
- Fill out a commitment contract to make your accountability stronger.
- If you want the help, contact us through MyProductivityCode.com.

APPENDIX B:
RESEARCH NOTE

In this appendix you'll find an overview and explanation of our research methods and analysis for the study that underpinned, influenced, and ultimately validated the 9 Habits of The Productivity Code. We collected all this data during the last decade as we've been studying, testing, and honing a series of habits and hacks that have driven not only our own productivity, but that of teams at dozens of our corporate clients worldwide. Most recently, over the course of several months in late 2018, our team collected data from 2,377 confidential assessments (as of this writing, now 5,000). The Extreme Productivity Assessment measured thirty-six productivity attributes, behaviors, and habits.

This Research Note mostly supplements findings shared throughout this book, but is also intended to stand alone; thus we may reiterate some of our commentary.

Research Overview and Demographics

Primary research data shared in this book was collected by the RAIN Group research team for our Extreme Productivity study. We conducted this global productivity research to better understand how to help people get the best results from their time and efforts, and achieve the greatest levels of motivation and accountability.

Data was analyzed through multiple lenses, including what The Extremely Productive (The XP) do differently than The Rest, which behaviors are correlated with Extreme Productivity, and which behaviors are the key drivers likely to have the greatest impact on productivity. Additionally, we analyzed productivity in conjunction with performance, job satisfaction, and happiness. We also analyzed the data in multiple demographic slices, including job function, role, industry, company annual revenue, and geographic region.

Data for the original study was collected from 2,377 confidential assessments completed by respondents across the Americas, Europe, the Middle East, Africa, and the Asia-Pacific region. Respondents were invited to participate via online links sent by the RAIN Group research team, as well as by RAIN Group partners. Before and after the quantitative portion of the study, we held over 250 conversations with company leaders about the productivity habits and performance of their teams to vet and validate the assumptions and quantitative conclusions.

Demographics Notes

There were no significant differences in productivity by job levels (role in organization) or functional area (e.g., sales vs. non-sales). There were slight differences in productivity by geography that may be accounted for with nuance differences in the survey sample. There were slightly (but not noteworthy) higher productivity scores in private company samples, possibly due to a minor and predictable Hawthorne Effect. In other words, the findings are generally applicable regardless of job focus, level, size of company, or geography.

Defining Extreme Productivity

As mentioned, in our analysis we placed respondents into two groups: The XP and The Rest. We also analyzed a subset of The XP to see what we could learn from people who, for all intents and purposes, don't waste time at work.

The Extremely Productive: This group responded to the prompt "I am extremely productive" with 5 out of 5, "Very much like me." To validate self-reported data, we reviewed (with permission) performer groups to confirm that those who labeled themselves as extremely productive and top performers versus their peers were categorized similarly by their managers.

The Rest: The Rest includes all other responses (1–4 on a 5-point scale) to "I am extremely productive." The Rest represents 86 percent of respondents.

TIME Champions: This is a subgroup of The XP who spend very little time during a typical workday on non-value-add activities (i.e., they do not waste time).

"I am extremely productive."

14% The Extremely Productive (5 out of 5)

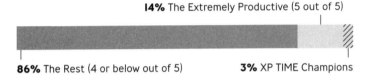

86% The Rest (4 or below out of 5)   **3%** XP TIME Champions

We did not write much about TIME Champions throughout ~~Not~~ *Today* as it was more detail than needed to support the conclusions, but note that from a research perspective, we found it instructive to look at the top-of-the-top in productivity to see if there was much difference. In fact, they looked quite like The XP, just an order of magnitude further down the path of reflecting the 9 Habits.

What Separates The XP and The Rest?

We were impressed at the large gaps between The XP and The Rest across all 9 Habits. The deep differences across the board between The XP and The Rest also demonstrate just how differently The XP work.

Study participants could score up to twenty points in each of the 9 Habits of Extreme Productivity through the XP Assessment instrument. The spider graph on the next page compares XP TIME Champions, The XP, and The Rest. Across the board, The XP scored significantly higher than The Rest for each Habit, with the biggest gaps in Habit 3: Reengineer Your Habits, Habit 4: Obsess over TIME, and Habit 5: Say No.

Overall, respondents, including The XP, scored the lowest in Habit 6: Play Hard to Get and Habit 5: Say No. While The Rest have the greatest amount of work to do to improve across all 9 Habits, even The XP have significant improvement potential.

Habit Mean Scores: XP Time Champions, The XP, The Rest

For those of you unfamiliar with statistical analysis techniques, here are two terms that will help you understand how we analyzed the results of our research.

Correlation: In statistics, a correlation describes whether a relationship exists between two variables. To be included in the 9 Habits, a habit or behavior that made up that habit as a whole had to be correlated with Extreme Productivity.

Key Driver: In statistics, a key driver indicates if a factor impacts the likelihood of a particular outcome. For this study, we analyzed habits and behaviors to determine whether or not they impact the outcomes of productivity, performance, happiness, and job satisfaction. A number of them did across the 9 Habits.

All 9 Habits positively correlate with Extreme Productivity. *Eight* of the 9 Habits are also either key drivers of Extreme Productivity in their own right or include a specific behavior that is a key driver. Seven of the 9 Habits include behaviors that represent the greatest *separation* between The XP and The Rest. Six of the 9 Habits include *low-frequency behaviors* (few respondents across all groups exhibit them) that have a greater than 2× difference between The XP and The Rest. In other words, while these low-frequency behaviors are uncommon, The XP are much more likely to exhibit them.

9 Habits of Extreme Productivity	Productivity			
I. Recruit Your Drive	★	●	◆	
2. Ignite Your Proactivity	★	●	◆	
3. Reengineer Your Habits	★	●	◆	■
4. Obsess over TIME	★	●	◆	■
5. Say No	★	●		■
6. Play Hard to Get	★			■
7. Sprint into the Zone	★	●	◆	
8. Fuel Your Energy	★	●	◆	■
9. Right the Ship	★	●	◆	■

★ Positively Correlated   ◆ Top Percentage Point Difference XP vs. The Rest
● Key Driver—Habit or Behavior   ■ Low Frequency, XP 2×+

Each of the 9 Habits is also correlated with top performance, job satisfaction, and happiness.

Extreme Productivity, Top Performance, Job Satisfaction, and Happiness Go Together

Due to their specific work habits, The XP are more likely to be top performers, satisfied with their jobs, and very happy compared to their peers.

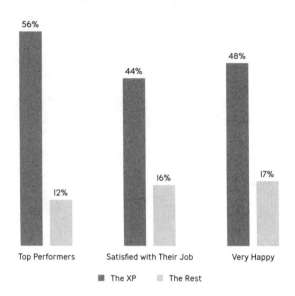

What's more, anywhere from three to five of the Habits are key drivers of happiness, job satisfaction, and top performance. The XP are significantly more likely to strongly agree (5 out of 5) that they're very happy, top performers, and satisfied with their jobs. These findings were surprising, with nearly half of The XP reporting they strongly agree they're very happy compared to only 17 percent of The Rest.

Productivity Quotient (PQ)

A Productivity Quotient (PQ) is a numerical measure of how productive a person is, derived from a cumulative score of productivity behaviors and attributes from our Extreme Productivity Assessment. First, statistically, PQ is valid. PQ is strongly positively correlated with Extreme Productivity (in statistical terms, it has a Pearson correlation coefficient of 0.631, which we considered to be a large effect). As your PQ goes up, so does productivity.

The average PQ is 129 across all respondents. The XP approach the upper quintile with an average PQ of 144, while The Rest have an average PQ of 126. If you or your team's PQ is below 144, a good first goal is to get it here. A second goal is 154, a score achieved by XP TIME Champions.

Productivity Quotients

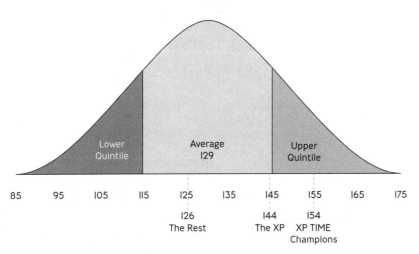

Possible score range is minimum of 36, maximum of 180. If you're looking at an assessment report, 129=72%, 144=80%, 126=70%, 154=86%.

Key Drivers of Productivity

To determine which attributes and behaviors are most likely to increase productivity, we performed a key driver analysis. In statistics parlance, a key driver is a factor that is likely to drive changes in a variable. In this case, the factors are attributes and behaviors and the variable is productivity.

We wanted to know:

1. Are any of the behaviors studied key drivers of Extreme Productivity? We knew thirty-six behaviors and attributes correlated, but was there something more? That is, could we identify behaviors with a predictable likelihood of increasing productivity?

2. Are behaviors clustered around any particular habits, such as with the low-frequency behaviors (see page 206)?

We found about one-third of the factors that correlated were also key drivers of Extreme Productivity. They're not clustered around a particular Habit. The behaviors and attributes largely span the 9 Habits of The Productivity Code. We're impressed at the large gaps between The XP and The Rest across all key drivers, suggesting that productivity improvement potential for most people and teams is both significant and widespread. The deep differences across the board between The XP and The Rest demonstrate just how differently The XP work.

Key Behavioral Drivers of Productivity by % Very Much Like Me

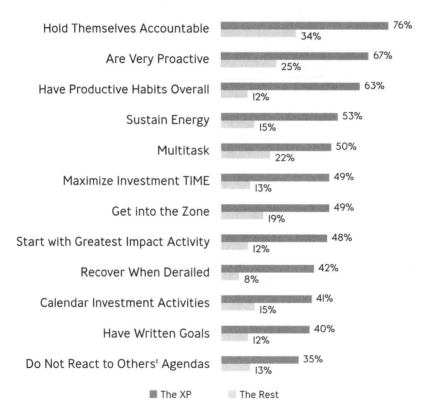

Driver	The XP	The Rest
Hold Themselves Accountable	76%	34%
Are Very Proactive	67%	25%
Have Productive Habits Overall	63%	12%
Sustain Energy	53%	15%
Multitask	50%	22%
Maximize Investment TIME	49%	13%
Get into the Zone	49%	19%
Start with Greatest Impact Activity	48%	12%
Recover When Derailed	42%	8%
Calendar Investment Activities	41%	15%
Have Written Goals	40%	12%
Do Not React to Others' Agendas	35%	13%

■ The XP   ▨ The Rest

The XP are 5.3 times more likely to have productive work habits compared to The Rest. Three-quarters (76 percent) of The XP say they hold themselves accountable for doing what they tell themselves they're going to do compared to just 34 percent of The Rest. The importance of accountability can't be overstated. Accountability is not only the most common behavior exhibited by The XP, but also the number-one key driver of Extreme Productivity.

The XP are 2.7 times more likely to be very proactive compared to The Rest. Indeed, The XP don't procrastinate or wait for others to tell them what to do. They take control of their time and day and maximize it for productivity, motivation, and happiness. Nearly half (49 percent) maximize their Investment time and 48 percent start with their Greatest Impact Activity each day. And when it's time to focus, they get into the zone (49%), a state of intense focus and productivity.

The XP are also able to regularly sustain energy for long periods of time (53% vs. 15%), indicating they have struck a balance between work and taking Treasured time to refill their tanks.

Productivity Can Be Learned

The number-one key driver most separating The XP from The Rest is productive work habits overall.

The XP are 5.3 times (!) more likely to have productive work habits compared to The Rest. This is the third most frequently exhibited behavior by The XP (63 percent).

Productive people don't seem to be born this way. They specifically employ the behaviors and habits set forth in this research. After our Extreme Productivity Challenge training, we've seen substantial increases in participants' PQ—one recent client team went from an average PQ of 124 to 142. And we've seen numerous changes to key company success metrics, from pipeline generated to account revenue and other areas. This goes to show that productivity can be learned and improved over time with the right behaviors.

Furthermore, The XP are also 5.3 times more likely than The Rest to quickly recover when derailed from being productive. We all lose focus every once in a while. The XP recognize this more quickly and are able to get back on track. Only 8 percent of The Rest agree they recover quickly.

Low-Frequency Behaviors Practiced Significantly More Often by The XP

We looked at low-frequency behaviors—behaviors that, across the board, aren't practiced very often. Despite their low frequencies, they all are correlated statistically with Extreme Productivity. What's striking is the large gaps between The XP and The Rest. These productivity behaviors, while practiced infrequently overall, are exceedingly more likely (ranging from 2.1 times to 5.5 times) to be exhibited by The XP.

Low-Frequency Behaviors by Percent Difference
% Very Much Like Me

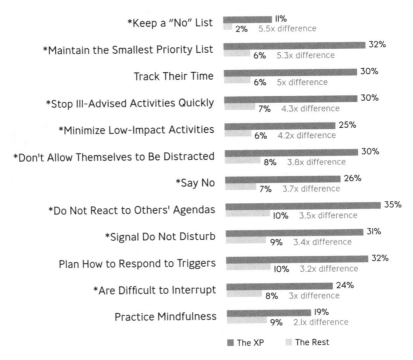

	The XP	The Rest	Difference
*Keep a "No" List	11%	2%	5.5x difference
*Maintain the Smallest Priority List	32%	6%	5.3x difference
Track Their Time	30%	6%	5x difference
*Stop Ill-Advised Activities Quickly	30%	7%	4.3x difference
*Minimize Low-Impact Activities	25%	6%	4.2x difference
*Don't Allow Themselves to Be Distracted	30%	8%	3.8x difference
*Say No	26%	7%	3.7x difference
*Do Not React to Others' Agendas	35%	10%	3.5x difference
*Signal Do Not Disturb	31%	9%	3.4x difference
Plan How to Respond to Triggers	32%	10%	3.2x difference
*Are Difficult to Interrupt	24%	8%	3x difference
Practice Mindfulness	19%	9%	2.1x difference

■ The XP   The Rest

*Themes corresponding to Habit 5: Say No and Habit 6: Play Hard to Get

Interestingly, nine of the twelve low-frequency behaviors either correspond directly with or are similarly themed to two Habits: 5 (Say No) and 6 (Play Hard to Get); these are noted with an asterisk. While only 11 percent of The XP keep a "no" list, they are 5.5 times more likely than The Rest to do so. Furthermore, nearly one-third of The XP report they maintain the smallest priority list compared to only 6 percent of The Rest. One-quarter of The XP minimize low-impact activities compared to only 6 percent of The Rest.

Many of these behaviors are about avoiding distractions and time wasters. Across the board, The XP do a much better job of this than The Rest.

---

9 Habits Correlate with Extreme Productivity

The thirty-six factors on the following page correlated statistically with Extreme Productivity. Typically, correlation by itself is enough to be noted as important in research like this. Beyond the correlations, we were struck by the following facts about each that stood out to us from the data.

---

9 Habits

Recruit Your Drive	**Are Very Driven** XP 2.2x more frequently than The Rest; #2 most frequent behavior of the XP	**Plan Actions Weekly** XP 2.9x more frequently than The Rest	**Track Progress Weekly** XP 3.4x more frequently than The Rest	**Have Written Goals** Key driver of XP
Ignite Your Proactivity	**Are Very Proactive** Key driver of XP; #3 most frequent behavior of the XP	**Use Positive Self-Talk** Top 10 behavior of happiness and job satisfaction	**Calendar Investment Activities** Key driver of XP	**Begin Immediately** XP 3.5x more frequently than The Rest
Reengineer Your Habits	**Have Productive Habits Overall** #1 key driver most separating XP from The Rest	**Have a Productive Work Environment** XP 3.3x more frequently than The Rest	**Follow a Consistent Morning Routine** Top 6 most frequent behavior of XP; Top Performers, Satisfied with Job, Very Happy	**Plan How to Respond to Triggers** XP 3.2x more frequently than The Rest
Obsess over TIME	**Maximize Investment TIME** #3 key driver of XP; XP 46% more Investment TIME per day than The Rest	**Start with Greatest Impact Activity** Key driver of XP	**Track Their TIME** XP 5x more frequently than The Rest	**Minimize Low-Impact Activities** XP 4.2x more frequently than The Rest
Say No	**Do Not React to Others' Agendas** Key driver of XP	**Maintain the Smallest Priority List** XP 5.3x more frequently than The Rest	**Say No** XP 3.7x more frequently than The Rest	**Keep a "No" List** XP 5.5x more frequently than The Rest

Play Hard to Get	**Signal Do Not Disturb** XP 3.4x more frequently than The Rest	**Do Not Allow Themselves to Be Distracted** XP 3.8x more frequently than The Rest	**Are Difficult to Interrupt** XP 3x more frequently than The Rest	**Turn Off Alerts** XP 1.8x more frequently than The Rest
Sprint into the Zone	**Get into the Zone** Key driver of XP	**Devote Undivided Attention** XP 2.3x more frequently than The Rest	**Concentrate for Long Periods of Time** XP 3.8x more frequently than The Rest	**Multitask** Key driver of XP
Fuel Your Energy	**Sustain Energy** Key driver of XP	**Are Active and Fit** Key driver of happiness	**Take Treasured TIME** Key driver of happiness; XP 2.2x more frequently than The Rest	**Practice Mindfulness** XP 2.1x more frequently than The Rest
Right the Ship	**Hold Themselves Accountable** Key driver of XP; #1 most frequent behavior of XP	**Break Down Large Tasks into Smaller** Top 12 most frequent behavior of XP; Top Performers, Satisfied with Job, Very Happy	**Recover When Derailed** Key driver of XP	**Stop Ill-Advised Activities Quickly** XP 4.3x more frequently than The Rest

A New Mindset About TIME

We asked participants about how they spend their time each workday. The implications of our findings are, we believe, profound. These are overall response frequencies. In the next few pages, we dig deeper into how the various productivity groups fare.

It's astounding that 47 percent of all respondents spend a significant amount of time on activities that are either non-value-add (Mandatory) or are outright wasting time (Empty) during a typical workday.

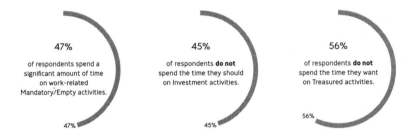

47%
of respondents spend a
significant amount of time
on work-related
Mandatory/Empty activities.

45%
of respondents **do not**
spend the time they should
on Investment activities.

56%
of respondents **do not**
spend the time they want
on Treasured activities.

We wondered if The XP would be focused on more Investment time now so they could have more Treasured time for later, but this wasn't the case. It seems they maximize *both* Investment and Treasured time *now*. The majority of The XP (62%) reported they spend the amount of time they want on Treasured activities, while only 42 percent of The Rest do.

I Spend the Amount of Time I Want on
Treasured and Investment Activities.
STRONGLY AGREE/AGREE

Potential to Increase
Investment Time

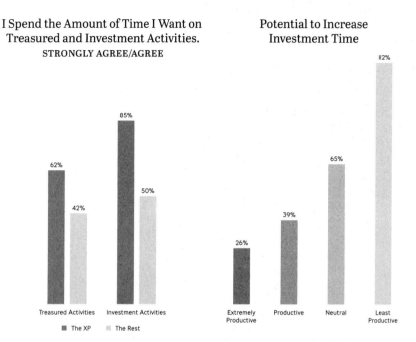

Extremely productive people accumulate Treasured and Investment time and proactively resist dwelling in the Mandatory and Empty
time zones. Yet even the most productive of us struggle with this:
37 percent of The XP admit they spend a significant amount of time
during a typical workday on Mandatory and Empty activities compared
to nearly half of The Rest.

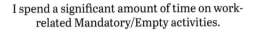

I spend a significant amount of time on work-related Mandatory/Empty activities.

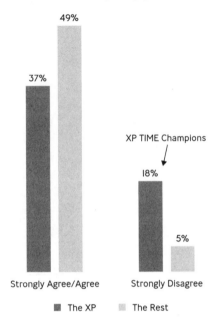

For Organizational Managers and Leaders: Add 46 Percent Productivity Without Adding Employees

We know The XP and TIME Champions spend more of their time on Investment activities, but we wanted to know exactly how much time they spend. We asked respondents: (1) On an average workday, how many hours do you spend on your highest priority (Investment) activities, and (2) how many hours per day could this increase to with strong effort, focus, and support?

The XP report spending 5.7 hours per day on Investment activities compared to just 3.9 hours that The Rest spend. In a five-day work-week, that represents 28.5 hours for The XP versus just 19.5 hours for The Rest. Imagine if you're among The Rest and you spent nine more hours a week on the activities that get you an outsized return. That's 46 percent (!) more time on Investment activities each week.

When it comes to hours they could devote to Investment activities, all performance groups report the potential to increase:

- The Rest: 2.1-hour average daily increase available to 6 hours (54 percent)

- The XP: 1.5-hour average daily increase available to 7.2 hours (26 percent)

- XP TIME Champions: 1.8 hour average daily increase available to 8.7 hours (26 percent)

If The Rest improved even partway to what they think is possible, they would match The XP. This would be like increasing your highly productive workforce by 46 percent without adding any actual employees.

Investment Time Analysis
Current # of Hours and Potential to Increase
HOURS SPENT PER WORKDAY

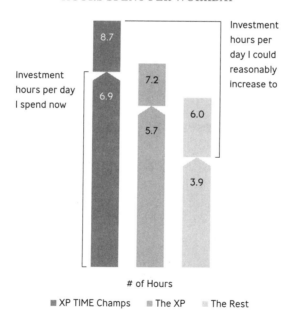

And as previously noted, The XP are significantly more likely to be satisfied in their jobs (44%) compared to The Rest (16%).

Finally, The XP and The Rest can decrease non-value-add TIME at work by 41 percent and 44 percent, respectively.

- The Rest: 1.9-hour average daily decrease available to 2.4 hours (44 percent)
- The XP: 1.4-hour average daily decrease available to 2 hours (41 percent)

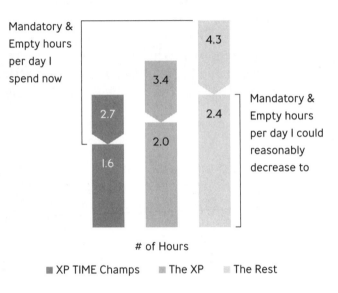

Mandatory & Empty hours per day I spend now

Mandatory & Empty hours per day I could reasonably decrease to

4.3

3.4

2.7

2.4

2.0

1.6

# of Hours

■ XP TIME Champs ▨ The XP ▨ The Rest

Research Conclusion

While the statistical analysis was quite technical in nature, the conclusion turned out to be refreshingly straightforward. To the extent people adopt the 9 Habits of The Productivity Code, their Productivity Quotients go up, and their productivity soars.

NOTES

Prologue

1. Denise Grady, "Operation on Fetus's Heart Valve Called a 'Science Fiction' Success," *New York Times*, February 25, 2002.

2. Rahul H. Rathod, MD, "Hypoplastic Left Heart Syndrome: Management And Outcome," UpToDate, 2018, www.uptodate.com/contents/hypoplastic -left-heart-syndrome-management-and-outcome.

Not Today

1. Brené Brown, *Rising Strong: How the Ability to Reset Transforms the Way We Live, Love, Parent, and Lead* (New York: Random House, 2017).

2. Productivity definition, Lexico, www.lexico.com/definition/productivity.

3. Steven Spear and H. Kent Bowen, "Decoding the DNA of the Toyota Production System," *Harvard Business Review*, September–October 1999, hbr .org/1999/09/decoding-the-dna-of-the-toyota-production-system.

4. Habit definition, Merriam-Webster, www.merriam-webster.com/dictionary /habit.

A New Mindset About TIME

1. Polly LaBarre, "Marcus Buckingham Thinks Your Boss Has an Attitude Problem," *Fast Company*, July 31, 2001, www.fastcompany.com/43419 /marcus-buckingham-thinks-your-boss-has-attitude-problem.

The Productivity Code Key #I: Manufacture Motivation

1. William James, *The Principles of Psychology* (New York: Henry Holt and Company), 1890.

2. Charles Duhigg, *Smarter Faster Better* (New York: Random House), 2016.

3. Motivation definition, Business Dictionary, www.businessdictionary.com /definition/motivation.html.

4. Geoff Colvin, *Talent Is Overrated: What Really Separates World-Class Performers from Everybody Else* (New York: Portfolio/Penguin Group), 2008.

Habit I: Recruit Your Drive

1. Erika Patall, Harris Cooper, and Jorgianne Civey Robinson, "The Effects of Choice on Intrinsic Motivation and Related Outcomes: A Meta-Analysis of Research Findings," *Psychological Bulletin* 134, no. 2 (2008): 270–300, www.researchgate.net/publication/5554527_The_Effects_of_Choice _on_Intrinsic_Motivation_and_Related_Outcomes_A_Meta-Analysis_of _Research_Findings.

2. "The Art of Choosing," *Executive Talent*, Association of Executive Search and Leadership Consultants, www.aesc.org/insights/magazine/article/art -of-choosing.

3. Stephen X. Doyle and Benson P. Shapiro, "What Counts Most in Motivating Your Sales Force?" *Harvard Business Review*, July 1980, hbr.org/1980/07 /what-counts-most-in-motivating-your-sales-force.

4. Morten T. Hansen, *Great at Work: The Hidden Habits of Top Performers* (New York: Simon & Schuster, 2019).

5. Teresa Amabile and Steven Kramer, *The Progress Principle: Using Small Wins to Ignite Joy, Engagement, and Creativity at Work* (Brighton, MA: Harvard Business Review Press, 2011).

6. Sarah Gardner and Dave Albee, "Study Focuses on Strategies for Achieving Goals, Resolutions," news release, Dominican University of California, February 1, 2015, scholar.dominican.edu/news-releases/266.

Habit 2: Ignite Your Proactivity

1. Susan T. Fiske and Shelley E. Taylor, *Social Cognition: From Brains to Culture* (Thousand Oaks, CA: Sage, 2013).

2. Heather Murphy, "What We Finally Got Around to Learning at the Procrastination Research Conference," *New York Times*, July 21, 2017, www .nytimes.com/2017/07/21/science/procrastination-research-conference .html.

3. Leila Valizadeh, et al., "Comparison of Clustered Case with Three and Four Procedures on Physiological Responses of Preterm Infants: Randomized Crossover Clinical Trial," *Journal of Caring Sciences* 3, no. 1 (March 2014): 1–10, www.ncbi.nlm.nih.gov/pmc/articles/PMC4134166.

4. Sarah Milne, Sheina Orbell, and Paschal Sheeran, "Combining Motivational and Volitional Interventions to Promote Exercise Participation: Protection Motivation Theory and Implementation Intentions," *British Journal of Health Psychology* 7 (May 2002): 163–84.

5. E. J. Masicampo and R. F. Baumeister, "Consider It Done! Plan Making Can Eliminate the Cognitive Effects of Unfulfilled Goals," *Journal of Personality and Social Psychology* 101, no. 4 (2011): 667–83. The evidence in this study indicated that unfulfilled goals are mental clutter, distracting us from our ability to execute on our intentions.

6. KJ Green, "Navy SEALs Mental Training," YouTube video, 16:22, February 15, 2012, www.youtube.com/watch?v=Ju4FojRkEKU.

7. Lynne Twist, *The Soul of Money: Transforming Your Relationship with Money and Life* (New York: W.W. Norton), reprint edition 2017.

8. Jason S. Moser, Adrienne Dougherty, Whitney I. Mattson, et al., "Third-Person Self-Talk Facilitates Emotion Regulation Without Engaging Cognitive Control: Converging Evidence from ERP and fMRI," *Scientific Reports*, July 3, 2017, selfcontrol.psych.lsa.umich.edu/wp-content/uploads/2019/09/Third-person-self-talk-facilitates-emotion-regulation-without-engaging-cognitive-control_-Converging-evidence-from-ERP-and-fMRI.pdf.

9. Antonio Damasio, *Descartes' Error: Emotion, Reason, and the Human Brain* (New York: Penguin Books, 2005).

10. Mel Robbins, *The 5 Second Rule: Transform your Life, Work, and Confidence with Everyday Courage* (Brentwood, TN: Savio Republic, 2017).

Habit 3: Reengineer Your Habits

1. Phillippa Lally, Cornelia H. M. van Jaarsveld, Henry W. W. Potts, and Jane Wardle, "How Are Habits Formed: Modelling Habit Formation in the Real World," *European Journal of Social Psychology*, July 16, 2009.

2. Ian Brown, et al., "Enhancing Antiepileptic Drug Adherence: A Randomized Controlled Trial," *Epilepsy & Behavior* 16 (2009): 634–39, www.researchgate.net/profile/Paschal_Sheeran/publication/222676740_Enhancing_antiepileptic_drug_adherence_A_randomized_control_trial/links/5c06cca6a6fdcc315f9dcc18/Enhancing-antiepileptic-drug-adherence-A-randomized-control-trial.pdf.

3. University of Illinois at Urbana-Champaign, "Will We Succeed? The Science of Self-Motivation," *ScienceDaily*, June 1, 2010, www.sciencedaily.com/releases/2010/05/100528092021.htm.

The Productivity Code Key # 2: Control Your TIME

1. "TV Viewing Time 'Underestimated,'" *BBC News*, March 5, 2011, www.bbc.com/news/entertainment-arts-12651728; "Weekly Time Spent Watching TV in Canada 2016–2019, by Age," Statista, www.statista.com/statistics/234311/weekly-time-spent-watching-tv-in-canada-by-age-group/.

2. "Carleton Study Finds People Spending a Third of Job Time on Email," April 20, 2017, newsroom.carleton.ca/archives/2017/04/20/carleton-study-finds-people-spending-third-job-time-email/.

3. "American Couples Spend 5.5 Days a Year Deciding What to Eat," *New York Post*, November 17, 2017, nypost.com/2017/11/17/american-couples-spend-5-5-days-a-year-deciding-what-to-eat/.

4. Adam Levy, "People Still Spend an Absurd Amount of Time on Facebook," *The Motley Fool*, February 6, 2018, www.fool.com/investing/2018/02/06/people-still-spend-an-absurd-amount-of-time-on-fac.aspx.

5. "Mobile Matures as the Cross-Platform Era Emerges," Comscore, March 31, 2017, www.comscore.com/Insights/Blog/Mobile-Matures-as-the-Cross-Platform-Era-Emerges.

Habit 4: Obsess over TIME

1. Meir Kay, "A Valuable Lesson for a Happier Life," May 4, 2016, www.youtube.com/watch?v=SqGRnlXplx0&sns=em.

2. Annie Dillard, *The Writing Life* (New York: HarperCollins, 1989).

3. Jenn Savedge, "What Is Sleep Yoga?" Treehugger.com, updated January 16, 2018, www.mnn.com/health/fitness-well-being/blogs/sleep-yoga-or-yoga-nidra.

4. Niraj Chokshi, "Want to Be Happy? Buy More Takeout and Hire a Maid, Study Suggests," *New York Times*, July 27, 2017, www.nytimes.com/2017/07/27/science/study-happy-save-money-time.html.

5. Abby Ohlheiser, "You Want to Quit Facebook, but Will You Really Click the Button? These Folks Tried," *Washington Post*, March 21, 2018, www.washingtonpost.com/news/the-intersect/wp/2018/03/21/its-easy-to-hate-facebook-its-much-tougher-to-quit.

6. Nolan G. Pope, "How the Time of Day Affects Productivity: Evidence from School Schedules," *The Review of Economics and Statistics* 98, no. 1 (2016): 1–11.

7. Simon Folkard, "Diurnal Variation in Logical Reasoning," *British Journal of Psychology* 66, no. 1 (February 1975): 1–8.

8. TH Monk, ML Moline, JE Fookson, and SM Peetz, "Circadian Determinants of Subjective Alertness," *Journal of Biological Rhythms* 4, no. 4 (Winter 1989): 393–404.

9. Singh Shailendra, et al., "Differences Between Morning and Afternoon Colonoscopies for Adenoma Detection in Female and Male Patients," *Annals of Gastroenterology* 29, no. 4 (October–December 2016): 497–501; M. C. Wright, et al., "Time of Day Effects on the Incidence of Anesthetic Adverse Events," *Quality and Safety in Health Care* 15, no. 4 (2006): 258–63; Folkard, "Diurnal Variation in Logical Reasoning."

10. Kaiser Permanente, "Keeping a Food Diary Doubles Diet Weight Loss, Study Suggests," *ScienceDaily*, July 8, 2008, www.sciencedaily.com/releases/2008/07/080708080738.htm.

11. Peter Drucker, *The Practice of Management* (New York: HarperBusiness, 2006).

12. Art Markman, "This Is Why Your Brain Sucks at Time Management," *Fast Company*, July 11, 2017, www.fastcompany.com/40438349/this-is-why-your-brain-sucks-at-time-management.

Habit 5: Say No

1. William Leith, "Say 'No' and Change Your Life," *The Guardian*, March 18, 2018, www.theguardian.com/global/2018/mar/18/the-power-of-saying-no-change-your-life-psychology-william-leith.

2. Jackie Swift, "How Much Influence Do We Have over Others?" Cornell University, accessed September 3, 2020, research.cornell.edu/news-features/how-much-influence-do-we-have-over-others.

3. Dave Kurlan, "The Best Salespeople are 2733% More Likely to Have This Than the Worst Salespeople," OMG Hub, July 11, 2019, www.omghub.com/salesdevelopmentblog/topic/need-to-be-liked.

4. The Oracles, "Warren Buffett Says the Secret to Success Is Saying 'No.' Do Experts Agree?" *Money*, May 8, 2019, money.com/money/5643705/warren-buffett-says-no-to-everything/.

5. Jillian D'Onfro, "Steve Jobs Used to Ask Jony Ive the Same Question Almost Every Day," *Business Insider*, October 8, 2015, www.businessinsider.com/this-is-the-question-steve-jobs-would-ask-jony-ive-every-day-2015-10.

6. David Maister, "Strategy Means Saying 'No,'" 2006, accessed September 28, 2020, davidmaister.com/articles/strategy-means-saying-no/.

7. Roy F. Baumeister and John Tierney, *Willpower: Rediscovering the Greatest Human Strength* (New York: Penguin Books, 2012).

8. Peg Streep, "7 Foolproof Ways to Doom Your Resolutions," *Psychology Today*, December 29, 2014, www.psychologytoday.com/us/blog/tech-support/201412/7-foolproof-ways-doom-your-resolutions.

9. Brian Halligan, "The Art of Strategy Is About Knowing When to Say No," *Harvard Business Review*, January 26, 2018, hbr.org/2018/01/the-art-of-strategy-is-about-knowing-when-to-say-no.

10. Darlene Lancer, "What Are Personal Boundaries? How Do I Get Some?" *Psych Central*, October 8, 2018, psychcentral.com/lib/what-are-personal-boundaries-how-do-i-get-some/.

Habit 6: Play Hard to Get

1. Nir Eyal, *Hooked: How to Build Habit-Forming Products* (New York: Penguin, 2014).

2. "Global Mobile Consumer Survey: US Edition," Deloitte United States, May 25, 2018.

3. "Mobile Matures as the Cross-Platform Era Emerges," Comscore, March 31, 2017, www.comscore.com/Insights/Blog/Mobile-Matures-as-the-Cross-Platform-Era-Emerges.

4. Bob Sullivan and Hugh Thompson, "Brain, Interrupted," *New York Times*, May 5, 2013, www.nytimes.com/2013/05/05/opinion/sunday/a-focus-on -distraction.html.

5. Sullivan and Thompson, "Brain, Interrupted."

6. Bailey Johnson, "Study: 3-second distractions double workplace errors," *CBS News*, January 15, 2013, www.cbsnews.com/news/study-3-second -distractions-double-workplace-errors.

7. Gloria Mark, Daniela Gudith, and Ulrich Klocke, "The Cost of Interrupted Work: More Speed and Stress," *CHI '08: Proceedings of the SIGCHI Conference on Human Factors in Computing Systems* (April 2008): 107–110, www .ics.uci.edu/~gmark/chi08-mark.pdf.

8. Shamsi T. Iqbal and Eric Horvitz, "Disruption and Recovery of Computing Tasks: Field Study, Analysis, and Directions," *CHI '07: Proceedings of the SIGCHI Conference on Human Factors in Computing Systems* (April 2007): 677–86, erichorvitz.com/CHI_2007_Iqbal_Horvitz.pdf.

9. Mark et al., "The Cost of Interrupted Work."

10. Tia Ghose, "Heavy Multitaskers Are the Worst at Multitasking," *LiveScience*, January 23, 2013, www.livescience.com/26528-multitasking -bad-productivity.html.

11. David Pierce, "Turn Off Your Push Notifications. All of Them," *Wired*, July 23, 2017, www.wired.com/story/turn-off-your-push-notifications/.

12. Susan Weinschenk, "Why We're All Addicted to Texts, Twitter and Google," *Psychology Today*, September 11, 2012, www.psychologytoday.com/us /blog/brain-wise/201209/why-were-all-addicted-texts-twitter-and-google.

13. Melissa Fares, "Do You Suffer from Smartphone Anxiety? (And if So, What the Hell's Your Problem?)," *Daily Beast*, July 12, 2017, www.thedailybeast .com/do-you-suffer-from-smartphone-anxiety-and-if-so-what-the-hells -your-problem.

14. Martin Pielot and Rello, Luz, "Productive, Anxious, Lonely: 24 Hours Without Push Notifications," *MobileHCI '17: Proceedings of the 19th International Conference on Human–Computer Interaction with Mobile Devices and Services*, September 2017, dl.acm.org/doi/10.1145/3098279 .3098526.

15. Andrew D. Blechman, "Citizen Simon: Author, Journalist, OBE, Sage of Sandisfield," *The Berkshire Edge*, September 9, 2018, theberkshireedge .com/citizen-simon-author-journalist-obe-sage-of-sandisfield/.

The Productivity Code Key #3: Execute in the Zone

1. Steven Kotler, *The Rise of Superman: Decoding the Science of Ultimate Human Performance* (New York: New Harvest, 2014).

Habit 7: Sprint into the Zone

1. Mihaly Csikszentmihalyi, *Flow: The Psychology of Optimal Experience* (New York: HarperPerennial Modern Classics, 2008).

2. Adapted from Csikszentmihalyi, *Flow*.

3. Csikszentmihalyi, *Flow*.

4. Matthias Orgler, "7 Secrets to Master Timeboxing," Medium.com, April 21, 2016, medium.com/dreimannzelt-adventures/7-secrets-to-master-time boxing-66a744ea9175.

5. "Brief Diversions Vastly Improve Focus, Researchers Find," University of Illinois at Urbana–Champaign, February 8, 2011, www.sciencedaily.com /releases/2011/02/110208131529.htm.

6. Steven Kotler, "Create a Work Environment That Fosters Flow," *Harvard Business Review*, May 6, 2014, hbr.org/2014/05/create-a-work -environment-that-fosters-flow.

7. Gregory Ciotti, "Why Better Energy Management is the Key to Peak Productivity," *Lifehacker*, October 29, 2012. lifehacker.com/why-better-energy -management-is-the-key-to-peak-product-5955819.

8. Steven Kotler, "The Science of Peak Human Performance," *Time*, April 30, 2014, time.com/56809/the-science-of-peak-human-performance/.

Habit 8: Fuel Your Energy

1. John Tierney, "Do You Suffer from Decision Fatigue?" *New York Times Magazine*, August 17, 2011, www.nytimes.com/2011/08/21/magazine/do-you -suffer-from-decision-fatigue.html.

2. Michelle Obama, *Becoming* (New York: Crown, 2018).

3. "How Meditation Can Reshape Our Brains: Sara Lazar at TEDxCambridge," YouTube, January 23, 2012, 8:33, www.youtube.com/watch?v =m8rRzTtP7Tc.

4. Dan Harris and Jeff Warren, *Meditation for Fidgety Skeptics: A 10% Happier How-to Book* (New York: Spiegel & Grau, 2017).

5. R. Ryan Patel, "Mental Health Benefits of Leisure Activities," The Ohio State University, September 22, 2017, u.osu.edu/emotionalfitness/2017/09/22 /mental-health-benefits-of-leisure-activities/.

6. University of Rochester, "Spending Time in Nature Makes People Feel More Alive, Study Shows." *ScienceDaily*, June 4, 2010, www.sciencedaily.com /releases/2010/06/100603172219.htm.

7. Boston University, "Yoga May Elevate Brain GABA Levels, Suggesting Possible Treatment for Depression," *ScienceDaily*, May 22, 2007, www.science daily.com/releases/2007/05/070521145516.htm.

Habit 9: Right the Ship

1. Benjamin Libet, "Do We Have Free Will?" *Journal of Consciousness Studies*, 6, no. 8–9 (1999): 47–57.

2. Daniel M. Wegner, *The Illusion of Conscious Will* (Cambridge, MA: MIT Press, 2002).

3. Scotty Hendricks, "Free Will or Free Won't? Neuroscience on the Choices We Can (and Can't) Make," Big Think, September 30, 2016, bigthink.com /scotty-hendricks/free-will-or-free-wont-what-neuroscience-says-about -the-choices-we-can-and-cant-make.

4. Timothy A. Pychyl, "Free Won't: It May Be All That We Have (or Need)," *Psychology Today*, June 20, 2011, www.psychologytoday.com/us/blog/ dont-delay/201106/free-wont-it-may-be-all-we-have-or-need.

5. Cameron Huddleston, "How Much Would You Have If You Saved $1 a Day for Your Entire Life?" *GoBankingRates*, February 18, 2009, www .gobankingrates.com/banking/savings-account/much-would-saved-1-day -entire-life/.

6. Teresa Amabile and Steven Kramer, *The Progress Principle: Using Small Wins to Ignite Joy, Engagement, and Creativity at Work* (Brighton, MA: Harvard Business Review Press, 2011).

7. Lauren Sommer, "Think Tiny: The Science of New Year's Resolutions," *KQED Science*, December 28, 2012, ww2.kqed.org/quest/2012/12/28 /think-tiny-the-science-of-new-years-resolutions.

8. Xavier Gine, Dean Karlan, and Jonathan Zinman, "Put Your Money Where Your Butt Is: A Commitment Contract for Smoking Cessation," PsycEXTRA Dataset, 2009.

INDEX

A

Abagnale, Frank W., 119
accountability, 174
    Track Progress Weekly, 44–46
accountability partner, 42, 45–46
achievement, xxv
actions, 4–5
activation energy, 51–52
alerts, 123–125, 130
Amabile, Teresa, 45, 171
anti-charity, 175
Ari. *See* Schultz, Ari Francis "Danger"
Ari's Tournament, 29–30
attitude, 158

B

batching, 50–51
Baumeister, Roy, 112
Be Free from the Shackles of Alerts,
    123–125
Be Someplace Else, 127–129
Becoming (Obama), 157
beginner's mind, 14
behaviors, xxxiv
body, 153, 159–160, 167
Bohns, Vanessa, 109
Boston Children's Hospital (BCH),
    xxi
boundaries, 110. *See also* Say No
breathing, 162
Brown, Brené, 2, 105, 109
Brown, Ian, 73
Buechner, Frederick, xxix
Buffett, Warren, 111
business, xvi. *See also* RAIN Group

C

calendaring Investment Time, 52–56,
    64, 157
capture list, 145–147
cardiac surgery, xxi
catalysts for proactivity, 51–52
    Calendar Your Investment Time,
        52–56
    Say "3 . . . 2 . . . 1 . . . Go!" 61–63
    Talk to Yourself, 56–61
change, 20
    micro changes, 170–173
Change Your Environment, 75–77
choice, 32, 88. *See also* Choose Your
        New Reality
choice architects, 71, 73
Choose Your New Reality, 31, 32–36, 46
clustering, 50–51
Cohen, Dan, 14
Colvin, Geoff, 24
commitment contract, 174–175, 176
concentration, 100. *See also* focus
consequences, strong, 142
Control Your Time
    Obsess over TIME, 83–104
    Say No, 105–117
creativity, 128
Critical Decision Window, 56
Csikszentmihalyi, Mihaly, 138, 139

D

Damasio, Antonio, 62
decision making, 156–157, 169
delegating, 93–94. *See also* Mandatory
        time

diet, 159–160
Dillard, Annie, 6, 89
distraction capture list, 145–147
distractions, 121–123
    changing environment and,
        127–129
Do Less, 114–115
Doerr, John, 33–34, 95–97
dopamine, 124
drive. *See also* Recruit Your Drive
    choice and, 32
    happiness and, 31
    Plan Actions Weekly and, 38
Drucker, Peter, 102
Dyer, Wayne W., 13

E
efficiency, maximum, 14
effort, xxv, xxvi
Einstein, Albert, 157
email alerts, 123–125, 130
employees, engaged, 19
Empty time, xxxi. *See also* TIME,
    levels of
    changing, 101
    eliminating, 98
    happiness and, 94
    tracking time and, 103
    vs. Treasured time, 20
    during typical workday, 17
    wasted time vs. downtime, 14–15
energy, 99–100
    body and, 153–155, 159–160
    Fuel Your Energy, 149–163
    happiness and, 153
    mind and, 153–155
    morning and, 156–157
    morning routines and, 78
    planning and, 157
    spirit and, 153–155
    sustaining, 152–153
energy direction, 154
energy quality, 154
engagement, 19
environment
    changing, 127–129
    zone-conducive, 142–143
environmental factors, 75–77
ESPN, 179–180
Execute in the Zone, 131–176
    Right the Ship, 165–176
    Sprint into the Zone, 135–147
exercise, 160, 167
exhaustion, 1, 2, 150

Extreme Productivity Assessment,
    9, 12
Extreme Productivity Challenge
    training, xxx
Extreme Productivity Morning
    Routine, 79–80, 82, 158
Extremely Productive (The XP), xxxiii
    difference from The Rest, 8
    drive of, 30–31
    job satisfaction, 19
    PQ of, 9
    system to become, xxxiv
    time spent on Mandatory and
        Empty time, 17
    time spent on Treasured activities,
        18
    tracking progress weekly and, 44
    weekly action plan and, 43
Eyal, Nir, 121

F
Fast Company, 19
Fields, W. C., 65
5 Second Rule, The (Robbins), 62
5-Step Extreme Productivity Morning
    Routine, 79–80, 82, 158
flow. *See* zone
focus, 137. *See also* concentration;
        Sprinting; zone
    interruption minimizers, 126–127
    losing, 11
    New Reality and, 33
    zone and, 143
Fogg, BJ, 172
food, 159–160, 167
Ford, Henry, 57
Four-Three-Four Plan, 39–44
Fuel Your Energy, 149–163
    Body, 159–160
    Mind, 156–159
    Spirit, 160–162
fulfillment, xxvii, 3. *See also* meaning
fun, xvi. *See also* Treasured time

G
Get in the Zone, 140–147
GIA (Greatest Impact Activity). *See*
        Greatest Impact Activity (GIA)
gifts, xxix
goals
    Annual Goals, 35
    benefits of, 43
    Big Picture Goals, 34–36
    defining, 19

Four-Three-Four Plan, 39–44
  framework for, 35
  Investment time and, 92–93
  quarterly priorities and, 41
  Three-Year Goals, 35
  written, 31, 33–36. *see also* Choose
    Your New Reality
golf, xxxii, 160–161
golf tournament, 29–30, 35
Good Morning Tour, 66–67
Greatest Impact Activity (GIA)
  described, 50, 55
  energy and, 157
  focus on, 49
  New Reality and, 33
  odds of completing, 80–81
  putting first, 99–100
  starting with, 80
grief, xxvi–xxvii, 150–152

H

Habit 1: Recruit Your Drive. *See*
  Recruit Your Drive
Habit 2: Ignite Your Proactivity. *See*
  Ignite Your Proactivity
Habit 3: Reengineer Your Habits. *See*
  Reengineer Your Habits
Habit 4: Obsess over TIME. *See*
  Obsess over TIME
Habit 5: Say No. *See* Say No
Habit 6: Play Hard to Get. *See* Play
  Hard to Get
Habit 7: Sprint into the Zone. *See*
  Sprint into the Zone
Habit 8: Fuel Your Energy. *See* Fuel
  Your Energy
Habit 9: Right the Ship. *See* Right the
  Ship
Habit Change Blueprint, 82
habit formation, 172
habits, xxxiii, xxxiv–xxxv, 168–169.
  See also 9 Habits of Extreme
  Productivity; routine
  changing, 71, 167
  definition of, 6, 74
  driving "automaticity," 72–73
  elements of, 69, 71
  of productive people, 7
  productivity and, 6
  Reengineer Your Habits, 65–82
  thought and, 68–70, 74, 168–169
  work habits to change/start, 70
hacks, xxxii, xxxiii, xxxiv
Halligan, Brian, 114

Hallowell, Ned, 132
happiness, xxv, xxvii, xxx, 5, 7, 34
  drive and, 31
  energy and, 153
  minimizing Empty time and, 94
  minimizing Mandatory time and,
    94
  morning routines and, 67
  PQ and, 10
  proactivity and, 50
  Treasured time and, 92
Harris, Dan, 159
Harrison, George, 87
Hawthorne Effect, 101
Headspace app, 159, 173
health insurance, xxiv
Hirshfield, Jane, 128
HLHS (hypoplastic left heart
  syndrome), xviii–xix, xx–xxii
hobbies, xvi
house, xvi, xxvii, xxxii
how, 4–5
hypoplastic left heart syndrome
  (HLHS), xviii–xix, xx–xxii

I

Ignite Your Proactivity, 47–64, 170
  Calendar your Investment time,
    52–56
  Say "3 . . . 2 . . . 1 . . . Go!" 61–63
  Talk to Yourself, 56–61
ikigai, 14, 17, 20, 32, 34, 90. *See also*
  why
important things, xxx, xxxi. *See also*
  Treasured time
in utero fetal balloon valvuloplasty,
  xx
interruption minimizers, 126–127
Investment activities, increasing
  average time spent on, 17
Investment time, xxxi, 14–15, 16, 17,
  40, 92–93. *See also* TIME, levels
  of
  calendaring, 52–56, 64, 157
  described, 55
  vs. Mandatory time, 16
  maximizing, 18
Ive, Jony, 112
Iyengar, Sheena, 32

J

James, William, 24
job satisfaction, 10, 19
Jobs, Steve, 112

K

Kafka, Franz, 129
Karlan, Dean, 174
Kay, Meir, 89
Keep a To-Don't List, 111–113
Key 1: Manufacture Motivation. *See* Manufacture Motivation
Key 2: Control Your Time. *See* Control Your Time
Key 3: Execute in the Zone. *See* Execute in the Zone
Kleitman, Nathaniel, 141
Kotler, Steven, 132
Kramer, Steven, 45, 171

L

Lally, Pippa, 72
Lancer, Darlene, 115
Laozi, 47
Lavie, Peretz, 144
Lazar, Sara, 158–159
lean manufacturing, 2
leisure activities, 162. *See also* Treasured time
Libet, Benjamin, 168–169
Limb, Charles, 146
Lindberg, Jessica, 150
Ethan M. Lindberg Foundation, 29, 35, 106–107, 150
Lindbergh, Anne Morrow, 129
Lock, James, xxi

M

Maister, David, 112
Make a Commitment Contract, 174–175
Make-A-Wish, xxiii
management, productivity and, 2
Mandatory time, xxxi, 14–16. *See also* TIME, levels of
changing, 98–99, 101, 170
vs. Investment time, 16
mindset and, 20. *see also* Obsess over TIME
minimizing, 93–97
tracking time and, 103
during typical workday, 17
Manufacture Motivation, 23
Ignite Your Proactivity, 47–64
Recruit Your Drive, 27–46
Reengineer Your Habits, 65–82
meaning, 3, 5, 162. *See also* fulfillment; why
medical bills, xxiv

meditation, 151, 152, 159
Meditation for Fidgety Skeptics (Harris), 159
mental energy
mindfulness and, 158–159
minimizing decisions, 156–157
positive self-talk and, 157–158
mental fatigue, 156–157
mental health, Treasured time and, 162
mental resistance, 49. *See also* starting
mental toughness, 56–57
micro changes, 170–173
Milne, A. A., 165
Milne, Sarah, 53
mind, 153, 156–159
mindfulness, 158–159, 169, 173
mindset, 20, 158
Mohr, Tara, 151
morning, 99–100, 156
morning routines, 67, 78–80, 82, 158
motivation, 23–25. *See also* Manufacture Motivation; Recruit Your Drive
choice and, 32
definition of, 50
environmental factors, 76
New Reality and, 33
Plan Actions Weekly and, 38

N

nature, 162
Navy SEALs, 57
Nietzsche, Friedrich, 36
9 Habits of Extreme Productivity, xxxiv, 7, 11. *See also* habits
90-Day Extreme Productivity Challenge, 11
no, saying, 105–117
"No for Now" list, 115
noise-canceling headphones, 130
now, focus on, 169

O

Obama, Barack, 157
Obama, Michelle, 157–158
Obsess over TIME, 15, 16, 20, 87–104
Put Your GIA First, 99–100
Take T, Increase I, Minimize M, Eliminate E, 90–99
Track Your TIME, 101–104
Orgler, Matthias, 140

outdoors, 162
outlook, 38

P
passion, 24
peace, 151, 154
pediatric cardiology, xxi
performance
    choice and, 32
    PQ and, 10
personal spiritual path, 162
Picasso, Pablo, 128
Plan Actions Weekly, 31, 36–44, 46, 176
planning
    calendaring Investment time,
        52–56, 64, 157
    energy and, 157
    Productivity Code Planner, 46
    sprints, 141–143
planning fallacy, 103
Play Hard to Get, 119–130
    Be Free from the Shackles of
        Alerts, 123–125
    Be Someplace Else, 127–129
    Signal "Do Not Disturb," 125–127
Porter, Michael, 112
PQ (Productivity Quotient), 9–10
Practice Free Won't, 168–170
Practice Saying No, 115
present, being, 88, 99, 158–159
priorities. *See also* Say No
    Four-Three-Four Plan, 39–44
    "No for Now" list, 115
    number of, 40–41
    quarterly, 41
proactivity, 49. *See also* Ignite Your
        Proactivity; starting
    catalysts for, 51–63
    happiness and, 50
procrastination, 49, 53
productive stamina, 155
productive work time units, 143–144
productivity, xxx, xxxi
    assessment of, 7
    changing conversation about, 2
    definition of, 2
    fulfillment and, 3
    habits and, 6
    learning, 11
    management and, 2
    Plan Actions Weekly and, 38
    research study., 7–8
    as self-worth, 2
    typical approach to, xxxiv

Productivity Code, xxxiv, 5, 7. *See also*
        9 Habits of Extreme Productivity;
        3 Keys
Productivity Code Planner, 46
Productivity Quotient (PQ), 9–10
progress, 171
    Track Progress Weekly, 31, 44–46
    Progress Principle, The (Amabile and
        Kramer), 45, 171
purpose, xxvii, xxx, 4, 46. *See also*
    why

R
Rackham, Neil, 142
RAIN Group, xvi, xxx. *See also*
    business; work
Rapid Activation Talk, 62–63
reason for being, 14, 90. *See also*
    ikigai; why
recovery, 167–176
Recruit Your Drive, 21, 27–46, 50, 63
    Choose Your New Reality, 31,
        32–36
    Plan Actions Weekly, 31, 36–44
    research findings, 31
    Track Progress Weekly, 31, 44–46
Reengineer Your Habits, 65–82
    Change Your Environment, 75–77
    Make Your Morning Routine
        Sacred, 78–80
    Say, "When I, Then I." And Ask,
        "Will I? ," 73–75
relays, 143–145
research study of productive people,
    7–8
Rest, The, xxxiii
    PQ of, 9
    time spent on Mandatory and
        Empty time by, 17
    time spent on Treasured activities
        by, 18
rest-activity cycle, 141
Restoring a Mother's Heart, 151–152
reward, long-term, 63
Right the Ship, 165–176
    Make a Commitment Contract,
        174–175
    Micro Changes, 170–173
    Practice Free Won't, 168–170
Rinaldi, Tom, 180
Robbins, Mel, 62
routine, 66. *See also* habits
    Extreme Productivity Morning
        Routine, 79–80, 82, 158

routine (*continued*)
    Good Morning Tour, 66–67
    morning routines, 67, 78–80
    Sprinting, 141–143
Ryan, Richard, 162

S
Say, "When I, Then I." And Ask, "Will
    I? ," 73–75, 172
Say "3 . . . 2 . . . 1 . . . Go!" 61–63, 64
Say No, 105–117
    difficulty of saying no, 109–111
    Do Less, 114–115
    Keep a To-Don't List, 111–113
    Practice Saying No, 115
schedule, 89–90. *See also* calendaring
    Investment Time; Obsess over
    TIME; planning
Schultz, Ari Francis "Danger," xxxv
    birth of, xxii
    as catalyst, xxxv
    death of, xxvi–xxvii, 150–152,
        180–181
    diagnosis, xviii–xix
    eighteen-week ultrasound,
        xvii–xviii
    gifts of, xxix
    Good Morning Tour, 66–67
    heart catheterization, 36–37
    heart transplant, 29, 37, 88, 179
    hospital stays, xix–xx, xxiii
    open-heart surgeries, xxii–xxiii
    sports and, xxiii, xxxii
Schultz, Eli, xxiv, xxvi, xxxii
Schultz, Lexi, xxiv, xxvi, xxxii
seeking behavior, 124
seiryoku-zenyo, 14, 90
self-talk, 56–61, 64
    energy and, 157–158
    Say, "When I, Then I." And Ask,
        "Will I? ," 73–75
self-worth, productivity as, 2
shoshin, 14
Signal "Do Not Disturb," 125–127
sleep, 166–167
social media, 6
solitude, 128–129
Soul of Money, The (Twist), 58
spark, 47. *See also* Ignite Your
    Proactivity
spirit, 153
spiritual energy, 157, 160–162, 167
Sprint into the Zone, 135–147
    Block Distraction, 145–147

Do Four Successive Sprints in a
    Relay, 143–145
Establish a Daily Routine of
    Obsessed, Planned Sprints,
    141–143
Get in the Zone, 140–147
Sprinting, 140–147, 158, 171
    described, 55
    planning, 141–143
stamina, productive, 155
starting, 49. *See also* proactivity
    activation energy, 51–52
    calendaring and, 54
    mental toughness, 56–57
    Rapid Activation Talk, 62–63
Steiner-Adair, Catherine, 124
Stevens, Brad, xxxii
Stickk, 176
success, xxv, xxvii, 3

T
tactics, 4–5
Take T, Increase I, Minimize M,
    Eliminate E, 90–99
Talent Is Overrated (Colvin), 24
Talk to Yourself, 56–61
task clarity, 142
    Plan Actions Weekly and,
        38–44
Terrapure Environmental, xxx
Tesla, Nikola, 128
thought, habits and, 68–70, 74,
    168–169
"3 . . . 2 . . . 1 . . . Stop!" 170
3 Keys, 10
    Key 1: Manufacture Motivation.
        see Manufacture Motivation
    Key 2: Control Your Time. *see*
        Control Your Time
    Key 3: Execute in the Zone. *see*
        Execute in the Zone
Tierney, John, 112
time
    Ari's, xxix
    manufacturing more, 18–19
    as mindset, 19–20
    model of thinking about, xxix
    new mindset about, 13–21
    questioning use of, 4
    tracking, 21, 101–104, 117
TIME, levels of, xxxi, 14–15, 91. *See*
    also Empty time; Investment
    time; Mandatory time; Treasured
    time

Time for Action, 46
    Choose Your New Reality, 46
    Control Your Time, 117
    Extreme Productivity Assessment, 12
    Fuel Your Energy, 163
    Ignite Your Proactivity, 64
    Obsess over TIME, 104
    Plan Actions Weekly, 46
    Play Hard to Get, 130
    Reengineer Your Habits, 82
    Right the Ship, 176
    Sprint into the Zone, 147
    Track Progress Weekly, 46
time log, 101–104
timeboxing, 55. *See also* Sprinting
To-Don't List, 111–113, 117
Toyota Production System, 2
Track Progress Weekly, 31, 44–46
tracking time, 21, 101–104, 117
Treasured activities, time spent on, 18
Treasured time, xxxi, 14–15, 17, 91–92, 116. *See also* TIME, levels of
    vs. Empty time, 20
    maximizing, 18
    mental health benefits of, 162
    tracking time and, 103
Twist, Lynne, 58
Tworetzky, Wayne, xix, xx, 37

W
weekly action plan. *See* Plan Actions Weekly
Weinschenk, Susan, 124
what, 4–5
"When I, Then I" statements, 73–75, 172
Whillans, Ashley, 94
why, 14, 21, 36, 46. See also *ikigai*; meaning; Recruit Your Drive

long-term, 5
spiritual energy and, 157
tying actions and tactics to, 4–5
willpower, 169
Willpower (Baumeister and Tierney), 112
Winchester, Simon, 129
Winnfield, Jules, 135
withdrawal, from alerts, 124
work, xvi. *See also* RAIN Group
    in hospital environment, xxiv–xxv
    inability to take leave of absence from, xxiii
work behaviors, xxxiii
work environment, productive, 77
workshops and online learning programs, 7
Writing Life, The (Dillard), 6, 89

X
XP, The (Extremely Productive). *See* Extremely Productive (The XP)
XP TIME Champions, 8, 17
    PQ of, 9
    time spent on Mandatory and Empty time, 17

Y
yen, 27, 30, 50
yoga, 151, 152, 162, 167, 173

Z
Zinman, Jonathan, 174
zone, 131–176
    conditions for getting into, 142–143
    Get in the Zone, 140–147
    productive work time units, 143–144
    productivity and, 158
    timeboxing, 140–147

IF YOU WANT TO CONTINUE YOUR JOURNEY WITH US

The 9 Habits of Extreme Productivity course is an online self-paced course designed to help you take what you've learned in this book to the next level.

With twenty-seven more videos and lessons, seventeen exercises and tools, and eleven training modules, the course is designed to build your understanding and know-how through practical application of The Productivity Code's 9 Habits.

You'll learn how to master the 3 Keys and 9 Habits of The Productivity Code to get more out of the time to you have to:

- Crush your career and work goals
- Spend time with your family and friends
- Do more of what you love
- Pause to refuel your tank

The 9 Habits of Extreme Productivity is the go-to online course for anyone serious about taking back control of their time, achieving their goals, and becoming unstoppable. It will help you live a more productive, happier, more fulfilled life. It's a proven system that works time and again to help people make lasting change in their habits and feel better day in and day out.

Learn more about the 9 Habits of Extreme Productivity course and enroll at myproductivitycode.com.

ABOUT THE AUTHORS

Erica and Mike Schultz are Ari's parents. This is their greatest life achievement. They are also leaders of RAIN Group, an award-winning sales training company with offices around the globe. Erica, Mike, and the team at RAIN Group have worked with organizations such as Toyota, Monitor-Deloitte, Harvard Business School, Oracle, Fidelity Investments, Ryder, UL, Navigant Consulting, Hitatchi, Lee Hecht Harrison, Lowe's, and thousands of others to unleash sales performance.

Under their leadership, RAIN Group has been recognized as a Top 20 Sales Training Company by *Training Industry* and *Selling Power*; won Multiple Stevie Awards for Sales Training Program of the Year, Business Development Achievement of the Year, Sales Training Professional of the Year, and Sales Training Practice of the Year; and they've won a Brandon Hall Group Excellence Award for Innovative Sales Training Program of the Year for the Extreme Productivity Challenge.

Sought-after experts in marketing, sales, and productivity, Erica and Mike's work has been featured in *Entrepreneur Magazine*, *Business Week*, *Forbes*, *ATD*, *CRM Magazine*, *American Express Open Forum*, *LinkedIn Sales Blog*, and hundreds of other publications. They've appeared in ESPN, *People* magazine, MSNBC, and *ABC World News Tonight*.

They are passionate about raising awareness for congenital heart defects (CHD) and organ donation and were recognized by the American Heart Association, receiving the Heart of Gold Award.

To interview Erica and Mike or invite them to speak at your conference or event, reach out via raingroup.com.

ABOUT RAIN GROUP

RAIN Group is an award-winning sales training and performance improvement company that helps leading organizations improve sales results through in-person and virtual training, coaching, and reinforcement. We've helped hundreds of thousands of salespeople, managers, and professionals in more than seventy-five countries increase productivity and sales significantly.

We help organizations:

- **Implement Training that Delivers Real Results**: RAIN Group's training system inspires real change and delivers real results that last. Our rigorous approach includes self and team evaluation, tailored training programs, robust reinforcement, and coaching to help you and your team develop skills and maximize results.

- **Deliver High Impact Virtual Instructor-Led Training**: Training a remote and dispersed team is a challenge for many leaders. We use a mixture of virtual instructor-led training, interactive digital reinforcement, eLearning, and virtual coaching to deliver award-winning training and results.

- **Grow Your Key Accounts**: At most companies there's a huge, untapped opportunity to add more value—and thus sell more—to existing accounts. We help clients capitalize on these revenue growth opportunities. Whether it's simply increasing cross-selling and upselling or implementing a major strategic account program, we can help.

- **Implement World-Class Coaching**: We coach professionals, managers, and leaders individually and in groups to achieve the greatest and fastest increases in productivity and results. We also train and certify leaders and managers in the Extreme Productivity Coaching system. Often, it's the coaching that truly unlocks the team's potential and keeps them motivated to produce the best results consistently.

Headquartered in Boston, the company has offices across the U.S. and internationally in Bogotá, Geneva, Johannesburg, London, Mexico City, Mumbai, Seoul, Sydney, and Toronto.

To learn more about RAIN Group, visit raingroup.com.